Human Spatial Computing

Human Spatial Computing

REGINÉ GILBERT

JAMES WELDON JOHNSON PROFESSOR,
NEW YORK UNIVERSITY

DOUG NORTH COOK

CEO AND CREATIVE DIRECTOR,
CREATURE, PITTSBURGH

Great Clarendon Street, Oxford, OX2 6DP,
United Kingdom

Oxford University Press is a department of the University of Oxford.
It furthers the University's objective of excellence in research, scholarship,
and education by publishing worldwide. Oxford is a registered trade mark of
Oxford University Press in the UK and in certain other countries

Published in the United States of America by Oxford University Press
198 Madison Avenue, New York, NY 10016, United States of America

British Library Cataloguing in Publication Data
Data available

Library of Congress Control Number: 2025947653

ISBN 9780192870094
ISBN 9780192870100 (pbk.)

DOI: 10.1093/9780191966477.001.0001

The manufacturer's authorized representative in the EU for product safety is
Oxford University Press España S.A. of Parque Empresarial San Fernando de Henares,
Avenida de Castilla, 2 – 28830 Madrid (www.oup.es/en or product.safety@oup.com).
OUP España S.A. also acts as importer into Spain of products made by the manufacturer.

CONTENTS

Foreword vii
Introduction ix

1. Why Should We Care about Ethics? 1

2. The Story of Human–Computer Interaction 41

3. What Connects Us All 63

4. Universal Design for Spatial Computing 103

5. Merging Human Creativity with Technology 127

6. The Body 151

7. Affordances of Immersive Technology and the Future
   of Computing 175

8. Spatial Computing and the Brain 197

9. Where Do We Go From Here? 227

Acknowledgments 251
References 253
Index 265

When I saw the movie *Tron* in 1982, I was starting high school. I was so excited by 3D graphics, but I couldn't find any books on how it was done (no Google, YouTube, or TikTok for 20–30 more years). So, I reverse-engineered what I saw using the trigonometry I'd learned in school. After a week, I made a 3D cube rotate on my little Commodore 64. I was ecstatic. I had no idea I could even make a living doing that.

At an engineering-focused college, our main grounding in ethics and design came from reading Science Fiction. Civil engineers, doctors, and even lawyers received ethics training and later swore oaths in the ethical application of their fields to avoid harming people. But those of us who came of age with computers, 3D games, the Internet, virtual reality, and spatial computing had to figure it all out on our own. And we made some big mistakes.

I'm so excited that my distinguished colleagues Reginé Gilbert and Doug North Cook have written this book. You can learn from our mistakes as well as our triumphs. You can obtain the grounding needed to surge ahead so you can figure out new areas we could never reach. It's all here in a comprehensive resource covering this remarkable set of technologies.

Just as computer mice and windows dominated the last 50 years, spatial computing (including AI and XR) is poised to change the way we interact with computers for the next 50 and beyond. We're still beginning this next major transformation, and there's still much more to uncover and grow.

Let's never forget what we have learned about ethics so far—what I'd call the science of how to do and be our best—in that technology and design must always be in service of fundamental human needs. Harms come in many ways unseen, and our job is to listen and see them. By doing so we can turn past mistakes into proactive principles, to guide us ahead and make our work as valuable and exciting as possible for everyone.

Avi Bar-Zeev

Spatial computing is now deeply integrated into daily life. It guides us through cities, daily use of social media filters, and virtual environments with seamless precision. Since remote work became mainstream in the early 2020s, hybrid collaboration has redefined how we communicate and create together. Our interactions with technology have evolved from external control to immersive engagement, using wearables, mixed-reality headsets, and spatial interfaces. This maturing era of embodied computing continues to expand how we experience reality and inspires new possibilities that push beyond our current understanding.

The potential for embodied computing is vast, including treatments, remote work, training, entertainment, and exploration. However, it is up to us to determine whether these technologies are used for good or bad. As we continue to develop and advance these devices, we must consider their impact on our perceptions, emotions, values, and narratives.

This book is an attempt to explore the complexity of navigating these steps in a direction that embraces the best of us. We want to ask difficult questions, be curious about other perspectives, and engage as many people as possible in this work. Authors Reginé and Doug have 15 years of combined experience working with AR and VR. Doug is a developer, educator, and creative director, while Reginé is an educator, researcher, and consultant. We wrote this book to shed light on the technological shift taking place, and emphasize the importance of ethics, human–computer interaction, storytelling, technology, privacy, accessibility, and universal design.

Throughout the book, we tell stories about projects we worked on. We have created it for educators, students, and spatial computing practitioners, specifically in augmented and virtual reality. Each chapter ends with reflective questions and activities for practice to guide people to make more ethical and equitable spatial computing experiences. The following are summaries of each chapter in this book.

Chapter 1 discusses the challenges that spatial computing presents regarding privacy, safety, and balancing harm versus benefit. It explores the concepts within design and how we can create inclusive narratives to support technology development that will shape our shared future.

Chapter 2 provides a brief history of human–computer interaction (HCI) and explains the importance of new approaches to HCI for spatial computing. It delves into how personal computers have redefined work and how spatial computing can potentially define the future of what it means to be human.

Chapter 3 highlights the importance of storytelling and how it connects us all. It covers the history of storytelling, its impact on the brain, and how we can tell stories using spatial computing.

Chapter 4 explores the concept of universal design and how it can be adapted to virtual and augmented settings. It invites us to think about creating experiences that are accessible to as many users as possible and working to remove barriers to access.

Chapter 5 explores the impact of technology on human life, emphasizing the need for inclusive and practical designs in spatial computing to drive progress and innovation.

Chapter 6 investigates how we can use our entire bodies as input devices for spatial computing. It discusses designing systems for various body types and backgrounds and how embodied computing can make us more human.

Chapter 7 examines how our experiences in the physical world define our interactions with objects and environments in spatial computing experiences. It considers how we can change these relationships and the challenges of replicating real-world objects in virtual environments.

Chapter 8 covers the brain's function and various types of bias and how they impact spatial computing. It emphasizes the need to understand discrimination and its impact on this technology.

Chapter 9 concludes the book by discussing the potential of spatial computing and its intersections with other cutting-edge technologies like artificial intelligence and advanced sensors. It encourages us to embrace innovation, ethical considerations, and forward thinking to shape a positive future where spatial computing plays a defining role.

The book covers various perspectives on systemic issues and how to apply that knowledge to spatial computing experiences. Spatial computing has become crucial in daily life, from Instagram filters to virtual reality for gaming and training, especially since the COVID-19 pandemic spread in 2020. This technology has allowed us to stay connected with others and transformed our experience of reality. Embodied computing has many applications, from therapy to remote work, training, and entertainment. However, the ethical implications of these technologies are still developing and depend on human intent.

As we navigate this transformative landscape, we must take responsibility for the impact of simulated experiences on emotions, ethics, and storytelling. The book tackles the complexities of this journey and aims to prioritize human considerations in technology. The domains of ethics, human–computer interaction, storytelling, privacy, accessibility, universal design, and the synergy of nature and technology underscore the importance of this discourse as we shape the future of humanity and technology.

Throughout the book, you may encounter some key terms related to spatial computing. Here are some essential definitions:

- *Depth sensing* is a technology that measures distances to objects, enabling more precise placement of AR objects in the environment.
- *Field of view (FOV)* is the extent of the observable environment in a single glance through an AR device.
- *Gestural interaction* refers to using hand movements or gestures to interact with AR content.
- *Haptic feedback* provides sensory feedback, such as vibrations or force, that corresponds to interactions within a virtual environment.

- *Heads-up display (HUD)* presents information or graphics on a transparent screen that doesn't block the user's view of the real world.
- *Immersion* is feeling surrounded and engaged in a virtual environment.
- *Marker-based AR* relies on markers like QR codes or images to trigger digital content display in a specific location.
- *Markerless AR* uses computer vision and other technologies to detect and track real-world objects without markers.
- *Motion tracking* is a technology that monitors the movement of the user's head and sometimes their hands to update the VR display accordingly.
- *Real-world anchoring* is the ability of AR content to stay fixed to a specific location in the real world.
- *Simulator (motion) sickness* is the discomfort or nausea some experience when using VR due to conflicting sensory inputs.
- *Spatial mapping* is creating a three-dimensional map of the physical environment to place AR objects accurately.
- *Telepresence* is the sense of being present in a remote location through VR technology, allowing users to interact with the remote environment.
- *Three-dimensional object scaling* is when augmented reality (AR) technology overlays digital information, such as images, videos, or text, onto the real-world environment.
- *Virtual reality (VR)* is a computer-generated simulation of a three-dimensional environment that users can interact with using specialized VR headsets.
- *VR content creation* involves designing and producing virtual environments, experiences, and interactions.
- *VR headset* is a device worn on the head that displays virtual environments and often includes sensors for tracking head movements.
- *VR interaction* describes how users engage with and manipulate objects and elements within a VR environment, often using hand controllers or gestures.

- *Virtual reality locomotion* refers to methods for allowing users to move within virtual environments, such as teleportation or natural walking.

It is essential to remember that spatial computing is a rapidly evolving field, and new terms and concepts will emerge as the technology develops.

The field of spatial computing extends beyond the scope of this book. Our primary focus is on augmented and virtual realities. These technologies have the potential to transport our bodies and minds to new worlds. We believe it is important to prioritize the human experience, rather than solely focusing on the technology itself.

1
—

Why Should We Care about Ethics?

"I just want to build cool things." That's what one of my students told me when I announced that we would be discussing ethics. This sentiment is common; many creators believe they should focus on innovation while leaving the ethical concerns to someone else. But who is that "someone else"? In my class of engineering students, I explored the fundamental question, "Why should we care about ethics, particularly concerning technology?" The students began writing their thoughts, expressing a variety of viewpoints. Some argued that technology itself is not inherently harmful, but can be when misused by people; it can potentially cause unintended damage. Others noted that while technology can be inclusive and accessible, issues of user privacy and trust remain significant concerns.

Our relationship with technology has fundamentally shifted over the past few decades. Before notifications, we only used technology when we needed; it was a way to get things done in a timely manner, as with word processing. In the early days of the Internet, we did not have the instant connection many of us have now; we waited to connect to a world bigger than the ones we knew. However, when I ask my students about their first action each morning, a sea of hands raises in affirmation of a common ritual: reaching for their phones before their feet even touch the floor. This simple gesture shows how technology has evolved from a tool to a companion; for many, it is now the silent architect of our daily lives.

Human Spatial Computing. Reginé Gilbert and Doug North Cook, Oxford University Press.
© Reginé Gilbert and Doug North Cook (2026). DOI: 10.1093/9780191966477.003.0001

We are inundated with information shortly after we begin our daily routines. Our relationship with technology has evolved beyond functionality into something more close and common. The algorithms that curate our morning news shape our worldview before we even have breakfast. Social media notifications direct our attention and emotions throughout the day. In recent years we have seen polarization in the media with a lot of uncertainty as regards the truth. AI systems influence decisions regarding our careers, loans, and even medical care—often in ways that operate beyond our awareness or understanding.

Do we control technology, or does technology control us? This question extends beyond just devices or applications; it pertains to how technology is deeply integrated into our fundamental human experiences. We have created systems that not only fulfill our needs but also shape our behaviors, alter our social connections, and influence our decision-making processes. That morning reach for the phone is not merely a habit; it reflects how technology has woven itself into the very fabric of our consciousness, affecting not just what we do but also who we are becoming.

The real question is not whether we control technology or it controls us; rather, we are engaged in a more complex dance, with each partner simultaneously leading and following. Understanding this relationship and consciously shaping it may be one of the most critical challenges of our time. After all, that morning reach for the phone is just the first step in a day filled with countless technological interactions, each shaping our human experience in ways we are only beginning to understand.

Spatial computing, including augmented reality (AR) and virtual reality (VR), has the potential to enhance creativity, education, and connection. However, these technologies must be designed responsibly. It is essential to consider who controls these tools, how they affect our minds, and whether they are used in fair and ethical ways. The choices we make today will shape the future of our interactions with technology—and with one another.

As spatial computing technologies emerge, they raise critical ethical questions. As technology becomes increasingly integrated into our daily lives, it impacts our privacy, fairness, and human dignity. While digital tools can empower creativity, foster connection, and drive innovation, they also pose risks, such as reinforcing biases, eroding attention spans, and undermining personal autonomy.

Our interaction with technology influences the information we encounter. Productivity software shapes our workdays, and AI-driven systems affect various aspects of life, including criminal justice and personal relationships. The consequences of these technologies extend beyond mere convenience; they fundamentally alter the fabric of society itself.

Let's begin with an example of the kinds of troubles people encounter with VR. In 2022, researcher Jess Sherwood of the BBC went into a virtual chat room and posed as a 13-year-old girl. During one of the sessions, she got into a virtual strip club, where she saw grown men running after a child and telling him to take off his clothes. In many of the virtual rooms she visited, Sherwood saw images of condoms and models of sex toys. In some cases, she saw situations where adult men and teenagers feign group sex. She also saw several cases of so-called grooming—when an adult develops a trusting relationship with a child for a long time for the purpose of sexual exploitation (Crawford & Smith, 2022).

One of the main issues with the VRChat app Sherwood used is that adults and children can interact with each other with no oversight. Additionally, applying ethical standards is difficult because the people who are visiting the virtual world could be located anywhere in the world. Different rules and regulations apply to different countries, and there is no standard set of rules for children and the use of technology.

Humans operate within systems that can be examined from various perspectives, such as social, cultural, and individual. In a capitalistic system that prioritizes speed and profit, the creation of safe spaces and a more measured approach may not seem to align with these values. It is rare to hear recommendations emphasizing safety and well-being over efficiency. Many organizations strive for maximum returns at minimal costs, and in technological fields, the idea of slowing down and establishing safe spaces often contradicts the "bottom line," which focuses on efficiency, productivity, and profit. The phrase "move fast and break things" was popularized by Mark Zuckerberg, who later revised his company's motto to "move fast with stable infrastructure" (Thompson, 2018). This shift highlights the tension between the urgency to advance and the necessity of fostering safe environments. Given the demands of global capitalism, how can we begin to address this conflict?

With the example of VRChat, one suggestion is that there should be a minimum age requirement to enter the social virtual reality (VR) space (Figure 1.1). However, it is easy enough for participants to lie in order to access information. Moreover, wearing a headset is different from playing a video game on television or a personal computer. In the latter, others can observe what is taking place on the screen. But if someone is using wearable technology to access an AR experience, those around them cannot see the experience. When it comes to protecting people, especially children, there are constraints to what consumers—including parents, guardians, and teachers—can do, despite their strongly felt responsibilities. Most of the responsibility for consumer privacy and safety is in the control of the organizations that create the technologies.

Figure 1.1 Rachel Franklin, Head of Social VR at Facebook.

Source: Reproduced from Maurizio Pesce (2017). https://www.flickr.com/photos/ 30364433@N05/34039625154. Licensed under a Creative Commons Attribution 2.0 Generic (CC BY 2.0).

As consumers, when we use specific applications, we agree to the companies' legal terms of service. These terms inform us about the rules of engagement and how our data and privacy may be utilized. When was the last time you actually read the terms of service for an app or game you downloaded? A 2017 Deloitte survey of 2,000 US consumers found that 91% of people consent to terms of service without reading them. Among individuals aged 18 to 34, this figure rises to 97% (Guynn, 2020).

Many people don't read the terms of service because they are often too long and written in legal vocabulary that is difficult to understand. Additionally, the small text size can make it hard to read without magnification. Typically, terms of service do not allow users to opt out, meaning they have to agree to them in order to use an application. Companies often fail to provide clear and simple explanations about their data collection, usage, and sales practices. As a result, users must navigate the terms on their own and decide whether to read them while also managing their privacy settings, most of which are set to share everything by default. A majority of the time the responsibility of settings falls on the consumer due to a practice of "privacy by default" where companies set the configurations that set data collection to their benefit (Norwegian Consumer Council, 2018). Consequently, users struggle to fully understand how their data is being used.

Would you allow a stranger to do the following: follow you home, record your conversations, track your purchases, monitor your friends, or store photos of your face? Most consumers sign up for services without fully understanding what they are agreeing to. If terms of service were presented as a stranger, we likely wouldn't allow someone to do these things. Yet, when we agree to certain terms of service, we often do just that (Figure 1.2).

Most people operate on trust and convenience. Because we cannot see what happens behind the scenes of the technology we use, we tend to overlook these concerns as long as the product or service meets our needs. In a real-world scenario, this would be similar to a business saying, "You can use my store, but I'll follow you home, watch you sleep, monitor your conversations, and tell others what you do. You just need to sign here."

Figure 1.2 Terms of Service.

Source: Reproduced from Kevin Hodgson (2020). https://www.flickr.com/photos/71805365@N00/49590883168. Licensed under a Creative Commons Attribution-ShareAlike 2.0 Generic (CC BY-SA 2.0).

Understanding the balance between corporate responsibility and consumer awareness is crucial. It determines whether technological advancements align with ethical standards and respect individuals' rights.

INNOVATION VERSUS RESPONSIBILITY

Facial recognition technology identifies individuals by analyzing their facial features, similar to how your phone unlocks when it recognizes you. However, it raises several significant concerns that we need to address.

First, this technology relies on sensitive personal information, such as facial data, which is highly private. Second, its design can sometimes lead to unfair outcomes, as it may not perform equally well for everyone. Lastly, the manner in which it is used is crucial—there are risks if it is applied inappropriately or unsafely.

The responsibility for determining how this technology is utilized typically falls on large companies or organizations. They establish the rules, so it is essential for them to ensure that it is used in a responsible and ethical manner.

As facial recognition technology is increasingly incorporated into spatial computing for purposes such as authentication, avatar creation, and eye tracking, it is crucial to recognize the potential risks and ethical challenges associated with it. A notable illustration of these challenges arose when one of the authors of this book participated in a hackathon.

Hackathons typically take place over a 24- to 48-hour period, providing an opportunity for programmers, designers, and others to collaborate on projects organized by major companies or institutions. The focus of this particular hackathon was a newly acquired facial recognition technology. The team aimed to leverage this technology to generate interest in shopping by analyzing facial features to attract potential customers into stores. The team consisted of individuals from various backgrounds:

- Two men of European descent
- Two men from Western Asia
- An Asian woman
- A Black woman (the author).

Each team member tested the technology by walking past a camera, which accurately identified most participants' gender and approximate age range. However, when a Black woman passed in front of the camera, the system either failed to recognize her or inaccurately described her. The team members noted the potential bias of the technology, labeling it "racist." This experience was the author's first encounter with the inherent biases present in facial recognition systems, highlighting that the technology tends to "see" and cater to certain groups and individuals while miscategorizing or failing to recognize others.

Over the past decade, issues with facial recognition technology have continued to emerge. Researchers at the National Institute of Standards and Technology (NIST) in the United States found significant racial disparities in the accuracy of facial recognition systems (Grother and Ngan,

2023). Their findings revealed that there were more errors when identifying individuals with darker skin tones. Additionally, the accuracy of these systems improved under good lighting conditions but decreased in dim lighting. This disparity can be attributed to training data that has historically favored lighter-skinned individuals, as well as camera technology being optimized for those same skin tones. Like all technologies, facial recognition comes with its own set of challenges and limitations.

In May 2024, Clearview AI, a facial recognition company that identifies individuals from photos for various organizations, faced significant legal repercussions for privacy violations in the European Union. The Dutch Data Protection Authority issued the company a fine of €30.5 million for failing to comply with GDPR regulations (Lakshmanan, 2024). The main violation was Clearview AI's practice of creating a vast facial recognition database by collecting billions of photos from the Internet without obtaining consent from the individuals depicted in those images.

We now have a much better understanding of the concerns surrounding facial recognition technology and its potential uses. These concerns include risks related to personal data protection, the extent of surveillance, and how much a person's movements can be monitored. Additionally, there is an overconfidence in the accuracy of this technology, which often misidentifies individuals. Furthermore, facial recognition data raises the possibility of lifelong tracking, since it relies on biometric data unique to each person (unlike a password, which can be changed); a person cannot simply change their face. While some view facial recognition as a means to enhance personalized experiences in immersive environments or improve security, others are worried about the associated privacy and data issues. The specific characteristics that facial recognition uses can be exploited for malicious purposes, including identity theft.

A related technology and set of challenges in spatial computing involves motion-tracking telemetry, which is the automatic collection and transmission of data from a device to a system for analysis. This process is essential for developing spatial computing experiences. It involves collecting movement and position data in real time and helps maintain proper alignment between virtual and physical spaces. However, recent studies show that this data can be used to identify VR users. Moreover, research reveals that private user information can be deduced by analyzing the collected motion data. Several researchers demonstrated that motion data from virtual reality (VR) devices has the potential to uniquely identify users when they surveyed 1,006 VR users while they played *Beat Saber* (Nair et al. 2023). The results indicate that basic machine learning models can accurately speculate various personal attributes from the motion data collected from these users. The study consistently found around 40 unique characteristics of the individual solely from VR motion data. Despite this significant privacy breach, many people are unaware of the implications of VR motion data, which reinforces the urgent need for privacy-preserving measures in multi-user VR applications.

Technology develops and evolves rapidly. In recent years, advancements have improved its ability to recognize people of color, as well as individual-specific movements in easily identifiable ways. However, corporations, individuals, and creators must acknowledge the limitations of technology and the potential risks it poses in order to create experiences that protect people's data.

To address ethical issues, corporations and creators can take several actions: They should conduct regular security audits, incorporate privacy considerations into their design and development processes, establish data-encryption standards, minimize data collection, and provide clear terms of service.

Individuals also have a role to play; they can read the terms of service, conduct regular privacy audits of the applications they use, support privacy legislation, and join advocacy groups. However, this can be challenging for many individuals who may have limited technical knowledge and face either/or choices.

Recognizing these risks is essential, as the challenges posed by spatial computing extend beyond data privacy. Existing social inequalities are exacerbated by biased algorithms and unequal access to technology.

Several examples highlight the problems that spatial computing presents to users, emphasizing how these technologies can reinforce sexual and racial hierarchies. A notable aspect of spatial computing is that virtual reality (VR) can allow users to experience life from someone else's perspective. This can lead to both positive and negative outcomes.

Design choices in technology encompass ethical decisions that influence privacy, accessibility, and social equality. Factors such as facial recognition accuracy and data-collection defaults play a crucial role, as each interface decision has real-world implications for users.

Similar to the real world, virtual environments can hold individuals and organizations accountable for their actions. In social situations, people generally strive to behave appropriately, particularly concerning children. However, in the virtual realm, the elements of virtuality and anonymity raise significant concerns about child safety, making it a critical issue for those involved in the field of spatial computing.

Child safety is a major issue on the Internet and poses additional risks with spatial computing due to the immersive nature of experiences and the inability of parents or guardians to see what children are exposed to. As with the Internet, the dangers to children include cyberbullying, inappropriate content, distortion of reality, privacy and safety issues, and more.

Sexism, racism, and bullying are prevalent issues on the Internet, and in immersive environments within spatial computing their impact on individuals can be even more significant than in the real world. Jordan Belamire, a user researcher, shared her experience with social VR, recounting a scenario in which she was virtually groped.

So, there I was shooting down zombies alongside another real-time player named BigBro442. The other players could hear me when I spoke, my voice the only indication of my femaleness. Otherwise, my avatar looked identical to them.

In between a wave of zombies and demons to shoot down, I was hanging out next to BigBro442, waiting for our next attack. Suddenly, BigBro442's disembodied helmet faced me dead-on. His floating hand approached my body, and he started to virtually rub my chest.

"Stop!" I cried. I must have laughed from the embarrassment and the ridiculousness of the situation. Women, after all, are supposed to be cool, and take any form of sexual harassment with a laugh. But I still told him to stop.

This goaded him on, and even when I turned away from him, he chased me around, making grabbing and pinching motions near my chest. Emboldened, he even shoved his hand toward my virtual crotch and began rubbing.

There I was, being virtually groped in a snowy fortress with my brother-in-law and husband watching.

(Belamire, 2016)

The sense of presence and realism that individuals experience in a virtual environment can exceed what they feel while sitting at a computer. People's mental health can be significantly affected by their interactions in these spaces, and as creators, we must consider the potential harm this technology can cause to individuals and society as a whole.

Jessica Outlaw and Beth Duckles conducted a study aimed at understanding the experiences of millennial and Gen-Z women when introduced to social VR platforms (Outlaw & Duckles, 2017). The participants had no prior experience with virtual reality. Their study examined how these women responded to social settings within VR to gain insight into the experiences of digitally savvy individuals on these platforms. Currently, there is limited systematic research on the experiences of women in contemporary social VR platforms, despite reports in the media regarding harassment and abuse in these environments.

Outlaw and Duckles worked with 13 women between the ages of 21 and 38. Each participant spent 30 minutes in social VR. The researchers discovered that participants had avoidant behavior, such as staying outside communal areas, limited interaction with others, and choosing non-gendered robots. The study concluded that women participants in social VR environments frequently experienced persistent unwanted attention, primarily from users presenting as male.

Spatial computing presents a remarkable opportunity for gaming, exploration, and social interaction. However, much like in the real world, some individuals misuse it to harm or annoy others. Harassment in virtual worlds—such as bullying or disturbing another person—can be just as painful as in real life. This is because, although virtual worlds exist in a digital space, the people within them are real, and their feelings are important.

What occurs in virtual environments is connected to broader issues in the real world, such as unfair treatment based on gender and the misuse of power to harm others. These problems do not vanish just because we are using exciting new technologies like spatial computing; rather, they take on new forms.

The creators of spatial computing platforms have a significant responsibility to maintain safety in these environments. They need to implement tools and rules to combat harassment, including features that allow users to block or report inappropriate behavior. However, addressing this issue goes beyond technology; we also need to change people's attitudes toward respect and fairness. Teaching individuals not to tolerate bullying or harassment in any environment—whether real or virtual—can contribute to a kinder world for everyone.

How might we ensure that everyone can feel safe, respected, and welcomed in spatial computing, regardless of their identity? Achieving this requires efforts in both technology and promoting respectful interactions among users.

SOCIAL IMPACT AND TECHNOLOGY

Our virtual interactions increasingly influence our lives and shape how we connect with one another. We rely on technologies that guide our experiences, from navigating our surroundings to accessing medical services. As we move forward with advancements in spatial computing, it is crucial to consider the cultural implications of these technologies.

Individual identities and cultural practices are largely determined by our origins and the ethical frameworks we have inherited and absorbed. Spatial computing technologies raise complex questions about what is right and fair across different cultures, legal systems, and social contexts.

In augmented reality (AR), adding digital content to real-world spaces can raise privacy concerns. These concerns include the unauthorized scanning of people's faces, altering significant cultural landmarks, or displaying advertisements that may conflict with local traditions. Additionally, there are issues regarding property rights when AR technology places digital objects in private or sacred areas without permission.

A group of Harvard students demonstrated how Meta's smart glasses, combined with artificial intelligence (AI), could enable real-time identity exposure, which raises significant privacy issues related to wearable technology (Song, 2024). The I-XRAY project uses existing technologies, such as facial recognition and public databases, to access personal information without consent. As Song points out, "The purpose of building this tool is not for misuse, their goal is to raise awareness that all this isn't some dystopian future."

This situation highlights important cultural and ethical tensions between technological innovation and privacy rights. As smart glasses become increasingly similar to regular eyewear, the potential for unnoticed surveillance in public spaces grows.

Virtual reality (VR) complicates these matters further, as individuals from different cultures share virtual environments that may operate under varying rules (Baba, 2023). For instance, if a person from a conservative culture enters a virtual world designed with more relaxed Western values, which set of rules should govern behavior? Legal questions also arise; if someone experiences bullying or harassment in VR, which country's laws should apply?

Both AR and VR pose safety challenges, such as guiding users in real-world hazardous environments or creating misunderstandings between cultures in virtual spaces. Additionally, personalized digital content may confine individuals in "bubbles" that reinforce their beliefs and hinder their understanding of others.

The biggest challenge is figuring out how to use these technologies while respecting the diverse cultures, laws, and values in both the physical and digital worlds. Different regulations and norms come into play in spatial computing, where users may be immersed in an environment vastly different from their physical and cultural contexts. This gap between virtual and physical cultural norms emphasizes the need to develop thorough ethical frameworks.

Where do we learn ethics? This question is not commonly asked and is rarely discussed publicly. We develop our understanding of ethics from various sources throughout our lives, including family, culture, religion, education, and personal experiences. From a young age, our parents and teachers help us understand right from wrong. We learn values such as honesty, fairness, and respect not only at home but also from the people around us every day. Just as cultural traditions, religious teachings, and societal traditions influence growth, they also play a role in shaping ethical standards. However, these same influences can sometimes lead to ethical dilemmas when different values conflict—for example, when loyalty to a group clashes with principles of fairness or justice. Ethics helps navigate these complexities by encouraging critical thinking and a broader perspective on moral responsibility.

The development of ethical or unethical behavior in individuals is often shaped by their upbringing and the systems that either promote or discourage specific actions. Ethical behavior is often reinforced when communities, families, and institutions promote values such as fairness, accountability, and empathy.

The opposite of good is harm. When harmful behaviors, such as discrimination, exploitation, or corruption, are accepted or even rewarded, individuals may adopt unethical practices, often without realizing it. This focuses on the importance of ethical education, strong legal systems, and personal reflection in guiding moral development toward principles that promote the well-being of the entire community.

While most of us may not have formal training in ethics, establishing ethical frameworks is essential for creating products and experiences that effectively meet the diverse needs and wants of customers, without causing harm. Developing this ethical foundation requires an awareness of cultures and practices beyond our own. Technology goes beyond borders and cultural divides, enabling us to connect with anyone, anywhere, at any time.

People adapt and change through our varied life experiences, social interactions, and exposure to diverse perspectives. This is what helps us refine our understanding of ethics over time. We are more connected than ever, and technology plays a significant role in our daily lives. The Internet enables people around the world to discuss privacy and ethics; however, the rules and actions of companies often determine how privacy, data rights, and user protections are implemented. This means that individuals must navigate both the company's policies and their country's laws, which can sometimes lead to confusion. For example, Meta (Facebook's parent company) has a uniform privacy policy for users worldwide, but individuals in the EU benefit from stronger privacy protections under the General Data Protection Regulation (GDPR), while those in other countries may not have the same rights. Under GDPR, Europeans have the right to access the data that companies hold about them, correct any inaccuracies, and request the deletion of their information, commonly referred to as the "right to be forgotten." They can also limit how companies use their data in specific ways (GDPR.EU, 2024). In comparison, the regulations in the US are less strict, allowing companies more freedom to collect and utilize personal data, often without needing explicit consent. As a result, Europeans have greater control over the management of their personal data.

This situation raises important questions about who is responsible for keeping user data safe. Companies play a significant role in protecting privacy, but countries also have their own privacy laws. At the same time, individuals need to be aware of how they can protect their own data. Different cultures may also have varying perspectives on what privacy means and how personal information should be handled.

Much of what dictates the way ethics is applied in organizations is through internal actions that eventually make their way to the public realm. Most of the world operates within a capitalist framework, which lacks a built-in ethical code. As a result, society must establish its own ethical standards. Furthermore, in the realm of technology, we're faced with more questions than answers regarding ethics. While capitalism functions within the ethical frameworks created by society, the rapid advancement of technology keeps introducing new ethical challenges that necessitate ongoing discussions and adaptive solutions.

Technology can do amazing things, like helping people connect all over the world. But not everyone has the same access to technology.

Right now, about 2.7 billion people don't have the Internet, especially in places where it's harder to get computers or phones (International Telecommunication Union, 2023). That means they miss out on learning, talking to others, and having fun online.

When people create new technology, they have to make important choices about how it works. For example, should a game share your personal information, or should it keep it private? Should a website be designed for ease of use by people with disabilities? Organizations like Harvard University's Berkman Klein Center for Internet & Society and Oxford's Digital Ethics Lab and Internet Institute focus on ensuring that technology is fair for everyone. Additionally, regulations regarding privacy help protect individuals' personal data.

Embracing an attitude of cultural sensitivity should be considered in technological designs. What is acceptable in one culture may not be acceptable in another. For instance, in some cultures direct eye contact, especially with older adults or authority figures, is seen as aggressive, confrontational, or disrespectful. This may also vary with gender, where prolonged eye contact can be considered inappropriate. Therefore, when designing technologies, it is essential for creators to consider what is fair and respectful to all individuals.

Despite the rapid growth of technology, some individuals are unable to utilize it due to financial constraints or a lack of access to the necessary tools. This limitation can significantly affect important areas such as job acquisition, healthcare access, and education. These issues are connected to the ethical principles of social justice, economics, and basic rights. Organizations like the Electronic Frontier Foundation strive to ensure that everyone has a fair opportunity to benefit from technology.

One aspect of our humanity is our limitations, specifically our abilities, time, and attention. These human constraints in processing information, managing emotions, and understanding complex systems directly shape our cultural ethics. Our limitations influence what we consider fair, reasonable, and morally acceptable in different societies.

These biological and cognitive limits create boundaries within which cultural traditions must operate. For example, our need for rest affects labor ethics, while our cognitive biases influence how we develop ethical frameworks for decision-making. Cultural ethics are deeply rooted in the values of a society, which in turn shape people's behavior regarding privacy, discrimination, bias, and inclusion. These values manifest in everyday life, affecting how privacy is respected in the workplace, how individuals adhere to rules, and how various cultures perceive authority, teamwork, and time. Additionally, larger systems such as laws and workplace policies reflect these cultural values.

The Institute for Global Ethics explains that ethical decision-making often involves balancing significant tensions, such as choosing between personal benefits and community welfare, being honest versus maintaining relationships, considering short-term versus long-term impacts, and following rules versus making compassionate exceptions (Mutan, 2023).

To make sound ethical decisions, it is essential to first understand your own cultural background and biases. It is also important to acknowledge the limits of your knowledge and the time available for reflection. Carefully evaluating each unique situation can help individuals make fair and thoughtful choices. By following these steps, individuals can better navigate ethical challenges while respecting cultural differences and recognizing human limitations. The ethical dilemmas involving individuality versus community in games highlight how players manage the tension between personal and collective benefits.

In every culture, people enjoy playing card games, and one of the most popular card games worldwide is poker. The rules of the game can vary based on the number of players or cards involved. Whether the game is played in a physical setting or virtually, a fundamental rule remains: cheating is unacceptable. Ethical dilemmas can arise during gameplay without players even realizing it. For instance, if you find yourself in a position where you can see another person's cards, do you choose to look away or take advantage of the information by examining their hand? What is the right choice? What is wrong? Ultimately, it is up to each player to make that decision.

Now, let's explore the comparison between poker and spatial computing through an ethical lens. The way ethics, culture, games, and new technology like VR and AR come together is all about how people make choices. In games like poker and in virtual worlds, people have to make quick decisions about things like sharing information, being honest, and using resources wisely. If someone loves playing poker and is introduced to it through spatial computing such as virtual reality, they can immerse themselves in the game without leaving the comfort of their home. They could find themselves sitting at a poker table, surrounded by players from all over the world.

However, if they notice something unusual, such as a player who never seems to lose, they might begin to wonder if that person is cheating. After conducting some research, they discover that the technology can track various movements, including eye tracking, breathing patterns, and small gestures. This realization leads them to question whether it is ethical to use such technology, as someone with the ability to track this information could potentially predict their opponents' moves.

The person starts to investigate whether advanced tools or AI could be employed to monitor this data. While this technology is fascinating when used fairly, it can also be exploited for cheating in certain circumstances.

In the world of digital design, there is a phrase that is often used: "It depends." Context is an important factor to consider when deciding the next right step, especially because spatial computing can distort reality. Designers should aim to create experiences that enhance reality rather than distort it, ensuring clear transparency about any augmentations. Additionally, it is essential to consider both the intended and the unintended effects on user perception and well-being across different contexts.

In games that mix the digital and real worlds, it is important to make sure everyone feels included and respected, no matter where they come from or what their interests are. Games should not trick people into playing longer than they want to, and they should be fun for everyone. Just like in real life, fairness and respect make games better for all. As technology grows and new ways to play are created, remembering these ideas will help make sure that gaming stays exciting, safe, and enjoyable for years to come.

The connection between game strategy—as in Sun Tzu's *The Art of War*—and ethics provides important lessons about making smart choices and playing fair. Sun Tzu, a renowned military strategist from ancient China, emphasized the importance of understanding in order to implement strategies involving deception, resource management, and timing (Sun Tzu cited in Crainer, 2003). These concepts are still relevant today in modern gaming, from strategy video games to VR and AR. In games, players often use tactics to outsmart their opponents, strategically manage their resources, and carefully consider their moves.

When addressing ethics, or the principle of doing what is right, games must strike a balance between fair play, honesty, and respect for others. This balance can sometimes become challenging, as competition may push players to test boundaries. This is particularly true in spatial computing, where it is vital to ensure that participants feel safe. Creators should aim to minimize risks of accidents or disorientation during immersive experiences, and respect players' personal space and data. Just as in traditional games, where following rules enhances enjoyment, digital games should clearly communicate what data they collect from players and how this information is used.

Furthermore, games should not manipulate players into spending more time than they intended and must be welcoming to everyone, regardless of their backgrounds or interests. Inclusion is especially critical as these games integrate the digital and physical realms in new and exciting ways. Fairness and respect are essential in making spatial computing enjoyable for all. As we develop innovative ways to play in mixed reality, adhering to these principles will help ensure that gaming remains a fun and safe experience for years to come, allowing us to explore incredible new avenues for play and learning together.

Extended Reality Safety Intelligence (XRSI) is an organization that aims to promote privacy, inclusivity, human rights, and safety in spatial computing. They have developed a framework comprising four crucial aspects: evaluation, assessment, management, and prevention. Understanding the root cause of a problem is essential for effective long-term solutions, which is why evaluation is so critical. Assessment and management give creators the necessary information to include privacy features in their experiences. Planning actions before problems arise is essential for ensuring safety, so prevention is a crucial aspect of their framework. The four areas are interdependent, for the following reasons:

One cannot effectively assess without first evaluating; management cannot be done without assessment data; future issues cannot be prevented without learning from management experience; and you cannot know if prevention works without evaluation.

Typically, Social VR platforms have general rules of use outlined in their terms of service. Unfortunately, many users do not read these terms. If people took the time to understand the terms of service, it could lead to greater awareness of what is allowed, establish accountability for breaking codes of conduct, and potentially open up for a cultural shift where people who follow the guidelines become more familiar with behavior. This, in turn, could make exploitative or harmful behavior less acceptable. One significant concern in Social VR is the potential for adults to pose as children in these spaces. This raises important questions about how we can ensure children's safety in virtual environments.

Privacy is a fundamental human right that empowers individuals to protect their identities, thoughts, and actions from unwanted intrusion or manipulation. It allows people to exist and interact in both physical and digital spaces without fear of surveillance, judgment, or exploitation.

Different cultures have distinct perspectives on the concept of privacy and its value. In Japanese culture, for example, privacy is largely about maintaining social harmony by establishing clear boundaries between public and private life, known as uchi/soto. Personal information is carefully guarded, with a strong emphasis on protecting collective privacy rather than focusing solely on individual privacy (Dornhege, 2019).

In contrast, many Northern European cultures, such as Germany and Sweden, prioritize individual privacy rights. This is reflected in strict data-protection laws, careful management of personal information, and well-defined boundaries around private spaces. These societies often view privacy as essential to individual autonomy and democratic freedom (DLA Piper, 2025).

In some Asian cultures, privacy is often viewed through the lens of family honor and collective responsibility. In these contexts, privacy is more about safeguarding family reputation and maintaining social structures than about individual rights. Personal information tends to be shared freely within family networks but is carefully controlled outside of them, leading to a layered understanding of privacy that contrasts sharply with Western individualistic models (Mishra and Basu, 2014).

Asking questions about privacy helps us understand the crucial choices that individuals and organizations make to protect information. It is important to differentiate between personal privacy and organizational policies so that we can comprehend how decisions are made and how information is utilized.

For example, individuals may hold beliefs or preferences or exhibit behaviors that do not align with those of their employers or affiliated organizations. This divergence could range from political views to lifestyle choices. The context in which an individual's actions occur and their implications for personal and organizational ethics highlight the intricacies of the modern privacy landscape.

Consider an employee using a company-issued head-mounted display for work, where all actions performed through the device could reflect the individual's and the company's reputation. In such cases, behavior that might seem personal or harmless in a different setting could have serious professional consequences. For instance, if an employee, while wearing the device in a public or mixed-reality environment, whistles at a woman on the street, it could be recorded, reviewed, or even broadcast within a workplace network. Such an action could be deemed harassment or misconduct, leading to disciplinary measures, including possible termination. Similarly, making an offhand joke or flirtatious comment toward someone of the same or opposite sex might not be inherently unethical. Still, it could be perceived as inappropriate, depending on cultural norms, company policies, or the context in which the interaction occurs.

This creates a complex ethical tension between personal freedoms and professional accountability, as actions performed in an augmented or virtual space can blur the boundaries between private and public behavior. An employee who casually places a bet on the outcome of a soccer match while using the device may believe it's a private action. Still, if the employer monitors or logs the device, it could be seen as violating workplace policies on gambling, financial ethics, or the use of company resources.

The challenge with such technology is that it expands the workplace beyond physical office spaces, making personal behavior more visible and subject to professional scrutiny in ways employees may not fully anticipate. This illustrates the complex interplay between individual privacy, personal values, organizational expectations, and ethical considerations. It emphasizes the importance of clarifying boundaries, understanding the potential consequences of one's actions, and creating an environment where personal and organizational ethics are respected and balanced.

As companies embrace spatial computing and mixed-reality tools, the question becomes: How much control should an employer have over an individual's actions when work and private life increasingly overlap?

TECHNOLOGY AND HUMAN EXPERIENCE

Technology has raised a series of questions that humanity has yet to address. These include: What are our ethical boundaries, and who defines them? What roles do the technologies we use daily play in our lives? What is the psychological impact of living in virtual environments? How do these technologies affect our relationships with others? Additionally, what is the environmental impact of technologies such as AI? Many of these areas are being researched thoroughly throughout the world. It is important to remember that everything is evolving, and changes in technology are happening rapidly. The best way to understand where we are headed is by exploring where we have been.

The history of technology reveals a clear pattern: Each breakthrough brings forth new ethical questions. We witnessed this with the Internet, where issues of privacy, security, and intellectual property rights emerged more quickly than we could address them. Now, spatial computing faces similar challenges. Currently, there are no established ethical guidelines for AR and VR, even as these technologies become increasingly integrated into our daily lives.

Different cultures have unique ways of understanding ethics, values, and morals. What is considered right or wrong in one country may not be viewed the same way in another. For example, in some cultures picking up a hat at an outdoor market without asking for permission and trying it on is acceptable, while in others it may be seen as rude. Additionally, the way people greet each other varies; in some places a handshake is customary, while in others people may greet each other with a kiss on the cheek. These cultural differences influence how individuals perceive honesty, respect, and fairness in everyday life.

However, some ethical concerns transcend cultural boundaries and impact everyone, regardless of their location. A significant example is how we behave and protect ourselves online. The Internet has highlighted the importance of personal data, privacy, and respectful communication everywhere. Regardless of cultural background, no one wants their personal information to be stolen or to be exploited online.

Developing ethical frameworks is not a straightforward task, as they must operate on three levels: personal choices, social relationships, and cultural norms. This presents a complex challenge that we need to address as technology continues to transform how we connect and interact with one another.

In 2016, a Snapchat lens created an overlay that depicted an animated caricature of an East Asian person, featuring slanted eyes and bucked teeth. This portrayal was widely criticized for promoting racist stereotypes. The historical roots of this depiction trace back to the early 1900s, associated with the concept of "Yellow Peril," which depicted East Asians using negative imagery such as apes, lesser beings, and madmen (Dower, 1986). This historical context is crucial for understanding many ethical decisions made by individuals, societies, and cultures. Some observers argued that Snapchat's decision to launch this lens perpetuated stereotypes that have existed for over a century.

Was it ethical to create such a lens? Did the responsible parties conduct adequate research before its launch? This situation highlights the crucial need for thorough research, diverse perspectives, and ethical review processes in technology design.

Many people found the Snapchat filter offensive because it promoted harmful stereotypes. This incident prompted Snapchat to reevaluate its policies regarding acceptable content. When assessing new features, it is

Figure 1.3 Snapchat.

Source: Reproduced from Adam Przezdziek (2015). https://www.flickr.com/photos/67683836@N02/16910572286. Licensed under a Creative Commons Attribution-ShareAlike 2.0 Generic (CC BY-SA 2.0).

essential to weigh the potential harm against the benefits, ensuring that users have an experience that is respectful and not offensive (Figure 1.3).

Due to the highly immersive nature of spatial computing, individuals may experience lasting effects from even a single encounter with AR or VR technologies, though this is rare. The surreal qualities of these technologies can create a sense of realism that can be particularly strong in younger individuals, who tend to be more open to such experiences. While many existing AR and VR tools are primarily designed for entertainment, there is a less obvious aspect of their potential long-term effects that deserves further investigation.

WHEN PROGRESS MEETS CULTURE

French cultural theorist Paul Virilio (1999) once said, "When you invent the ship, you invent the shipwreck." Although technology has its advantages, this quote illuminates how the invention of something great can also have negative consequences. As we move forward with the increased use of technology, privacy and safety issues often appear.

Unlike a map, which clearly lays out the boundaries between countries, cultural lines are nonlinear. People can simultaneously belong to multiple cultures, and these cultural affiliations can evolve throughout their lives. This nonlinear perspective on culture provides us with a multidimensional view that involves various layers, including geography, profession, age-related perspectives, online communities, hobbies, and more. Each country has its own culture, along with subcultures within it. Depending on the specific culture, the handling of technology and ethical issues can vary significantly, particularly in areas such as data privacy and protection, AI and algorithmic bias, digital access and inclusion, cultural appropriation, and communication expectations.

As we progress with technologies within our various cultures, privacy continues to be a major issue. Many individuals do not fully understand what privacy entails or how their personal information can be misused. When data is leaked or stolen, it can result in identity theft, where someone impersonates you to access your accounts, funds, or private information. These risks apply to spatial computing and are especially alarming when it comes to our healthcare.

Another significant challenge is the variation in privacy regulations around the world. There is no universal set of standards, as every country—and even different cultures—has its own perspective on what privacy should involve. Some regions enforce strict laws to safeguard individuals' data, while others permit companies and governments greater access to personal information. This inconsistency complicates the creation of clear, global rules for online privacy and security.

Culture consists of patterns, explicit and implicit, of and for behavior acquired and transmitted by symbols, constituting the distinctive achievements of human groups, including their embodiment in artifacts; the essential core of culture consists of traditional (i.e., historically derived and selected) ideas and especially their attached values; culture systems may, on the one hand, be considered as products of action, on the other, as conditional elements of future action.

(Kroeber & Kluckhohn, 1952)

Different countries use the same technology but adapt it in ways that align with their cultural values. Cultural attitudes toward technology are shaped by the diverse social systems present in various societies. While examining individualistic versus collectivist mindsets provides one perspective on cultural differences, it is just one aspect of the complexities within cultures.

Individualistic cultures, such as those in the United States and many Western countries, prioritize personal freedom and independence. In these societies, technology is typically designed to enhance individual control. This is exemplified by personal smartphones, customized apps, and social media platforms that allow users to express their unique opinions.

In 2021, Apple introduced a feature focused on privacy and user control, called App Tracking Transparency (ATT) in iOS 14.5. This feature gives users the power to block apps from tracking their data across other apps and websites (Apple, 2025). This update aligns with Western individualist values by prioritizing personal control over data privacy rather than allowing companies to track users.

In collectivist cultures, individuals prioritize working together as a group rather than focusing solely on themselves. These cultures can be found in regions such as Africa, Japan, and China. In these societies, technology is developed to benefit the entire community rather than just an individual. Instead of emphasizing personal choices and customization—like in the US—technology is typically utilized to improve the quality of life for everyone.

For example, Africa's mobile money revolution, M-Pesa, which launched in Kenya, has transformed how Africans send and receive money, especially in rural areas. Instead of relying on traditional banking, people use mobile phones for payments, loans, and savings (World Bank, 2018). Unlike Western digital payment systems that focus on individual transactions, M-Pesa supports family and community-based financial networks. Many users pool money together for communal needs, such as school fees and medical emergencies.

Cultures are shaped by numerous factors, including religious beliefs, social hierarchies, property rights, family structures, courtship practices, gender dynamics, conflict-resolution approaches, and deeply held convictions about unacceptable behaviors.

All these elements influence how societies perceive and adopt technology. While we often have high expectations for what technology can achieve, these expectations are filtered through our beliefs, traditions, systems, and social structures. The differences between individual and collective approaches to technology use become evident in how various cultures utilize digital tools and spaces, particularly regarding their attitudes toward privacy, data sharing, and security measures.

This distinction can be observed through different privacy regulations, such as the European Union's General Data Protection Regulation (GDPR) and China's Personal Information Protection Law, which seeks to balance collective and individual interests. For example, technology like WeChat, a popular messaging app in China, emphasizes shared social features, while Western apps like WhatsApp prioritize individual privacy and offer end-to-end encryption. These differences reflect varying attitudes toward data sharing.

Human behavior is shaped by lived experiences, and culture plays a significant role in influencing that behavior. However, the complexities of culture depend on the context of a situation, including factors such as migration from people's places of origin, personal experiences, and the impact of technology.

Research into cultural variations shows significant differences in how personal information is valued and protected across different societies. A comprehensive study on cross-cultural privacy behaviors by Fleming et al. (2021) identifies complex patterns regarding the valuation and protection of personal information. The study analyzed participants from the UK, the US, and India, demonstrating that cultural background significantly influences how individuals value their personal data and how they take steps to protect it.

Participants from India, representing a more collectivist society, displayed stronger links between the value placed on data and their privacy protection behaviors compared to participants from the UK and US. Additionally, the research went beyond national comparisons to examine individual cultural values. It found that individuals who prioritize group harmony and the desire to "fit in" are more likely to actively protect their valuable personal data, regardless of their nationality. This indicates that privacy behaviors are influenced by both broader societal culture and individual cultural values, with collectivist orientations generally resulting in a stronger relationship between data-valuation and -protection efforts (Fleming et al., 2021).

While Western companies, such as Google, Meta, and Apple, currently lead in global technology development, there is a pressing need to explore how these technologies can be adapted to better reflect and respect diverse cultural practices. As we create virtual worlds through spatial computing, we must consider what it means to have a safe experience—both individually and collectively. Is safety reserved for a select few, or should it be accessible to everyone? What implications does this have for intercultural communication and interactions within spatial computing? The answers to these questions can vary depending on the context.

Several ethical dilemmas arise when dealing with different cultures. For example, scanning an environment is often used in spatial computing for various uses; for example, the scanning of religious sites may be allowed in some places and not in others. In 2015, advanced laser scanning technology allowed art historian Andrew Tallon to create a virtual clone of Paris's Notre-Dame Cathedral. This digital twin captured the medieval building's entire structure with remarkable 5-millimeter accuracy, documenting everything from its massive architectural features to its tiniest ornamental details. The scanning process produced a perfect virtual copy that preserved every aspect of the cathedral's design (Church Heritage EU, 2023). The scan was instrumental in rebuilding the church after a 2019 fire destroyed a large part of the building. The three-dimensional scan was allowed because France has relatively open policies regarding three-dimensional scanning of historical buildings and many European landmarks have been scanned without significant pushback.

In Japan, various companies and tourists have sought to take photographs of temples but often encounter restrictions imposed by temple authorities (Japan National Tourism Organization, 2024). Additionally, Japan's Act on the Protection of Cultural Properties mandates that visitors obtain a permit to photograph certain designated cultural properties (Japan Center for International Cooperation in Conservation, n.d.). Temples are viewed as sacred spaces, and any reproduction of these images may be considered disruptive or disrespectful. The concept of sacred space in Japanese culture differs significantly from Western perspectives. In Japan, the physical and spiritual realms are often regarded as interconnected, which makes the act of reproducing sacred spaces through photography or digital scanning a complex cultural issue. The ethical implications of this situation extend beyond mere legal restrictions to encompass more profound cultural considerations regarding respect, spirituality, and the suitable use of technology in sacred spaces. This perspective contrasts with Western views, where documentation is generally seen as a form of preservation rather than a potential source of disruption.

Given these cultural differences, determining ethical behavior can be challenging. It is essential to consider what constitutes unethical conduct in this context. Unethical actions are those that violate social norms or are deemed unacceptable in public settings, whereas ethical actions typically align with social standards and are publicly acceptable.

One aspect to consider with spatial computing is the intercultural aspect of who might be using or creating an experience. If you are in a VR environment, you could be in Los Angeles, California, and interacting with someone in Accra, Ghana. Understanding various cultures is important when creating experiences in spatial computing because the last thing you want to do is insult or demean an entire culture.

DECEPTIVE USER EXPERIENCES

In a virtual space where users interact through avatars, social interactions and gameplay are essential features that contribute to the immersive experience on popular platforms. Imagine joining an environment but unable to leave a specific area because a recurring call to action keeps pulling you back. In a 2023, leak by Frances Haugen, internal research from Meta revealed that the company intentionally designs its platforms to enhance user retention, prioritizing the time users spend in the virtual environment over their well-being (Milmo, 2021).

This isn't the first documented case of deceptive user experiences. The ethical implications of such practices include tricking users into actions they did not intend to take, exploiting human psychology, and providing users with fewer choices—often without their awareness of being manipulated. When people recognize a pattern, they frequently begin to document it, as demonstrated by Dr. Harry Brignull.

Dr. Brignull, who holds a PhD in cognitive science and has consulted with major organizations worldwide, popularized the term "deceptive patterns." He created a website called Deceptive Patterns to identify those who purposely manipulate their customers. Many users encounter deceptive patterns when attempting to cancel a subscription, facing difficulties that prevent them from completing tasks easily. These patterns are seen as unethical, and Brignull established his site to raise awareness and give names to these tactics, such as disguised ads.

Immersive technologies are bringing familiar design practices from web and mobile environments into uncharted territory, creating new opportunities for deception. While traditional misleading tactics like visual interference still exist in Extended Reality (XR) and virtual worlds, the distinct characteristics of immersive technology enable more sophisticated manipulation. Research indicates immersive technologies present new opportunities for manipulative design patterns (Future of Privacy Forum, 2024).

The enhanced realism and the blending of virtual and physical elements in immersive environments make it easier to subtly influence users' perceptions and behaviors. This effect is particularly potent when these technologies are combined with AI that mimics human interaction. Moreover, immersive technologies collect new types of personal data, such as eye tracking, which users may not fully understand, leading to potential privacy vulnerabilities. The innovative interfaces and increasingly realistic AI-generated content in these spaces create fresh opportunities for deceptive design patterns.

The features that make immersive technologies valuable for fields like healthcare, education, and entertainment also heighten their potential for manipulation. The multi-modal nature of these experiences—combining visual, audio, and haptic elements—offers more avenues for persuading users or obscuring information. Advanced devices, such as neurotechnology (which encompasses systems that directly interface with the brain or nervous system to monitor, analyze, or influence neural activity), could monitor and alter mental states.

To mitigate these risks, organizations should:

(1) design clear disclosures that leverage the strengths of immersive technology;
(2) help regulators and the public understand the potential for manipulation techniques; and
(3) support further research on how users can be deceived in immersive environments.

The risks become even more pronounced when AI is involved, as immersive environments provide rich data for creating highly targeted influence campaigns. For example, research has demonstrated that subtle AI-driven modifications to facial expressions can impact voting behavior. Combining AI's real-time learning capabilities with immersive technology's ability to generate convincing physical experiences could significantly enhance the effectiveness of manipulative design.

Data collection can be a deceptive pattern when people don't know that it is being collected or what it is being used for—when people are not given transparency, they are not being told that the data may be used against them. For example, private data leaks happen quite frequently. In addition, someone's data could be used to form a discrimination and bias against them when they want to make a major purchase such as a home.

Deceptive patterns are incorporated by design to gain something from the people using the product. There is an opportunity within spatial computing to move forward without deceiving others so they don't experience data breaches, loss of privacy, mistrust from consumers, or negative experiences. There are choices to be made when creating an experience, and people can choose to be ethical.

VIRTUAL SPACES, REAL IMPACT

Interactions with technology can have both positive and negative impacts on people's lives and mental well-being. On the positive side, technology provides access to information, medical resources, connection, and communication. However, it can also lead to negative effects such as cognitive overload (when our brains receive too much information at once), excessive screen time, and instances of cyberbullying or harassment.

A notable study conducted by Facebook and leaked by former data scientist Frances Haugen showcased the impact of social media on young girls. Known as the Instagram Teen Annotated Research (2021), the study utilized data from focus groups, diary studies, and online surveys. *The Wall Street Journal* reported on these findings:

> Among the most concerning findings was that among users who reported suicidal thoughts, 13% in the UK and 6% in the US traced them back to Instagram. Another transatlantic study found more than 40% of Instagram users who reported feeling "unattractive" said the feeling began on the app; about a quarter of the teenagers who reported feeling "not good enough" said it started on Instagram.
>
> (Gayle, 2021)

Building on Facebook's findings, NYU Professor Jonathan Haidt's 2023 book, *The Anxious Generation* argued that social media is a major factor in rising mental health issues among Gen Z. Everything is done by design, and Haidt's research suggests that these effects are not accidental but result from business models designed to maximize engagement, often at the expense of people's well-being. Knowing that most people pick up their device first thing in the morning before they get out of bed is alarming. Within spatial computing environments where people may immersed, their sense of presence can produce new mental and social side effects (Haidt, 2024).

MINIMIZING UNCERTAINTY

In project management, a risk register identifies and mitigates risks. When a concept is created for spatial computing, a risk register is one way to examine ethical issues through multiple lenses. The first step is describing the risk. For example, in social VR, children risk being exposed to content inappropriate for their age. Therefore, the next step is to categorize the chance of children's exposure to content unsuitable for a young audience, whether technical or environmental. After categorization, the register should identify who would handle the risk, and whether it would be an individual or a team. For example, knowing that online harassment is an issue on the Web, an organization could assess that harassment might be similar in an XR environment, such as in the VR chat example. Therefore, the likelihood of these types of situations would need to be evaluated. And lastly, there would need to be a way to mitigate the risks identified and include strategies and plans for the best- and worst-case scenarios. For example, as there is more than likely a high incidence of harassment in the XR environment, recordings may offer some solution to the issue.

EMERGING TECHNOLOGIES

Spatial computing is an emerging field with the potential to transform many aspects of our lives, including education, healthcare, entertainment, and gaming. However, it is crucial to establish culturally relevant and sensitive principles within local contexts to ensure that spatial computing serves the needs of its users. It is important to recognize that the world is diverse, with cultures where people hold different values and beliefs based on their backgrounds and experiences.

The use of computer technology in our daily lives began with the Web, and now we have the opportunity to explore possibilities through spatial computing that we never could have imagined.

Organizations can effectively implement technology by establishing clear principles and guidelines, monitoring compVliance, and enforcing consequences for violations. By providing training, incentives, and leadership modeling, ethics can be integrated into daily operations rather than treated as separate or secondary issues. The introduction of guidelines in the Web industry, such as the General Data Protection Regulation (GDPR), which was implemented in 2018, has imposed limitations on the use of personal data. This regulation requires businesses and organizations that process personal data to ensure greater transparency and provide users with more control over data collection and usage within the European Union. Additionally, the European Accessibility Act, enacted in 2025, mandates that products and services be made more accessible to older adults and people with disabilities. By connecting the Web to spatial computing, we can draw insights into how to apply these lessons and develop more immersive technology.

Learning from web development and usage, we can create better virtual environments that promote equity and fairness. A fundamental principle that emerged from web development is the importance of having an open and accessible platform that facilitates easy sharing and collaboration. Similarly, in spatial computing it is crucial that technology is accessible to all individuals, regardless of socio-economic status or technical expertise.

Another vital lesson from the Web industry is the necessity for transparency and accountability in how data is collected, stored, and used. This is especially important in spatial computing, where vast amounts of data are generated and processed. Therefore, establishing clear guidelines and policies regarding data privacy and security is essential to protect users and ensure that their data is used ethically and responsibly.

By establishing culturally relevant principles and learning from the development and use of the Web, we can create better virtual environments that are equitable, fair, and accessible to everyone. Achieving this will require collaboration and cooperation among industry, academia, government, and civil society to ensure that spatial computing is implemented in a way that reflects the needs and values of the people in each region where it is used.

DIVERSITY, EQUITY, INCLUSION AND ACCESSIBILITY

Imagine a future where diversity, equity, inclusion, and accessibility are outlawed in the US, but that the European Accessibility Act (EAA), which mandates digital accessibility, remains in full force across Europe. This creates a paradox: In one part of the world, laws suppress discussions around systematic barriers, while in another, regulations require designing for inclusivity. Without DEIA policies, US tech companies may stop prioritizing inclusive design, leading to AR/VR spaces that ignore race, gender, disability, and other marginalized identities. This could mean the world would be fractured where access depends on geography. This could lead to the erasing of representations of marginalized communities where there could be a ban on creating AR history overlays of civil rights protests, for example.

The future of digital identity, history, and inclusion depends on our daily choices because, in spatial computing, what isn't represented might as well not exist. We have to ask, will digital reality become a mirror of oppressive laws reflecting exclusion and inequality? Or will people find ways to embed ethics into accessibility frameworks to ensure diverse voices remain a part of the digital world?

Building an Ethical House

With over 8 billion people living on the planet, speaking more than 7,000 languages, and representing diverse cultures and beliefs, our ways of living and the technologies we use are shaped by our unique experiences. If we compare the field of spatial computing to building a home, the most necessary aspect is the foundation. A weak foundation results in an unstable structure, regardless of how advanced or beautiful the house may appear. Similarly, if spatial computing is not built on a foundation of ethics, privacy, and inclusivity, it risks collapsing under mistrust and inequity.

ETHICS AS THE FOUNDATION

Spatial computing goes beyond technology; it involves people and their physical environments. When using AR or VR, users often need to scan their surroundings, disclose their location, and provide data such as height and movement patterns. This process is akin to surveying land before constructing a home, ensuring every detail is mapped out before the building begins. However, just as a home should offer security and privacy to its residents, spatial computing must protect users from intrusion and misuse.

FRAMING THE WALLS: MAPPING AND MOVEMENT

When a person uses spatial computing devices, the technology must understand their environment to function properly. Imagine the device as an architect, meticulously creating a detailed three-dimensional map of the room. It utilizes cameras and sensors to detect walls, furniture, and objects, all while tracking how the user moves within that space. This scanning process results in a digital replica of one's physical world—a virtual blueprint that enables interaction but raises ethical concerns.

DOORS AND WINDOWS: ACCESS TO PERSONAL SPACES

A home has doors and windows that control what is visible to outsiders and ensure security for those inside. In spatial computing, scanning an environment may grant companies access to personal details such as what a person owns, how they arrange their space, and even their behaviors within it. The critical question becomes: Who holds the keys to this digital house? If a company accesses this data, how is it used, stored, and protected? Without ethical safeguards, users may find themselves in a home where the walls are transparent instead of protective.

A House for Everyone: Designing for Diversity

Not all homes look the same. Cultural, geographical, and personal preferences influence architectural styles, layouts, and materials. Similarly, spatial computing should not offer a one-size-fits-all experience. It must respect cultural norms, accessibility needs, and individual comfort levels. An ethically built system ensures that people from diverse backgrounds and of diverse abilities can navigate and interact with spatial computing in ways that resonate with their experiences.

Building a Future-proof Home

A well-constructed home endures the test of time because it is designed with care, intention, and a solid foundation. The same principle applies to spatial computing. It can become a safe, adaptive, and empowering space for all if constructed with ethics at its core in order to ensure privacy, inclusivity, and respect for human diversity. However, if built carelessly, it risks becoming a structure that alienates, exploits, and erodes trust. The foundation is everything. How we build determines how we live.

QUESTIONS FOR REFLECTION

1. What risks are associated with spatial computing for children?
2. How does your application ensure cultural sensitivity, inclusivity, and privacy while complying with relevant regulations in different regions?
3. Can you identify any ethical dilemmas that could arise in your projects?
4. Suppose a designer is allowed to work on a project with the military. They are asked to create a three-dimensional world with realistic scenes of war, including imagery of a dog being exploded by a bomb. The request made the designer feel uneasy, and they decided they were not the person for the job because the project did not align with their ethics and morals. What might you do if you were in this scenario? Would you do the work, or turn down the assignment and potentially lose your job?

PROJECT FOR CONSIDERATION

Case Study: Ethical Considerations for VR/AR Research Project

Research Proposal: A researcher proposes studying how VR and AR affect memory and learning. The study involves participants using immersive technologies for educational content while collecting data on their performance and experiences. How would you evaluate and ensure ethical practices in this VR/AR research project?

Key Ethical Concerns:

1. **Psychological Impact**
   - VR/AR can strongly affect emotions and mental state
   - Risk of causing anxiety or discomfort
   - Need for monitoring participant wellbeing

2. **Privacy and Data Security**
   - Protection of cognitive performance data
   - Secure storage of personal information
   - Prevention of unauthorized access
   - Data anonymization requirements

3. **Informed Consent**
   - Clear communication of study purpose
   - Explanation of potential risks
   - Participant rights and withdrawal options
   - Data usage transparency

Required Safety Measures:

1. **Participant Protection**
   - Regular monitoring during sessions
   - Clear support mechanisms
   - Easy withdrawal process
   - Well-being checks

2. **Data Security**
   - Encryption protocols
   - Secure storage systems

- Access controls
- Anonymization procedures

3. **Consent Process**
   - Detailed information provision
   - Question-and-answer opportunities
   - Clear documentation
   - Ongoing consent checking

Key Questions for Review:

1. How will personal data be protected?
2. What specific security measures are planned?
3. How can participants control their data?
4. What privacy risks exist with these technologies?
5. How will data collection balance with privacy?

By considering the potential harms, suggesting mitigation measures, and seeking additional information from relevant stakeholders, you can ensure the project meets the highest ethical standards and provide valuable feedback to the researcher to address any ethical concerns.

2

The Story of Human–Computer Interaction

WHY DID WE BUILD COMPUTERS?

At the start, computers were built for research purposes, calculations, cracking codes, and sending a man to the Moon. Today computers affect more of us (and even resemble us), and the things of which they are capable (and how they work) are still understood by very few. Most of us use computers daily. The computerized world designed for us decades ago has capabilities that increase each year. Though its future is very uncertain, computers will play a pivotal role and likely become even more deeply intertwined with our physical spaces, our bodies, and our relationships. How did we get here? Why did we come here? What do we do now? And where are we going? These are the questions this chapter attempts to answer as we seek to understand our relationship with the next wave of computers: computers with spatial awareness that are able not only to send us into new worlds but also to fundamentally alter our relationship with the world we live in now.

The 1940s saw the first explorations into what computing could be. Early systems built prior to the Second World War were created to explore a variety of mathematical models, assist in the development and monitoring of other systems, and conduct research. Spurred by competition between Germany and the United States (US) during the war, computing became an essential part of the conflict as both sides sought

Human Spatial Computing. Reginé Gilbert and Doug North Cook, Oxford University Press.
© Reginé Gilbert and Doug North Cook (2026). DOI: 10.1093/9780191966477.003.0002

to find new ways of using advanced computing systems to encrypt messages, plan air attacks and artillery output, and conduct research.

The US Army made heavy use of human "computers" in the 1940s, many of them women trained to solve difficult calculation problems using sets of predefined parameters and structures. Many of these women were tasked with working on complex calculations for the Ballistic Research Laboratory as the Army sought to increase the effectiveness of systems already deployed and to develop new systems with greater accuracy. The training of competent human workers capable of performing the complex work of computing was expensive and had to contend with the hard limits of human capabilities and output. The competitive drive to develop increasingly powerful and accurate weapons systems highlighted the need for governments around the globe to push to create more capable machines to replace the limited amount of human output that could be coordinated.

> A human being multiplying two 10-digit numbers by hand without any mechanical aids takes about 5 minutes. The traditional desk calculator of the 1940s spent about 10–15 seconds on this task, and thus such a machine provides a speed-up of between 20 and 30 times. This of course is the value of such a device. However, in both cases the human must then record the results by hand on paper, whereas all the automatic machines do this without human intervention.
>
> (Goldstine, 2001)

The era of human computation ended abruptly in the 1950s as a result of the rise of computers created by companies and laboratories around the globe. Researchers in India, Denmark, Russia, Norway, France, and many other countries were all working toward creating more powerful, affordable, and capable computing machines. Tasks that were difficult for humans became automatic and rapid, and allowed researchers to conceive of projects that would have been impossible for humanity to execute on its own. The desires for expanded human capabilities and automated work, as well as the competitive drive to win the "war of machines," put computer development on the fast track; development became a massive focus for government research dollars and consumer product development, resulting in eventual integration of computers into almost every area of life around the world. Over more than 70 years, computers have transformed from mainframes the size of a small home, capable of executing complex calculations over days and weeks, to pocket-sized wireless devices capable of running dozens of complex stand-alone applications simultaneously while taking a video call.

Billions of users each own a smartphone, making this handheld computer by far the most ubiquitous form of personal computing in the 2020s. In less than 30 years, smartphones have permeated almost every corner of the globe and caused massive shifts in how people relate to one another, date, bank, take photos, shop, listen to music, play games, learn languages, order pizza, and more. In 2023, most major technology companies are betting that spatial computing is the next step in personal computer use, as computers move from users' hands to users' faces. Meta, Google, Apple, Bytedance, Sony, HTC, Valve, and others are all competing to develop the world's leading computer hat—a joke moniker given to head-mounted displays after a typo in a tweet from YouTuber Marques Brownlee referencing the announcement on the Apple Vision Pro went viral (Brownlee, 2023).

Has the time arrived when humanity transitions to living in cyberspace, as depicted in many dystopian science fiction narratives? Or maybe this is another period like the 1990s, when virtual reality (VR) hype saw several companies crash and burn. We'll look through some of the narratives that have guided the development of these technologies; consider the companies, artists, and researchers that have driven these technologies to where they are today; and investigate ways that these technologies may actually help us to become more, rather than less, human.

THE STORIES OF SPATIAL COMPUTING

For as long as we have been able to conceptualize our relationship with machines, we have created fiction to explore how that relationship might evolve. Often, the stories depict how machines might—over time—separate from us the things that make us uniquely human; our souls, our individuality, and our connections to each other. These stories often show a path toward a future where humans have been designed out of existence.

In *Hamlet on the Holodeck*, Janet Horowitz Murray (1997) provides a powerful look into the narratives that have helped shape the development of spatial computing. She highlights the rift between dystopian and utopian narratives as they portray these technologies, what they might become, and how they might alter humanity.

> Which vision of digital storytelling are we to believe? Will the literature of Cyberspace be continuous with the literary traditions of the Beowulf poet, Shakespeare, and Charlotte Brontë as the *Star Trek* producers portray it, or will it be the dehumanizing and addictive sensation machine predicted by the dystopians? Is the optimistic *Star Trek* view too pat and sentimental to be credible at all in the light of Huxleyan criticism?
>
> (Murray, 1997)

By exploring some of these narratives, we may find answers to, warnings about, and insight into how we have arrived at this point in the history of technology where we have built immersive spatial computing systems. Many of these fictional narratives have direct links to later events that they either predicted, inspired, or avoided. By looking at the stories we have told ourselves about our relationship with technology, maybe we can write and explore new narratives that portray a more positive future that hopefully we can build together. The thread that runs through the fiction portraying these technologies runs alongside the history of their development—with some correlation.

In "The Machine Stops," E.M. Forster (1909) describes a world where all of humanity is connected through a single machine, with limited in-person interaction as a result. Humans in this world communicate through glowing "plates" (sound familiar?) and rarely go outside. Forster is one of the earliest writers to conceive of the world full of machines that mediate a significant number of our interactions and seek to mediate (or eliminate) even more. An early exchange between two characters gives a glimpse into the mindset of this world:

> "I want you to come and see me."
> Vashti watched his face in the blue plate.
> "But I can see you!" she exclaimed. "What more do you want?"
> "I want to see you not through the Machine," said Kuno. "I want to speak to you not through the wearisome Machine."
> "Oh, hush!" said his mother, vaguely shocked. "You mustn't say anything against the Machine."
> "Why not?"
> "One mustn't."
>
> (Forster, 1909)

Forster's machine world is one of constant and immediate connectivity to the machine world and simultaneous intense isolation and disconnection from the physical world and in-person connections. While perhaps a fantastical subject in 1909, in the 2020s this is reality. At the end of the story, Kuno and Vashti confront the machine, and as it shuts down, they reflect on how to move forward:

> "Oh, tomorrow—some fool will start the Machine again, tomorrow."
> "Never," said Kuno, "never. Humanity has learnt its lesson."
>
> (Forster, 1909)

As we reflect on the state of technology and human connection in the 2020s, we are heading deeper and deeper into the "machine" that Forster imagined—it is always on, it connects us all, it demands our time, and over time we conform to it. There are few places in the world that have not been connected by smartphones, cellular networks, and personal computers. Spatial computing devices are slowly starting to find their own foothold, and with this comes great existential risks, many of which appear in 20th-century fiction. Spatial computing's development over the last several decades has been a conversation between that fiction and the engineers, designers, and artists who have built the actual technology.

There are plenty of troubling portrayals of the future, like those in Forster's short stories, and also in William Gibson's 1984 novel *Neuromancer* and Neal Stephenson's 1992 novel *Snow Crash*.

Gibson reimagines Forster's "Machine" as a vast network of interconnected computers and systems. Gibson's network is so vast and complex that it is beyond human comprehension, leading to dangerous situations.

> Cyberspace. A consensual hallucination experienced daily by billions of legitimate operators, in every nation, by children being taught mathematical concepts. [. . .] A graphic representation of data abstracted from the banks of every computer in the human system. Unthinkable complexity. Lines of light ranged in the nonspace of the mind, clusters and constellations of data. Like city lights, receding.
>
> (Gibson, 2000)

We must ask ourselves how much we should continue to try and understand the machines that augment our behaviors. No one person can hold all the knowledge needed to build the complex systems we have today—it is a great effort of the collective to develop increasingly complex systems that then help to accelerate their own development. While some scientists, engineers, programmers, and designers have a low-level understanding of current computing systems, most people simply accept the situation. In *Snow Crash*, Neal Stephenson (2000) captures the fatalistic sentiment of many of those who engage deeply with these technologies: "See, the world is full of things more powerful than us. But if you know how to catch a ride, you can go places." The distinction here between capable creators and capable users of technology begins to widen—those able to create powerful technology are not necessarily those who will wield it most powerfully. It is the intention of the user and the capability of the technologies that will dictate their use, not the intention of the creators. We have seen repeatedly throughout history how various technologies are co-opted for new uses.

Developing complex systems, such as the Internet and its protocols, requires the collaborative efforts of experts from various fields. For example, networking, programming, and cybersecurity specialists must work together, as each individual lacks the necessary comprehensive knowledge to understand the system.

Machine-learning algorithms are developed to improve their performance over time. The system can adjust itself as more data is processed, which leads to accelerated capability improvements without constant human intervention.

Most smartphone users do not know the intricate hardware and software components that enable their devices to function. They interact with user-friendly interfaces without needing to understand the underlying technical details.

Individuals who work directly in fields like artificial intelligence (AI), quantum computing, or blockchain technology possess deeper insights into the mechanics of these systems. In contrast, the public might only experience the end products of such technologies.

Despite the complexity of technology, learning to navigate and use it effectively enables people to achieve remarkable feats. Technology's creators might not necessarily be those who use it with the greatest impact.

Social media platforms are used for both positive and negative purposes. The intention and capability of the user determines the impact of the information posted on the platform.

Initially designed for military communication, the Internet is now a global information and communication tool. Technologies often find unexpected applications as users experiment with their possibilities.

Whether or not spatial computing ushers in a predicted dystopia will be partially contingent on legislation aimed at mitigating *unintended* consequences from good and neutral actors and closing as many pathways as possible for bad actors who aim to unleash *intended* consequences. Governments have a history of taking years, if not decades, to provide meaningful legislation regulating the use and adoption of new technologies. To date, most governments have adopted little to no legislation to regulate online privacy, social media use, and the safety of children using all varieties of computing devices. As we sit on the verge of the potential large-scale adoption of spatial computing devices and the mass adoption of advanced AI systems, it is more crucial than ever that legislators, companies, and users work together to push for safe use, ethical consumption, and age limits as we seek to understand the short- and long-term effects on physical and mental health of prolonged use of these devices. Often those capable of taking legislative action succumb to fear or their own insecurity, or never take the time to become knowledgeable enough to work on these complex problems. It is crucial that those who have the power to make significant changes in how these technologies are used overcome that fear, as its "unanticipated consequences should not lead to policy paralysis in this arena, where legislators or policy makers pursue no substantive technology policy or innovation policy to avoid making a mistake" (Cunningham & Link, 2021).

Legislation is not enough to steer us away from creating a dystopian society; we must make a coordinated effort to ensure that humanity takes a positive path. Spatial computing isn't the problem—we are. We choose our own path down this road. According to Murray in *Hamlet on the Holodeck*:

These accounts of a digital dystopia both eroticize and demonize the computer. Cyberpunk surfers are like cowboys on a new frontier or motorcycle hoodlums with a joystick in their hand instead of a motorcycle between their legs. They are outlaw pirates on an endless voyage of exploration throughout the virtual world, raiding and plundering among the invisible data hoards of the world and menaced by the stronger pirate barons who reach in and reprogram their minds.

(Murray, 1997)

PAINTING FOR PRESENCE

How did we end up here, and why did we decide to build spatial computing in the first place? While the developments of VR and augmented reality (AR) in the past 10 years have brought these technologies further into the cultural consciousness, we must go back much further to find the reason why this has happened. The search for more effective means of conveying experiences, memories, and ideas is ancient. We begin in 1400s Italy, where Leonardo da Vinci penned his notes on human perception and the limitations of painting—a treatise that in the 1800s inspired the development of the first stereo-image viewing device. For da Vinci, there was a clearly defined limitation to what painters were able to capture on a flat surface about the true nature of an object—he highlighted that two-dimensional images are incapable of conveying the reality of our three-dimensional world.

> Painters often despair of being able to imitate Nature, from observing, that their pictures have not the same relief, nor the same life, as natural objects have in a looking-glass, though they both appear upon a plain surface. They say, they have colours which surpass in brightness the quality of the lights, and in darkness the quality of the shades of the objects seen in the looking-glass; but attribute this circumstance to their own ignorance, and not to the true cause, because they do not know it. It is impossible that objects in painting should appear with the same relief as those in the looking-glass, unless we look at them with only one eye.
>
> (da Vinci, 2014/1802)

Da Vinci's remarks in *A Treatise on Painting* resonated hundreds of years later with Charles Wheatstone, an English scientist and inventor working in the mid-1800s. Wheatstone saw the potential to provide a new method of capturing the reality of objects in a way that preserved more of their essence in answer to how we can convey reality more clearly:

> It is impossible for the artist to give a faithful representation of any near solid object, that is, to produce a painting which shall not be distinguished in the mind from the object itself. When the painting and the object are seen with both eyes, in the case of the painting, two *similar* pictures are project on the retinae, in the case of the solid object the pictures are *dissimilar*; there is therefore an essential difference between the impressions on the organs of sensation

in the two cases, and consequently between the perceptions formed in the mind; the painting therefore cannot be confounded with the solid object. After looking over the works of many authors who might be expected to have made some remarks relating to this subject, I have been able to find but one, which is in the *Trattato della Pittura* of Leonardo da Vinci.

(Wheatstone, 1838)

It was this inspiration from da Vinci that led Wheatstone to invent the first stereoscopic image viewer in 1838—a device that used stereo photograph cards with two images taken from slightly different perspectives and a panel that blocks each eye from seeing the image on the opposing side of the card (Figure 2.1). This creates an effect that gives the

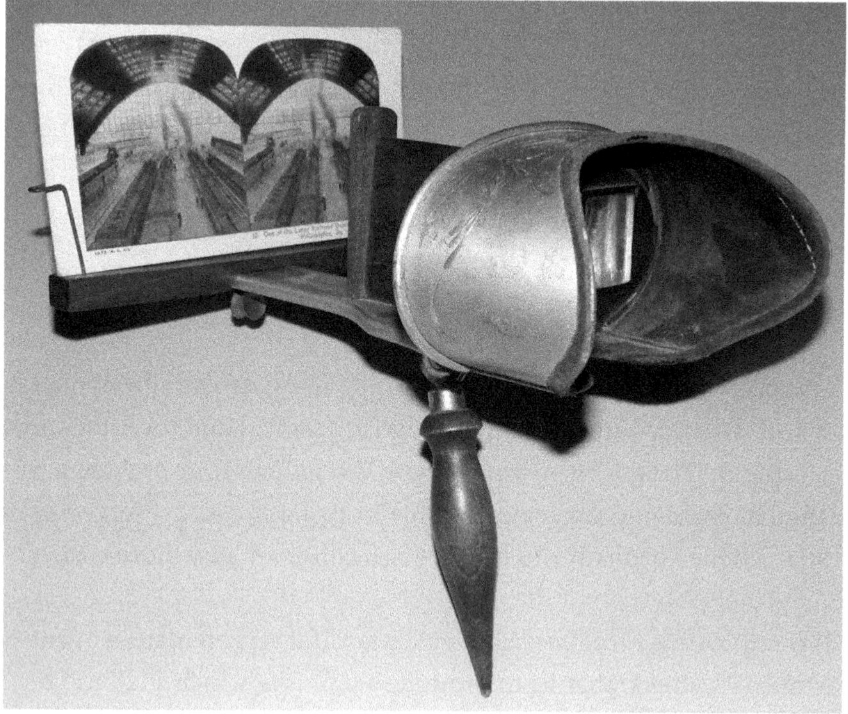

Figure 2.1 Vintage Perfecscope Stereoscope Viewer, 1897 Patent Date.

Source: Reproduced from Joe Haupt (2014). https://www.flickr.com/photos/51764518@N02/15751836930. Licensed under a Creative Commons Attribution-ShareAlike 2.0 Generic (CC BY-SA 2.0).

impression of depth to the viewer and allows them to reconstruct the image in their mind in a way that more closely resembles reality.

When writing about his experience with stereoscopic images, Holmes described them as a revelation—and the next answer to the question posed by da Vinci:

> The first effect of looking at a good photograph through the stereoscope is a surprise such as no painting ever produced. The mind feels its way into the very depths of the picture. The scraggy branches of a tree in the foreground run out at us as if they would scratch our eyes out. The elbow of a figure stands forth so as to make us almost uncomfortable. Then there is such a frightful amount of detail, that we have the same sense of infinite complexity which Nature gives us. A painter shows us masses; the stereoscopic figure spares us nothing—all must be there, every stick, straw, scratch, as faithfully as the dome of St. Peter's, or the summit of Mont Blanc, or the ever-moving stillness of Niagara. The sun is no respecter of persons or of things.
>
> (Holmes, 1859)

In his reflections on the dawn of the stereoscope, Holmes points out that there is magic in the sharing of the infinite complexity of moments, memories, and ideas. Where the stereoscope allowed the sharing of images to move a significant step forward toward a more faithful representation of a moment in time, spatial computing offers the potential not only to present moments in time in even greater detail, but also to move an image beyond faithful representation and into acts of creation. A VR headset puts someone "inside" a simulation of their own home, showing them playback of a 360-degree video, or in a three-dimensional rendering of a new environment, such as exploring an inaccessible or difficult-to-reach site—but we can also use the same device to place a user inside of a synthetic dream world, an imagined alien world, or anything else from our imaginations.

The experiences we can create using modern spatial computing devices go far beyond the attempt of photography to capture a moment in time, and beyond painting and the limitations of the painter's ability, imagination, and skill in abstraction. A painter can capture the idea of a place in a way that can unlock new perspectives, even if it is not photo-realistic. A VR experience can take the user to an entirely new environment or a world that does not exist and allow them to form memories there in the same way that they might form memories in their home. The drive and reasons for the creation of spatial computing devices, software, and experiences are as varied as the experiences themselves.

Some creators seek to entertain, some to enlighten, some to scare, some to line their own pockets, some to manipulate, and some to fulfill a personal fantasy. The creator of the first head-mounted display reveals his own desire in his hope for what he calls "the ultimate display." On the heels of Morton Heilig developing the Sensorama, research engineer Ivan Sutherland began developing head-mounted displays with his team at MIT in the early 1960s:

> Morton Heilig, through a combination of ingenuity, determination, and sheer stubbornness, was the first person to attempt to create what we now call virtual reality. In the 1950s it occurred to him that all the sensory splendor of life could be simulated with "reality machines." Heilig was a Hollywood cinematographer, and it was as an extension of cinema that he thought such a machine might be achieved. With his inclination, albeit amateur, toward the ontological aspirations of science, Heilig proposed that an artist's expressive powers would be enhanced by a scientific understanding of the senses and perception. His premise was simple but striking for its time: if an artist controlled the multisensory stimulation of the audience, he could provide them with the illusion and sensation of first-person experience, of actually "being there."
>
> (Jordan & Packer, 2002)

Heilig was interested in how you might start to incorporate more of the senses into the re-creation of moments in time. Using his background in film, he reimagined the film viewing experience as a multisensory one. His creation, the Sensorama, was a coin-operated machine that simulated multisensory experiences, including one where you ride through New York City, feeling wind generated by the machine, scents to convince your nose, stereoscopic film viewing, and stereo sound. Heilig created an experience that would still be powerful today—even with its limited fidelity, it captures more of the senses directly than any spatial computing device currently in mass production. What Heilig understood very early on is that communicating meaningful input to multiple senses can deepen the viewer's immersion in an experience.

Sutherland would take a very different approach—rooted in the development of advanced display technology. His 1965 text "The Ultimate Display" gives a glimpse into what he hoped to build:

The ultimate display would, of course, be a room within which the computer can control the existence of matter. A chair displayed in such a room would be good enough to sit in. Handcuffs displayed in such a room would be confining, and a bullet displayed in such a room would be fatal. With appropriate programming such a display could literally be the Wonderland into which Alice walked.

(Sutherland, 1965)

A few years later, Sutherland and his team introduced the world to the Sword of Damocles (Figure 2.2), a head-mounted display that relied on a mechanical arm to suspend it from the ceiling to track the head movements of the user, but also because its weight made it too heavy to wear. This first display was essentially a pair of augmented reality glasses that allowed a user to perceive rudimentary three-dimensional line drawings and forms and confirmed that the development of Sutherland's ultimate display was not only possible, but inevitable—we were on our way to Wonderland.

Tom Furness, developer of some of the US Air Force's early head-mounted displays in the late 1960s and into the 1970s, highlights his own desires for the development of more advanced display and multisensory transfer methods for new computing systems. In his 1995 opening to

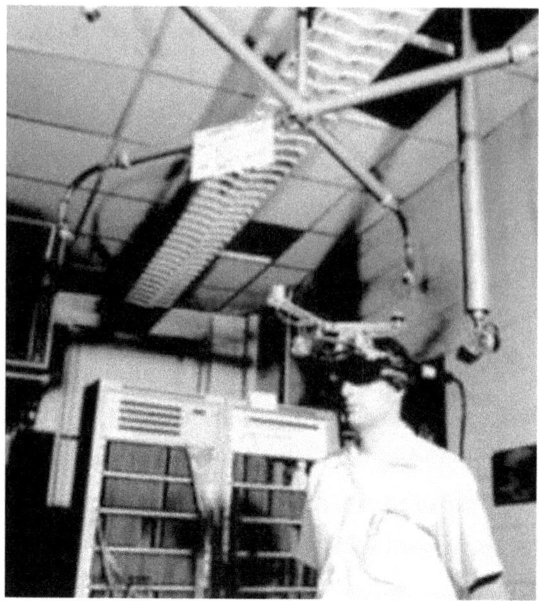

Figure 2.2 Sword of Damocles.

Source: Reproduced from Rosenfeld Media (2020). https://www.flickr.com/photos/
rosenfeldmedia/50511175133. Licensed under a Creative Commons Attribution 2.0
Generic (CC BY-SA 2.0).

Introduction to Virtual Environments and Advanced Interface Design, he
writes:

> Typically, the computer, via a display monitor, only allows a lim-
> ited two-dimensional view of the three-dimensional world we
> live in. For example, when using a computer to design a three-
> dimensional building, what we see and interact with is often only
> a two-dimensional representation of the building, or at most a
> so-called 2½D perspective view. Furthermore, unlike the sounds
> in the real world which stimulate us from all directions and dis-
> tances, the sounds emanating from a computer originate from a
> stationary speaker, and when it comes to touch, with the exception
> of a touch screen or the tactile feedback provided by pressing a key
> or mouse button (limited haptic feedback to be sure), the tools we
> use to manipulate symbols are primitive at best.
>
> (Barfield & Furness, 1995)

During the same time period that Sutherland was working on his head-mounted display, Brazilian artists Lygia Clark and Hélio Oiticica were developing installations and art pieces that explored multisensory experiences using similar forms and ideas and exploring how these forms mediate relationships between multiple viewers—again, exploring the range of how we might gain a greater sense of perception of reality. Simone Osthoff's insightful article on the two artists highlights that there is a clear connection between them and Sutherland's project. She remarks that there are significant "visual and conceptual parallels between Clark's and Oiticica's sensorial creations from the 1960s and 1970s—masks, goggles, hoods, suits, gloves, capes and immersive environments—and early virtual-reality experiments from the 1960s and 1970s, such as Ivan Sutherland's head-mounted display" (Osthoff, 1997).

Clark's and Oiticica's work explored the body's relationship to devices, how interactions mediated by devices alter our perceptions of each other, and how we might find deeper connectivity through full-body interactions. Clark was looking for ways to express deeper truths about the nature of the human experience. In a 1968 letter to Oiticica, Clark identifies the primary nature of embodied experiences: "In all that I do, there really is the necessity of the human body, so that it expresses itself or is revealed as in a first [primary] experience" (Bishop, 2006, p. 110). In this way, Clark's own work connects to Sutherland in its attempt to access the primordial essence of human experience and translate that through something created by a human. Clark's own work resonates with the approaches of Max Bill, the Swiss designer hunted by the Nazis during the Second World War as an anti-fascist artist. As Bill spent significant time in Brazil working with artists, educating designers, and learning from them, it is unsurprising to see connections between Clark's and Bill's work as two artists seeking to create immersive experiences that alter the perception of one's body in the universe. On applying mathematics to art, Bill writes:

As the artist has to forge his concept into unity his vision vouch-safes him a synthesis of what he sees which, though essential to his art, may not be necessarily mathematically accurate. This leads to the shifting or blurring of boundaries where clear lines of division would be supposed. Hence abstract conceptions assume concrete and visible shape, and so become perceptible to our emotions. Unknown fields of space, almost unimaginable hypotheses, are boldly bodied forth. We seem to be wandering through a firmament that has had no prior existence; and in the process of attuning ourself to its strangeness our sensibility is being actively prepared to anticipate still further and, as it were, as yet inconceivable expanses of the infinite.

(Emmer, 1993)

It is this expanse of the infinite that drove Max Bill to construct infinite Möbiuseque forms out of stone. The Möbius strip is a shape that can be imagined simply as the shape formed by attaching the ends of a strip of paper together after a single half-twist. It is a shape with no end and no orientation. Clark constructs those same shapes as a form of handcuff in her own performances and installations. It is that same form that users see when they log in to their Meta Quest VR headsets—the logo of Meta, itself a Möbius strip. In all of this, there is the search for a way to transcend the mundane and find within us something profound by using a device created for that explicit purpose.

THE EYEPHONE MOMENT

There have been several moments during the development of spatial computing devices when developers have been hopeful the technology might become a mass-market device capable of connecting users in new ways. One of those early optimists was Jaron Lanier, who cofounded VPL Research with Thomas Zimmerman, where they created the EyePhone. Jaron Lanier designed and built the first most complete commercially available virtual reality system. It included the Dataglove and the EyePhone head-mounted display. The Dataglove would evolve into the Nintendo Powerglove. The Dataglove was able to track hand gestures through a unique trait of fiber optic cable. If you scratch a fiber optic cable, and shine light through it while it is straight, very little of the light will escape. But if you bend the scratched fiber optic cable, light will escape, and the more you bend it, the more light escapes. This light was measured and then used to calculate finger movements.

(Williamson & Palmer, 2018)

Lanier and his team at VPL picked up the work of their predecessors and packaged it into a complete device—though this was still too early for the quality of experience (and price point) that would lure companies and consumers to purchase such a device. Lanier, reflecting on the skepticism of many of his friends and peers, remembers:

[I]n the 1980s, when the internet was only available to small number of pioneers, I was often confronted by people who feared that the strange technologies I was working on, like virtual reality, might unleash the demons of human nature. For instance, would people become addicted to virtual reality as if it were a drug? Would they become trapped in it, unable to escape back to the physical world where the rest of us live?

(Lanier, 2010)

The closure of VPL in 1998 also marked the end of a potential chapter in the history of spatial computing, where the early company developing these technologies was one with a culture of building tools for creativity and expanded consciousness. In his book *You Are Not a Gadget*, Lanier (who still actively writes about the current state of technology) gives an important reminder about the state of the world, the need for prioritization, and the danger of ignoring digital culture:

We need to address global warming, shift to a new energy cycle, avoid wars of mass destruction, support aging populations, figure out how to benefit from open markets without being disastrously vulnerable to their failures, and take care of other basic business.

But digital culture and related topics like the future of privacy and copyrights concern the society we'll have if we can survive these challenges.

(Lanier, 2010)

THE DAWN OF OCULUS

In March 2011, researchers Mark Bolas, Evan A. Suma, David M. Krum, and J. Logan Olson presented a paper for the Institute of Electrical and Electronics Engineers that showcased an innovative approach to the head-mounted display. Citing Sutherland's work in their writing, almost 60 years later they combined several technologies that had enjoyed rapid development in consumer video games and mobile phone technology.

We have demonstrated how to integrate stereoscopic lens assemblies, game engine software, and smartphones to create a head mounted display. This smartphone-based head mounted display is a unique platform since it combines a virtual reality display and powerful graphic computers into a single unit. With an appropriate tracking technology, this head mounted display can be wireless. By sharing the specifications and techniques that we have used, we hope to enable and encourage others to build and improve on such displays.

(Olson et al., 2011)

A few months later Bolas would receive an inquiry from someone eager to learn from their team—looking for a job, an internship, offering to do anything they needed around the lab—and in July 2011, he offered Palmer Luckey (who would then go on to found Oculus) a job as lab technician in his Mixed Reality Lab at USC's Institute of Creative Technologies (Harris, 2019). It was this job that gave Luckey—who at the time was living in a trailer on his parent's driveway—the access, mentorship, and network that he needed in order to build the Rift (Figure 2.3), which kicked off the first wave of consumer spatial computing devices. Luckey took inspiration from the work of Bolas and his colleagues and built a device that brought all the current advancements in display technology and real-time computer graphics together, in the process building a VR company that Facebook purchased for $2 billion. In *The History of the Future*, Blake Harris describes Luckey as pursuing a grand vision:

> [T]he only "limit" to the limitless possibilities of VR was computing power. The faster computers got, the better the graphics would be and the more real virtual worlds could feel. And if it felt real enough—if you could bestow users with a true sense of presence— then VR could achieve almost anything. It could reinvent how we communicate, educate . . . not even the sky was a limit.
>
> (Harris, 2019)

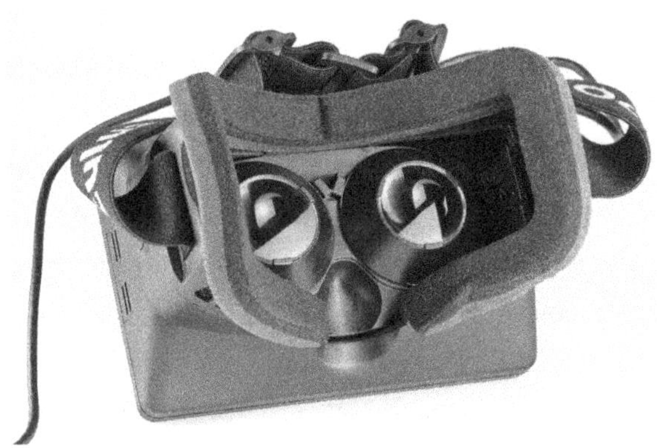

Figure 2.3 Oculus Rift—Developer Version—Back.

Source: Reproduced from Sebastian Stabinger (2013). https://commons.wikimedia.org/ wiki/File:Oculus_Rift_-_Developer_Version_-_Back.jpg. Licensed under a Creative Commons Attribution 3.0 Generic (CC BY-SA 3.0).

THE ARRIVAL OF SPATIAL COMPUTING

In the 14 years since the launch of the first Oculus Rift developer kit (DK1), there have been huge successes, massive failures, and great concerns as companies all over the world wrestle with what this new computing platform might look like. Facebook rebranded to Meta to steer its entire company toward the creation of a new digital layer that exists in parallel to the physical world. Apple released the Apple Vision

Pro in early 2024, its first consumer head-mounted display. By 2025 several other companies, including Google, have a strong hardware offering or planned to launch one in 2026–2027. There is still uncertainty regarding whether or not these devices can eclipse the space occupied by smartphones to become the primary personal computing device. However, these devices are no longer theory or a tool relegated to hobbyists and researchers, as tens of millions of users around the world own modern VR headsets, and even more still use AR features on their smartphones.

WESTERN INFLUENCE AND THE SHIFTING CULTURE

Note that much of the development of spatial computing was centered in the United States and was bolstered by military research spending and the drive for new advanced computing systems capable of providing new capabilities for training and enhancement to armed forces. This process is still well underway with Microsoft developing for the US Army a head-mounted display that has suffered from a variety of difficulties. As Microsoft and the US Army continue to explore what role spatial computing devices will have for soldiers on and off the battlefield, they continue to wrestle with long-standing issues related to comfort and long-term use. A US Army report details that soldiers reported feeling physically ill and that using the devices made them more vulnerable to harm in a variety of situations (Harding, 2022).

The United States was able to capitalize on its military-backed research efforts, a strong economy in the wake of the Second World War, and an aggressive stance on market-driven research:

The United States emerged as a global leader in science and technology in the second half of the 20th century. During this period, U.S. public and private investments in R&D grew rapidly and helped to propel the United States to a position of global economic leadership. By 1960, the United States accounted for approximately

69% of the world's R&D funding. By 2020, however, the U.S. share
of global R&D expenditures had fallen to about 31%.

(Congressional Research Service, 2022)

This allowed the United States to be the global leader in technology
development for decades—a trend that continues as many global companies struggle to penetrate the US and other lucrative Western markets.
This is changing. As new markets continue growing, so does their influence. Chinese company ByteDance, founded in 2012, developed TikTok
for Western markets, which rapidly became one of the largest platforms
used around the world. ByteDance then acquired Pico, a leading Chinese
VR headset manufacturer in 2021. After years of failed VR ventures by
companies outside of the United States (like Sega's attempt to create a
VR system in the 1990s and Nintendo's failed Virtual Boy device), there
is now significant competition not only for market share but also for
which company will steer the cultural shifts that these technologies will
bring.

THE SEARCH FOR A NEW REALITY

Engineers, artists, and designers have been looking for new ways to
create experiences that engage users with something that goes beyond
painting, books, and film—something more than software. What sits before us now is a class of devices that can generate meaningful levels of
presence, immersion, and output unlike anything possible before. These
technologies have the potential to take us to the wonderland described
by Sutherland, to imprison us in cyber hellscapes described by Gibson
and Stephenson, or to provide us with a path out of the hours most people spend on their phones—a small window into the digital world—and
instead invite us to make the digital world a more normal and embodied part of our physical world. The real question here is: Who do we
want to become? We can look back at some of the people who helped
guide us to where we are now and we can see some of what they wanted:
the ability to create new kinds of art; the chance to educate in a fully

immersive environment; the ability to spend time with someone in a way that feels like they are *with* you when they aren't; the opportunity to access the infinite complexity of the universe. So many hopes are tied up in something that also has many uncertain and unintended consequences. Those who want to actively contribute to the development of these technologies must first ask themselves why.

QUESTIONS FOR REFLECTION

1. As you consider the development of spatial computing, what stands out to you as the most exciting potential for how it could positively change the human experience? What about negatively?
2. What are problems that spatial computing is uniquely equipped to help solve?
3. What improvement to spatial computing hardware do you think might encourage a more diverse group of users to buy head-mounted displays?

PROJECT FOR CONSIDERATION

1. Make a detailed list of every activity in your day on a regular weekday and then on a weekend day. Be sure to list mundane moments, usage of technologies, interactions in person and on a device, time spent at home, etc.
2. Go back through both lists and annotate them with interventions for potentially using a spatial computing device for that activity or during that moment.
3. Then, write a short narrative stringing the moments of the day together and describing in detail the ways that a spatial computing device is used throughout the day. What does it feel like? What is the device like? How does it change those moments?

What Connects Us All

Our human experience is interwoven with stories that touch every aspect of our lives. From the bedtime stories that put us to sleep as children, to the news stories that shape our understanding of the world as adults, stories and narratives have an unshakable influence. They fuel our imagination, evoke empathy, and inspire change. Our personal stories shape our identities and influence our beliefs, values, and aspirations. Our cultural narratives connect us to our roots and foster a sense of belonging and shared history.

From the ancient campfires where stories were shared under the starlit skies to the modern digital age where stories spread across the globe in an instant, storytelling has been an essential tool in our survival kit. Tales of bravery and caution, love and loss, triumphs and trials have provided a roadmap for navigating the complexities of life. These narratives have equipped us with the collective insights of our ancestors to offer guidance on how to adapt, overcome, and thrive in the face of adversity.

Each interaction, decision, and emotion is colored by the stories and narratives that have shaped us. The choices we make are often influenced by the stories we've internalized, whether they are tales of caution that guide our actions or stories of hope that spur us to dream bigger. Even in the mundane moments of daily life, narratives play a role to provide context and meaning to our experiences.

Human Spatial Computing. Reginé Gilbert and Doug North Cook, Oxford University Press.
© Reginé Gilbert and Doug North Cook (2026). DOI: 10.1093/9780191966477.003.0003

The power of stories lies not only in their ability to transport us to different worlds but also in their capacity to make us reflect on our own lives. They challenge us to confront our fears, question our assumptions, and explore the depths of our emotions. Through stories, we can explore the human condition in all its complexity and forge connections between our personal experiences and the broader tapestry of humanity.

As we delve into the realm of storytelling, we embark on a journey of self-discovery and connection. There is a wealth of narratives waiting to be explored that can offer insights into the human psyche, the intricate web of relationships, and the diverse tapestry of cultures that populate our planet. Each story is a thread that contributes to the rich tapestry of our existence and helps us make sense of our past, navigate our present, and envision our future.

"IN BLOOM"

"Am I the demons inside my head? Is that critic me?" These questions emerge when one enters "In Bloom," an exhibition launched in the summer of 2023. This inspiring exhibit tells the story of Estella Tse, an artist and 2023 summer fellow at Oxford University, who used immersive technology and art to overcome complex post-traumatic stress disorder and severe depression. Originally from Oakland, CA, Tse combines cutting-edge virtual and augmented reality technologies with visual storytelling to create a unique artistic experience.

She has performed and spoken at global events as an artist in residence with Google, Adobe, and Cartoon Network Studios. Through her work in creative innovation, Tse aims to inspire new ways to connect, educate, and foster empathy. Her achievements have been highlighted in various publications, including Forbes, CNET, and *The Australian*.

During a challenging period in Tse's life, she decided to take a step back from her creative pursuits in order to focus on her well-being. Before creating "In Bloom," Tse worked at a plant nursery as part of her healing process. She focused on addressing her childhood wounds, past trauma and grief, allowing herself the necessary space and time to recover. This experience, along with her connection to nature, greatly influenced her work for "In Bloom," which beautifully illustrates the natural cycles of life, death, and renewal. The exhibit highlights the remarkable healing power of art and its ability to foster growth and resilience. It is divided into four phases, each reflecting distinct experiences, emotions, and artistic expressions from Tse's life (Figure 3.1).

Grief is an inescapable part of life, often manifested through the death of a loved one. On an ordinary day, as Tse was going about her typical routine, she received the unexpected news of the death of her best friend, a friend she had just messaged before the tragedy. In an instant, that ordinary day transformed into one where the sun seemed to stop shining, leaving Tse to navigate the unfamiliarity of life without someone who had brought so much brightness to her existence. This marked the beginning of her darkest days.

Figure 3.1 "In Bloom" Exhibition (2023), Estella Tse (University of Oxford). *Source*: Photo courtesy of Ian Wallman.

Grief can lead to trouble sleeping, difficulties with concentration, a lack of interest in activities, and a persistent sense of sadness (National Institute on Aging, 2024). It can create both physical and emotional pain. Time alone does not heal grief; instead, confronting and processing the emotions we experience is essential to learning how to live with our loss.

Through photographs, stories, and immersive storytelling Tse's first phase of "In Bloom," titled "The Darkest Days," not only highlighted her grief over losing a lifelong friend but also shared her journey of rebuilding her life and identity after experiencing relationship abuse and housing instability. We cannot recognize darkness without understanding light, and this leads to the next phase of her story: recovery. This phase showcases how Tse worked through her grief with the help of therapy and nature, ultimately inspiring her to return to her creative practice.

When the wind blows, some tree roots grow deeper. Similarly, humans must also delve deeper to heal, which involves exploring our foundational learning and strengthening our core connections. People often gain strength from their hardships, and this process is not undertaken alone. Just like tree roots that intertwine with neighboring trees through mycorrhizal networks, humans also rely on support from others (Holewinski, 2024). This is what Tse experienced during her healing journey through therapy, finding support, and working in a plant nursery. For many, grief can trigger a process of opening up, reminiscent of how nature responds after destruction. Adaptation occurs, allowing for repair and the development of new capabilities through healing. To grow, old layers must be shed to make way for new growth. The second phase, "Recovering and Working Hard," highlights the turning point where Tse's dedication to her artistic craft became crucial to her recovery.

The recovery process has both active and passive elements. This is reminiscent of orchids, which may appear dead during their lengthy juvenile period. Just as it takes years for humans to reach adulthood, orchids grow slowly and have a limited ability to photosynthesize, making them less efficient at converting sunlight into energy

(Zhang et al., 2018). Similarly, healing from grief takes time and requires gentle transitions. Like the nature of orchids, Tse took time to grow slowly and rebuild her life by adapting and seeking nourishment in supportive environments. The third phase, "Rebuilding," emphasizes the transformative journey of reconstructing her life after facing adversity.

When a flower appears in a crack in the sidewalk, think about what it must have gone through to reach that point. Picture a tiny seed finding just enough soil in the darkness to begin pushing through a crack, gathering the strength it needs to grow fully and flourish despite its challenges. The crack symbolizes the obstacles to growth; somehow, the seed found enough resources to sustain itself and grow toward the light, all while overcoming barriers. In doing so, it created beauty in an unexpected place.

Tse underwent a similar journey to heal, confront uncertainty in the darkness, and grow toward the light to thrive. In the final phase, "Thriving," Tse radiates a profound sense of achievement and resilience. Struggles can create deep roots and strengthen the stem of a flower. Like Tse, who faced challenges, this effort brought unexpected strength. Healing and growth can happen anywhere, and often in the most unlikely situations.

"In Bloom" invites visitors to explore spatial computing technologies such as AR and VR. Through these experiences, guests can witness Tse's journey from darkness to light and understand the concept of being "In Bloom." Tse, who faces complex post-traumatic stress disorder and depression, shares her personal stories in the hope of helping others feel less isolated.

At the end of the exhibit, visitors were invited to share their own stories—what challenges they've recently overcome, who supports them in their personal ecosystems, and what nourishes their growth and sense of self. The goal is to inspire others with these messages. Some of the anonymous messages left are shared here:

"Focus on what makes your soul feel at peace because you are your biggest accomplishment—Just keep shining like you do."

"Love yourself & be your own best friend."

"Happiness is the new rich. Inner peace is the new success. Health is the new wealth. Kindness is the new cool."

"Choose love. Connect with those around you. Be kind to yourself and others."

"Sometimes I feel like I'll never get better but then I remember it's the trying that heals you."

"Today might not be the day you 'succeed' but you've still lived and loved and just because of that TODAY matters."

Visitors are encouraged to embark on a transformational journey that showcases the evolution from pain to strength, darkness to light, and vulnerability to empowerment. Ultimately, Tse's exhibition celebrates her extraordinary artistic path, highlighting the idea that every journey from darkness to light offers valuable lessons, truths, and perspectives waiting to be explored. Tse's exhibit shows how storytelling has always been important across cultures for sharing knowledge and understanding the world. At its core, storytelling is fueled by curiosity—the desire to understand, explore, and share the depths of human experience.

STORYTELLING AND CURIOSITY

How curious are you? What does curiosity have to do with storytelling? In one word: everything. Curiosity is what compels us to ask, "What happens next?" Just as nature goes through its seasons and cycles, human stories reflect our need to connect, understand, and find meaning in the world.

A good story ignites curiosity. In "The Psychology of Curiosity," George Loewenstein (1994) outlines four ways to induce curiosity in people:

1. Posing a question or presenting a puzzle.
2. Exposing individuals to a sequence of events with an anticipated but unknown outcome.

3. Creating a violation of expectations that triggers a search for an explanation.
4. Indicating that someone else possesses information that we do not.

(Loewenstein, 1994).

When a story engages us, we want to discover what happens next. This instinct has contributed to our survival as a species, as we continually seek out problems to solve. While many of us don't live in the same survival mode as our ancestors, we are still wired to engage with information presented as stories. Do we truly have stories if there are no problems to solve?

Traditionally, stories have centered around conflicts or issues, creating narrative tension that captures the attention of readers, viewers, or listeners. Consider your favorite book, movie, video game, or social media story; the common threads include our emotional investment in the characters, cliffhangers, various plotlines, the time we dedicate to them, and our familiarity with the characters. While not every story revolves around a solvable problem, the most compelling narratives typically do, as they generate curiosity along the way.

Curiosity drives us to explore new experiences and find joy in the familiar. Spatial computing technologies enable millions of people around the world to share their stories daily through augmented reality on social media. Filters are often used to enhance visuals, whether it's showcasing distant landscapes, applying age-altering filters to babies, or allowing users to dance alongside their favorite performers. Spatial computing gives us the opportunity to enrich our storytelling.

Imagine a TikTok filter where random letters appear on the screen, and the storyteller must craft a funny narrative based on each letter. For instance, "E" might inspire a story about Elvis Presley, "D" could lead to a tale about dinosaurs, and "J" might prompt a story about jumping. This is what creators do on social media to tell stories, keeping viewers engaged as they eagerly anticipate what will come next. This approach taps into Loewenstein's curiosity gap theory, where people feel compelled to discover what others know that they don't.

Spatial computing redefines storytelling by breaking away from traditional frameworks. Instead of passive consumption, it invites audiences to step into the story by moving through it, shaping it, and experiencing it in immersive ways. Virtual reality (VR) is transforming storytelling by allowing individuals to step into the lives of others. Unlike traditional media, VR creates immersive experiences that enable users to truly feel what it's like to navigate someone else's daily challenges and experiences.

A notable example of this is a VR experience titled "1,000 Cut Journey," created by Dr. Courtney Cogburn, Elise Ogle, Jeremy Bailenson, Tobin Asher, and Teff Nichols. This experience, studying the psychosocial effects of cultural racism, was developed through a collaboration between Stanford's Virtual Human Interaction Lab and the Cogburn Research Group at Columbia University (Tribeca Festival, n.d.).

The concept behind "1,000 Cut Journey" is based on the idea of a simple paper cut. While a single paper cut might hurt slightly, imagine experiencing a paper cut every day for an entire year. Each cut is small, but cumulatively, they begin to add up. After weeks and months of daily paper cuts, the pain becomes significant, even though each individual cut seemed minor at first. This experience serves as a metaphor for systemic racism, illustrating how seemingly small incidents can accumulate over a lifetime. What may appear insignificant to some can have profound physical and emotional effects on those who experience it daily.

In 2018, "The 1000 Cut Journey" premiered at the Tribeca Film Festival. Directed by Courtney Cogburn and Elise Ogle, this immersive experience takes participants through three pivotal moments in the life of Michael Sterling, a Black man in the United States. Throughout the journey, participants encounter various instances of racism that Sterling faced from his youth into adulthood.

In this virtual reality (VR) experience, users step into the shoes of Michael Sterling, fully embodying his perspective. When they look into virtual mirrors, they see Sterling's reflection instead of their own, serving as a powerful visual reminder that they are experiencing the world through his eyes. This first-person viewpoint allows participants not only to observe Sterling's story but also to live it. They navigate through each scene as if they were him, experiencing his interactions, confrontations, and the cumulative impact of discrimination first hand. For 12 minutes, participants gain insight into what it is like to live a day in the life of Michael Sterling; however, the experience does not fully capture the breadth of his daily challenges.

As Michael Sterling, users experience not only overtly racist incidents, such as being racially profiled by police officers, but also more subtle forms of racism, such as being overlooked by job interviewers who do not expect a Black man to be an exceptional candidate. Although the story does not end happily and provides no resolution or justice, it leaves the user in a state of reflection about what they have witnessed. The intention behind this is to evoke a sense of empathy and awareness. The experience is designed to help users not only observe discrimination but also feel it personally, encountering microaggressions first hand rather than merely watching from a distance.

Design is often seen as a tool for solving problems, and the "1,000 Cut Journey" demonstrates this effectively. By immersing participants in the experiences of others, this project demonstrates how design can foster empathy, challenge perspectives, and inspire social change.

The ability to tell stories and address complex issues through spatial computing opens up new possibilities for transforming our engagement with the world. Unlike traditional storytelling, which is typically limited to screens or pages, spatial computing allows narratives to unfold in interactive and dynamic environments. This approach makes abstract or distant realities feel immediate and personal. In this sense, the entire world becomes a stage, one where stories can be experienced rather than just observed, and where design has the potential to bridge gaps in understanding, amplify marginalized voices, and create meaningful, lasting impact.

Immersive theater is a form of performance that breaks the traditional boundaries between actors and audience, inviting participants to engage directly within a carefully crafted environment. This approach transforms spectators into active participants, allowing them to explore the narrative and setting in a personal and often nonlinear fashion.

In 2019, the creative studio Tender Claws launched *The Under Presents*, a groundbreaking experience that combined immersive theater with VR. This innovative project allowed participants to embark on an otherworldly adventure, blending live and pre-recorded performances within a surreal, time-bending narrative.

Set in a space that wobbles between a vaudeville stage and the story of a ship trapped in time, players could interact with both the environment and other participants, uncovering stories at their own pace. A distinctive feature of *The Under Presents* was the inclusion of live actors who, during specific times, performed and interacted with the audience in real time. This added a dynamic and unpredictable element to the experience. The seamless integration of live performance within a persistent virtual world marked a significant evolution in immersive theater, expanding its possibilities beyond physical spaces into the digital realm.

Tender Claws hosted limited-run ticketed events that reimagined Shakespeare's *The Tempest*. During these events, a single live actor guided small groups of participants through various virtual environments. The actor encouraged participants to pantomime the actions of the characters in the play while narrating, performing lines, and controlling changes in the virtual setting. These events provided a glimpse into the creative potential that emerges when immersive and interactive theater productions, which some theatrical companies have been exploring for years, are combined with modern virtual technologies. This combination creates something entirely new: an opportunity for users to embark on grand adventures and engage in a dynamic, interactive storytelling experience.

While Tender Claws demonstrates a distinctive, commercially released experience, other types of storytelling involving other narrative traditions and cultures are emerging. If there is more diversification, the field of spatial computing will become more accessible. In turn, we see the inclusion of narratives that reflect diverse cultural traditions, storytelling methods, and community perspectives—similar to how social media platforms enabled new forms of digital storytelling from previously underrepresented voices.

In many virtual spaces, such as social VR environments, identity can be fluid, and the laws of physics can be defied. Unlike in the real world, where gravity keeps us grounded, avatars can float, and imagination knows no bounds. When users are free to present themselves in any form, the interactions and stories that emerge from these communities can be unique and endless. Allowing users to import their unique avatars means you can enter a room where a giant teddy bear is conversing with a man in a suit and a rain cloud. In this shared virtual space, users from around the globe interact with one another, each represented by their chosen avatar.

Virtual reality spaces may never be completely mainstream, but their appeal is undeniable for many users who seek connection, anonymity, and opportunities to meet new people—even if those individuals don't appear human. As smartphones and mobile applications have shifted most social interactions to passive and asynchronous forms, such as email, social media, and texting, there is something exciting about developing new ways to engage in embodied, synchronous, and active communication. These innovative forms of interaction allow us to connect in a way that is distinctly different from video calls, enabling us to create new memories, forge new connections, and share stories in ever-evolving ways.

HOW STORIES SHAPE THE MIND

What is happening in our brains when we hear a story? Why do stories make us feel strong emotions, like anger or happiness? Neuroscience helps explain.

Stories engage our brains differently than raw data or isolated facts. When we experience a story, multiple brain regions activate simultaneously, including those involved in sensory processing, emotion, memory, and meaning-making. This explains why we can genuinely feel happiness, anger, or fear from fictional events, and why we often remember stories more easily than statistics or abstract information. This connection between our brains and stories illustrates how we naturally organize and process information using narrative patterns. As a result, storytelling is an exceptionally effective way to communicate and remember experiences. While this explanation simplifies the neuroscience involved, it highlights why storytelling has been a crucial aspect of human communication throughout history.

When we hear a story, various regions of our brain become active—not only the areas responsible for language processing but also those linked to emotions, sensory experiences, and even motor functions. This occurs because our brains engage with narratives as if we are experiencing the events ourselves, rather than just passively receiving information.

Neurotypical and neurodiverse individuals often approach storytelling and technology in different ways. Neurotypical thinking typically favors linear narratives that have clear structures, easy recognition of social cues, and defined emotional arcs. In contrast, neurodiverse individuals may prefer nonlinear, fragmented, or highly detailed storytelling. They often prioritize logic, patterns, or unique perspectives rather than the conventional emotional arcs found in typical narratives.

Sensory processing varies between neurotypical and neurodiverse individuals. Neurotypical individuals typically engage with media in a standard manner, while neurodiverse individuals may experience sensory overload or interpret elements such as sound, color, and movement differently. People engage with stories in different ways; some naturally visualize them, while others, like those with aphantasia, may process narratives through concepts, structure, or other cognitive strengths instead of mental imagery.

When it comes to technology, neurotypical users typically adapt easily to standard UI/UX patterns, while neurodiverse users may prefer customizable, structured, or alternative interfaces, such as text-based designs over highly visual ones. Attention and focus also differ between these groups: Neurotypical users usually maintain consistent engagement with a storyline, whereas neurodiverse individuals may either hyperfocus on specific details or struggle with distractions.

In virtual and immersive environments, neurotypical users often enjoy predictable interaction models, while neurodiverse users may prefer deeply interactive, customizable, and immersive experiences. Recognizing these differences can help create more inclusive storytelling and technology experiences, ensuring that narratives and digital environments cater to diverse ways of thinking and engaging with content.

When neurotypical individuals hear a narrative presented in story format, multiple areas of their brains become activated. This activation is significantly greater than when they are exposed to facts, numbers, or generic information. When a story resonates with a person personally, it aligns their mind with that of the storytellers or the experiences of the characters.

It's important to note that some individuals with disabilities process narratives differently. For example, people may engage with and interpret stories through various cognitive pathways, and the connection with storytellers or characters can occur in ways that differ from traditional narrative processing.

The value and impact of storytelling remain significant, but the mechanisms and patterns of engagement can vary greatly among different forms of neurodiversity and disability. Here are a few examples:

Visual Processing Differences:

- Aphantasia refers to the condition where individuals cannot create mental images of scenes, characters, or events. Although they grasp narrative content, they process descriptions through conceptual understanding rather than visual imagery. This fundamentally alters their engagement with descriptive passages and visual metaphors (Ebeyer, 2025).
- Prosopagnosia, or face blindness, affects how people recognize and connect with characters. Instead of identifying characters by their facial features, individuals with prosopagnosia rely on other identifiers such as voice, clothing, or behavior patterns to understand character interactions and relationships in stories (NHS, 2024).
- Visual impairments can lead to rich alternative experiences of narratives through sound, touch, and spatial awareness.

Rather than limiting their story experience, these impairments often enhance attention to non-visual elements like dialogue, sound, and textural details (Lewis and Tolla, 2003).

Cognitive Processing Variations:

- Autism influences how social interactions and emotional cues in stories are interpreted. Many autistic individuals may focus more on specific details, patterns, or logical progression in narratives rather than social subtleties, engaging more deeply with technical aspects or systematic elements of stories (Ferretti et al., 2018).
- Memory processing conditions affect how narrative information is stored and retrieved, influencing how people connect different parts of a story, remember character details, or follow plot developments across time. Some might excel at remembering specific details while finding overall plot arcs more challenging (Vim & Vibe, n.d.).

Language and Audio Processing:

- Specific language impairments mean that stories might be processed through different neural pathways. While traditional narrative processing often relies heavily on language centers, these individuals might engage more with visual, spatial, or emotional elements of stories, finding movement, gesture, or visual sequences more engaging than text-based narratives (Flores Camas and Leon-Rojas, 2023).
- Auditory processing disorders affect how verbal storytelling is experienced. While the ears function normally, the brain processes sound differently, impacting how spoken narratives are understood. This can lead to stronger engagement with written text, visual storytelling, or stories told through movement and gesture (Cleveland Clinic, 2023).

Overall, storytelling holds significant value, but the way individuals interact with and understand narratives can differ widely based on their cognitive experiences.

When you hear a narrative presented in story format, several areas of your brain become activated, many more than when you hear or read facts, numbers, or generic pieces of information. When the story is personally relevant to you, it aligns your mind with the experiences of the storyteller or the characters. This phenomenon is known as neural coupling, where the brain activity of the listener synchronizes with that of the speaker or storyteller. This synchronization occurs in various brain regions, including the motor, sensory, and frontal cortices (Grover, Nguyen, and Reinhart, 2021). Essentially, during meaningful communication, the speaker's brain actively influences the listener's neural responses, creating a direct connection between their brain activities.

For example, consider a child being taught how to tie their shoes through the following story:

Once upon a time in a vast kingdom, there was a child who was the only one who knew how to tie shoes. People traveled from far and wide, and even the king relied on the child to tie his shoes each day, paying handsomely for this skill.

With great care, the child took the king's laces and formed the number 11. Then, they crossed the laces like an X, tucked one lace under the other, and pulled it tight. Next, they formed a loop, wrapped the other lace around their thumb, and gently pulled it through the opening. With one final tug, the shoe was tied!

The king was amazed and asked, "Can you teach me?" The child smiled and replied, "Of course! Anyone can learn with a little patience and practice." From that day on, the kingdom was filled with people tying their own shoes, one loop at a time.

Neural coupling activates multiple brain regions associated with emotion, memory, and anticipation, enhancing our understanding, engagement, and retention of information, and making storytelling and conversation more immersive and impactful.

Humans naturally think, communicate, and remember through stories, whether in the workplace, in personal life, or through entertainment. This ability explains why stories often create lasting impressions and are more memorable than raw data such as statistics (NLI Staff, n.d.). When stories are shared in a three dimensions, immersive environment, neural coupling helps users connect with the narrative. Additionally, mirroring, where individuals reflect the actions and emotions of the storyteller, strengthens their physical and emotional investment, making the experience feel more intuitive and participatory rather than purely observational.

When we become emotionally engaged in a story, experiencing a character's pain, struggles, and triumphs, our brains react as though the experience is real. This reaction occurs because of certain brain chemicals that affect our emotions. One of the key chemicals involved in our emotional responses is dopamine. Often referred to as the "feel-good" chemical, dopamine helps us feel engaged, excited, and motivated. When a story captivates us—especially if it contains suspense, surprises, or emotional moments—our brains release dopamine. This release enhances our focus on what happens next and improves our ability to remember the story.

Another important chemical is oxytocin, which is released when we connect with a character's emotions. Oxytocin is sometimes called the "bonding hormone" (Rutledge, 2022), because it fosters a sense of closeness to others. When we witness a character facing a difficult situation, such as a loss or significant challenge, and then ultimately finding resolution or a happy ending, our brains release oxytocin. This response helps us feel compassion, connection, and trust toward the character and their journey.

When we engage with stories, our brains create a chemical journey that mirrors a structured path from beginning to end. As characters encounter conflicts or challenges, our brains may release cortisol, the stress hormone, which heightens our attention and strengthens memory formation (Myers, 2022). This biological response makes us more alert and invested in the story's outcome. Then, as characters work through these challenges, our brains begin releasing dopamine, the reward chemical that keeps us engaged and wanting to know what happens next.

The resolution phase of stories often triggers the release of the bonding hormone oxytocin, essential for fostering empathy, trust, and emotional connections with characters.

So the structure of storytelling follows a classic pattern: tension (marked by cortisol), leading to engagement (linked to dopamine), and ultimately reaching connection and resolution (associated with oxytocin). This neurochemical progression helps explain why stories with clear conflicts and resolutions tend to be more memorable and emotionally satisfying than simple event descriptions. Our brains are literally wired to process and retain information presented in this way. The stress-to-resolution pattern creates a stronger neurological impact than information delivered without an emotional context.

When a story evokes feelings of excitement, sadness, inspiration, or relief, it's not just a product of our imagination—our brains are genuinely reacting! These chemicals engage us, enhance our emotions, and make stories more memorable and meaningful (Rantanen, 2020). In spatial computing, stories can be transformed into immersive experiences that allow you to physically inhabit a character's perspective. For instance, you might experience a love story through the eyes of the main character. Instead of passively observing their emotional journey, you actively move through their world, experiencing the neurochemical responses associated with attraction (such as dopamine), relationship conflicts (like cortisol), and reconciliation (involving oxytocin) through your own body's reactions to the virtual environment.

An immersive spatial computing experience could place users in the roles of the romantic leads within this narrative, enabling them to embody and experience these emotional complexities first hand. Through such an embodied storytelling experience, users could directly feel how love, conflict, and emotional chemistry unfold within the story.

Scientists are unraveling how narratives shape our cognitive processes, emotions, and neural pathways. Exciting discoveries lie ahead as we uncover storytelling's transformative power and its profound influence on the human brain. What we do know is that stories have traveled through time and will continue to do so. Those we tell ourselves and others will have an impact far beyond what we can see now.

As mentioned, many parts of the brain are activated when we hear stories. According to Pam Rutledge, storytelling affects the brain in various ways:

1. It synchronizes the listener's brain with the teller's brain through neural coupling.
2. It enables the listener to mirror an experience through mirror neurons.
3. Storytelling activates many additional brain areas, such as the motor, sensory, and frontal cortices, beyond the two areas activated when processing facts.
4. The brain releases dopamine in response to an emotionally charged event, resolution, or pattern recognition, creating a pleasurable response and ease of memory and recall.

How we tell stories influences who gets heard, whose experiences are validated, and how deeply audiences connect. While neuroscience indicates that storytelling engages the brain through mechanisms like neural coupling, mirror neurons, and dopamine-driven emotional resonance, the perspectives that dominate mainstream narratives often reflect Western, Eurocentric, and male-centered viewpoints. To create a richer and more inclusive storytelling landscape, we must reconsider who tells the stories, how they are presented, and what cultural frameworks influence them.

CULTURAL EXCHANGE: APPRECIATION VERSUS APPROPRIATION

In the 21st century, algorithmic bias shapes storytelling, often determining whose stories are told, heard, and amplified. Algorithms have shown bias regarding race, gender, and other demographic factors. Platforms like TikTok prioritize content from dominant cultural groups while erasing or sidelining creators from marginalized communities. Cultural appropriation can exist on a spectrum where it can be harmful or it can be positive when done with respect. When one culture profits or gains from another's traditions without giving credit, this can be a bad thing.

In 2019, a 14-year-old named Jalaiah Harmon created one of the biggest dance trends on the Internet. She choreographed the viral "Renegade" dance for K-Camp's song "Lottery" and posted it on Instagram in September 2019. However, when the dance became popular on TikTok in 2020, she received no credit as it spread. Other users, including influencers like Charli D'Amelio, adopted the dance without acknowledging Jalaiah's contribution. Her story highlights how the cultural contributions of Black teens are often appropriated without recognition and illustrates how viral Internet content can separate creators from their work. In the US and globally, there are very few regulations or laws to protect users. In fact, there is a law in the US that protects companies from liability.

Section 230 of the 1996 Communications Decency Act protects tech companies like Facebook, Twitter, and Google from being held liable for content posted by users. It also permits these platforms to moderate content in "good faith" without facing legal consequences (Ortutay, 2023). This section legally shields social media companies from liability, allowing cultural appropriation to flourish without accountability. Proposed reforms do not adequately address how algorithms influence which narratives gain visibility and which are suppressed. Without meaningful change, storytelling in digital spaces will continue to reflect existing power imbalances rather than showcasing diverse and authentic voices.

Learning from other cultures with respect and understanding can lead to positive outcomes and create something meaningful. In a paper titled "Cultural Appropriation in Computational Thinking Education," de Souza et al. (2014) explore how computational thinking acquisition (CTA) programs have been culturally adapted in Brazil from the original scalable game design (SGD) project in the USA. The SGD USA program encourages middle schools to engage in learning through game design, where educators have developed a curriculum aimed at enhancing student participation.

In contrast, the Brazilian initiative, SGD-Br, confronts unique socio-economic challenges that necessitate new strategies for technology development, teacher training, and student engagement. This adaptation of computational thinking programs in Brazil highlights how cultural and socio-economic differences impact the educational use of technology (de Souza et al., 2014).

At its core, education, especially in the realm of computational thinking, is a form of storytelling. The way knowledge is transmitted, adapted, and appropriated across cultures reflects how stories evolve over time. Education is not a one-size-fits-all narrative; it must be reshaped based on cultural and socio-economic contexts. The cultural adaptation of computational thinking in Brazil illustrates the need for educational technology to be localized in order to address socio-economic and pedagogical differences. There is a phrase commonly used in marginalized communities: "Nothing about us without us."

The research highlights that programming can serve as a powerful means of self-expression and social engagement, especially in underprivileged communities. The authors emphasize the importance of adapting educational technology to fit local contexts instead of merely copying Western models. They illustrate how cultural differences affect the teaching and learning of computational thinking. Programs developed in the USA cannot be replicated exactly due to socio-economic constraints and other factors. Therefore, it is crucial to consider the history and current circumstances of cultures when creating educational experiences and stories.

While creators have the ability to make anything about anyone, it is crucial for organizations and creators who do not share the cultural background of their subjects to conduct extensive research. Whenever possible, they should also involve the subjects in the project. Key factors in this research include mitigating the risk of using harmful language or presenting inaccuracies.

Understanding that people have real stories requires more than just empathy; it calls for a genuine effort to grasp their perspectives and to listen to what they are expressing, even if their views differ from your own. It is common for individuals to want to maximize their profits from a situation, so it is important to give proper credit to avoid cultural appropriation.

STORYTELLING AROUND THE WORLD

Today, stories told in spatial computing and other technologies often reflect the experiences and perspectives from a viewpoint that usually aligns with Eurocentricity and Western culture. When dominant narratives primarily feature white male protagonists, audiences are repeatedly conditioned to align their neural synchronization with that experience, often at the exclusion of others. Expanding storytelling means amplifying Indigenous, Black, Latinx, Asian, queer, disabled, and global perspectives. This approach allows people to connect their neural pathways with broader experiences. The dominant narrative often revolves around economic resources and access to transformative technologies. When these technologies are developed and controlled by a relatively small group, the stories that emerge primarily reflect the perspectives of these creators, which can lead to biases, exclusion, discrimination, reinforcement of stereotypes, and power imbalances.

Given these structural and systemic issues, it is essential to hear from non-Western voices. Examining experiences through a multicultural lens allows us to explore diverse ways to communicate with various audiences. Every culture offers unique stories to tell.

Creators and organizations tell stories with our technologies that are self-reflective, but who is the self that is reflecting? When dealing with cultures that are not your own, here are some questions to ask yourself.

- Am I properly crediting and compensating the original creators, especially those from marginalized communities?
- Do I understand the historical context of the cultural elements I engage in, and am I representing them authentically?
- Am I actively listening to and engaging with voices from the communities whose culture I am featuring?

- Are algorithms or recommendation systems unintentionally privileging certain voices while suppressing others?
- Am I profiting from a cultural tradition while its originators remain unrecognized or under-compensated?

Throughout history, storytelling has been a shared experience that serves the community in various ways. Humans have evolved from oral traditions to ancient myths, religious narratives, folklore, visual tales, and now digital storytelling. Additionally, forms such as dance, poetry, and puppetry represent storytelling across different cultures.

Spatial computing can present stories in creative and immersive ways, particularly highlighting non-Western storytelling traditions. It is essential that the communities who originate these stories have an active role in their ongoing creation. This active participation empowers communities to shape and develop their cultural heritage, ensuring that their stories accurately reflect their values, beliefs, and experiences.

Through AR and VR storytelling, cultures can creatively express their dance and musical traditions. Here are a few ways this can be achieved:

Calypso: Calypso music originated in Trinidad and Tobago in the mid-19th century and is an Afro-Caribbean musical tradition that is deeply rooted in resistance and social commentary (Notting Hill Carnival, n.d.). Through virtual reality, participants can be transported to historical Caribbean settings to experience the evolution of Calypso as both an art form and a tool for political expression. In this immersive environment, users can witness key moments in the development of Calypso, understand how musicians employed clever wordplay and rhythm to critique colonial power, and engage with interactive elements that showcase the interplay between music and political resistance.

Bharatanatyam (Bha-ra-ta-na-tyam): Bharatanatyam is an ancient classical dance form that originates from Tamil Nadu, India. Its name is derived from a combination of Sanskrit words: "Bha" (emotions), "Ra" (melody), and "Ta" (rhythm). While traditional film or video can capture performances, augmented reality (AR) offers a unique way to engage with this art form. With AR, learners can see life-sized holographic dancers in their own space, interact with the performance from a 360-degree perspective, and actively participate in learning the dance. Users can practice alongside virtual performers, receiving real-time feedback on their hand gestures (mudras), body positions, and rhythmic patterns. This technology transforms passive observation into an immersive learning experience, allowing participants to not only watch Bharatanatyam but also physically engage with its intricate movements and cultural significance.

Griots: In West Africa, a griot is a versatile and skilled individual who serves as a historian, storyteller, praise singer, poet, and musician. The primary role of a griot is to preserve and pass down the oral traditions of their people. Griots are highly respected for their knowledge and wisdom and often act as advisors to royalty, making them influential leaders in their communities. Due to their dual functions, they are sometimes referred to as bards. In this context, VR can create an immersive African landscape where participants can interact with virtual griots. They can listen to captivating stories, songs, and poetry, as well as engage in conversations with the griots to ask questions and learn more about the rich cultural history they represent.

Calligraphy: This art form involves creating visually appealing handwritten symbols through various techniques. The symbols are arranged to inscribe words that reflect qualities such as integrity, harmony, ancestry, and rhythm (Andre, 2016). AR can transform static calligraphy pieces into dynamic and interactive experiences. Users could explore the artistic strokes and meanings behind each letter, observe calligraphers at work, and even practice virtual calligraphy themselves, receiving real-time feedback on their technique.

Shadow puppetry: Shadow puppetry ("pi ying xi" or leather shadow play) emerged in China over 2000 years ago during the Han Dynasty, legendarily created to comfort Emperor Han Wudi after his empress's death. An advisor devised a way to project shadow figures that resembled the late Empress, pioneering an art form that would combine intricate puppet manipulation with light, music, and storytelling to bring Chinese folklore to life (Maxwell Museum, 2020). Through AR, this ancient art form can be reimagined: Users can project virtual shadow puppets onto any surface, using hand gestures to control the detailed jointed figures just as traditional puppeteers do. The AR experience preserves the essence of shadow play while allowing users to manipulate light sources, create shadows, and learn the traditional techniques of puppet manipulation without the need for physical leather puppets or a traditional screen setup.

Hula: Originally from Hawai'i, this alluring dance is performed while standing or sitting and involves undulating gestures to instruments and chants: "Originally, the hula was a religious dance performed by trained dancers before the king or ordinary people to promote fecundity, honor the gods, or praise the chiefs. Common ornaments included wristlets and anklets made of whale teeth or bone, as well as necklaces and fillets of leis (interwoven flowers). Women wore short skirts (pa'us) while men wore tapa loincloths (malos)" (Encyclopedia Britannica, 2020).

VR can transport participants to the Hawai'ian Islands, where they can witness the grace and beauty of hula performances. Users could learn the hand motions and gestures that accompany the dance, explore different chants and songs, and gain a deeper understanding of the stories and cultural significance behind each movement.

Yupik story knife: The Princeton University Art Museum (n.d.) explains that this object originates from south-western Alaska, where young Yupik girls used story knives to illustrate narratives on smooth, damp mud or sometimes on snow. These carvings were commonly shaped like birds. To carve and engrave ivory, the material was typically softened by soaking it, often multiple times, sometimes in urine. The engraved areas were then darkened using a mixture of gunpowder and blood (Oswalt, 1964). AR technology can enhance the traditional Yupik practice of story knife telling by projecting animated drawings onto physical surfaces. While historically, Yupik storytellers created tales by drawing in the snow or mud with ivory or wooden knives, with this new technology users can watch these virtual drawings come to life, interpret their meanings as traditional listeners would, and even create their own stories using virtual knives to draw in augmented space. This interactive experience maintains the essence of the Yupik story knife tradition while making it more accessible in various environments and seasons.

PRESERVATION USING DIGITAL TWINS

A digital twin is a detailed three-dimensional representation of a real-world object or space that closely resembles its physical counterpart. Digital twins have the potential to preserve physical locations by capturing the narratives embedded within their architecture and artifacts. Each site carries a layered history of how spaces have been used over time, along with cultural memories and community stories linked to that place.

One of the remarkable features of spatial computing is its ability to integrate real-time data into an immersive environment. The democratization of digital twin technology allows more communities to preserve not only their physical but also their storytelling heritage. Rather than relying on outside experts to document sites, local communities can now capture and share their narratives through these digital platforms, providing essential cultural context that might otherwise be overlooked.

Through spatial computing, cultural storytelling traditions can be preserved, shared, and experienced in innovative and engaging ways, connecting people to their heritage like never before. A notable example is the island nation of Tuvalu (Figure 3.2), which is threatened by rising sea levels due to climate change. In response, Tuvalu plans to create a digital representation of their island in the metaverse to safeguard their history. At the COP27 climate summit, Tuvalu's foreign minister, Simon Kofe, showcased this alternative method for protecting their heritage from the impacts of climate change (Fortis, 2022).

Tuvalu is actively working to redefine the concept of statehood in international law, particularly in light of cultural preservation. Currently, legal frameworks require a nation to have defined physical territory and a permanent population. However, as rising sea levels threaten to submerge Tuvalu, the government is exploring new avenues to maintain its recognition as a sovereign nation. By establishing a presence in the metaverse, Tuvalu aims to adapt to these changes. Future plans include the use of digital passports, blockchain-based governance systems, and virtual administrative functions that will help the nation sustain its statehood, even if its land becomes uninhabitable.

Figure 3.2 Tuvalu—Funafuti—Beach #1.

Source: Reproduced from Stefan Lins (2000). https://www.flickr.com/photos/
68467272@N00/304276123. Licensed under a Creative Commons Attribution 2.0
Generic (CC BY 2.0).

According to Yeo (2024), The Digital Nation project introduces a
new method of storytelling that preserves and presents a nation's identity, history, and cultural narratives through spatial computing. By
developing an interactive digital twin, Tuvalu ensures that future generations can connect with its landscapes, traditions, and governance,
even if the physical islands are lost to climate change. This approach
reinforces the transformative power of spatial computing, allowing
storytelling to go beyond physical boundaries. It enables people to
immerse themselves in lived experiences, historical memory, and national identity in ways that were previously unimaginable. The digital
twin also represents a significant advancement in the fight against climate change and could set a precedent for other vulnerable nations
worldwide.

Shifting our perspective can unlock opportunities for innovation and
creativity. Our shared stories connect us all and shape how we learn,
create, and understand the world around us. By embracing diverse

narratives and the technologies that convey them, we create new ways to engage with knowledge, cultivate empathy, and inspire discovery.

STORYTELLING AND TECHNOLOGY

Social media platforms like Twitter, Facebook, and Instagram have reshaped storytelling, allowing people to share personal narratives, experiences, and perspectives instantly with a global audience (Mendoza, 2015). While this has democratized storytelling, it has also amplified misinformation, as stories can spread quickly without verification. The same immersive and interactive technologies that enhance storytelling, such as spatial computing, digital twins, and AI-generated narratives, can also be used to manipulate perception, distort reality, and spread false narratives in more immersive ways than ever before.

Spatial computing offers opportunities for both education and the dissemination of misinformation. Misinformation, which refers to incorrect or misleading information, is prevalent in today's world. In 2020, the augmented reality game *Escape Fake* was released by Polycular. In this escape room-style game, players work to prevent a dystopian future from becoming a reality. The experience begins with players interacting with a character from the future who encourages them to explore deceptive news stories to save the world. Players collect puzzle pieces of additional information, enhancing their understanding along the way. The game's narrative entertains while also educating players about the dangers of misinformation. Although storytelling is primarily used for entertainment, it can also serve as a powerful tool for education.

Spatial computing is revolutionizing how we tell and experience stories, allowing users to step into digitally recreated places, historical events, or entirely new virtual realities. This offers new opportunities for education, cultural preservation, and empathy-driven experiences. However, when combined with misinformation, spatial computing can become a powerful tool for deception, where fabricated digital environments and AI-driven avatars simulate events that never happened, manipulate historical records, or mislead users through deep fakes and altered realities.

The blurring line between reality and digital storytelling means that critical thinking and media literacy are more important than ever. Just as books were once considered a technology for knowledge-sharing, today's digital platforms, AR/VR experiences, and interactive media are tools that shape public perception. Engaging with diverse narratives, fact-checking sources, and questioning digital experiences are crucial in an era where spatial computing and misinformation intersect, influencing how we see, remember, and experience the world.

Brown, Bailenson, and Hancock (2023) discuss a project where Stanford students developed a VR simulation of the 1969 moon landing as part of a class experiment. The authors use this example to illustrate the potential of VR to generate convincing misinformation. They argue that the unique features of virtual reality, such as spatial audio, a sense of embodiment, haptic feedback, and persistence, can make misinformation more persuasive compared to traditional media formats.

While VR and other immersive technologies can potentially amplify misinformation through powerful sensory experiences, the COVID-19 pandemic revealed a deeper truth: Technology served as a vital bridge for human connection when we needed it most, but it also highlighted our fundamental need for authentic storytelling and shared experiences. Even as we relied on digital tools to stay connected, we discovered that meaningful narratives emerge not just from the technology itself, but from our collective human experience of making sense of challenging times together. The fundamental human need to connect through storytelling, share experiences, create meaning together, and build community exists independently of any technological platform. Storytelling is a cherished gift that we possess, not something defined by technology.

The challenges of misinformation in emerging spatial computing platforms highlight the importance of adopting more responsible approaches to digital narrative spaces. Indigenous storytelling traditions are uniquely positioned to address this need, given their emphasis on contextual knowledge, intergenerational verification, and the inseparable connection between stories and the landscapes that shape them.

INDIGENOUS STORYTELLING

Lee Timutimu, a Māori storyteller from New Zealand, has been preserving and sharing oral traditions for over 15 years. His wife's grandfather's passing prompted him to create a storytelling collective, which has since traveled throughout Australia and New Zealand.

Combining his passion for technology and Māori storytelling, Timutimu founded Arataki Systems in 2016. The company specializes in location-based cultural storytelling and using technology to offer immersive experiences. Through partnerships with the Māori tech community, Timutimu's company has been able to innovate in cultural storytelling using technology.

Timutimu and his team collaborated with Meta to develop a digital platform for the Asia Pacific Economic Conference (APEC) 2021, held online in New Zealand. The objective was to offer participants an inclusive digital experience that highlighted the distinctive cultural heritage of New Zealand, especially the Māori culture. Timutimu spearheaded the initiative, featuring the Māori gods, or "Toa Māori," in the digital platform, employing his knowledge of cultural storytelling and Indigenous technology.

NGĀ ATUA MĀORI AR EXPERIENCE

> Every culture has its traditions about how the world was created. Māori have many of them, but the most important stories are those that tell how darkness became light, nothing became something, earth and sky were separated, and nature evolved. Through the spoken repetition of these stories, the world is constantly being recreated.
>
> (Royal, no date)

The Māori are the indigenous people of New Zealand, believed to have arrived between the 8th and 14th centuries, migrating from Polynesia in large canoes. In their language, they refer to New Zealand as Aotearoa and call themselves tangata whenua, meaning "people of the land," which highlights their deep connection to the Earth.

The Māori have a rich cultural heritage, including their language and various artistic expressions. One of the most famous cultural performances is the haka, a traditional war dance characterized by powerful movements. Their spiritual beliefs also play a significant role in their culture, connecting them to their ancestors and nature.

As of 2019, there were nearly 800,000 Māori individuals, with the majority residing in urban areas. The revitalization of the Māori language is evident through the establishment of kōhanga reo (preschool language nests) and schools that teach in Māori. Additionally, there are two Māori television channels, 21 radio stations, and 29 members of Parliament who identify as Māori. The Māori culture is also flourishing in the arts, with numerous creative projects in film, music, and visual arts (Royal, no date).

One noteworthy project that began in 2020 focuses on spatial computing and the stories of the Māori gods and was managed by Lee Timutimu. The Ngā Atua Māori AR experience features three-dimensional animated characters that bring to life the stories of five Māori gods to provide a digital overlay in a person's physical environment. Additionally, a two-dimensional AR face filter allows users to create their own Instagram stories inspired by the Māori creation narrative.

The experience begins with an introduction to Ranginui, the Sky Father, and Papatūānuku, the Earth Mother. It then highlights five of the most well-known Māori gods: Tangaroa, Rūaumoko, Tāwhirimātea, Tūmatauenga, and Tāne. These characters are just a few examples of the over 70 gods present in Māori storytelling (Haimona-Riki, 2021).

Timutimu shared his story in an interview with one of the book's authors, offering insight into the project. The project was a collaboration among various stakeholders and service providers, including Māori Studios, which focused on creating graphic visualizations and representations of Māori gods. While some negative comments raised concerns about partnering with large technology companies that have a history of crossing ethical boundaries, the overall response to the project was positive. Many LinkedIn users provided encouraging feedback and support for the collaboration. The launch of the Māori Experience received positive feedback and engagement from Timutimu's community, as well as online support from connections on LinkedIn. Timutimu (project creator and person of Māori descent) emphasized the importance of cultural safety and the significance of accurately representing Māori narratives.

Despite facing challenges, Timutimu felt a sense of pride in the project and the partnership with Meta. He recognized the importance of sharing Māori stories and appreciated the exposure gained from the platform's large user base. Although there were areas for improvement, such as involving Indigenous content producers, the project ultimately became something to be proud of. Timutimu reflected on the overall experience and its positive impact in showcasing Māori culture and Indigenous storytelling through technology.

The collaboration with Meta and the successful delivery of the Māori Experience (Figure 3.3) marked a significant milestone for Timutimu's small Indigenous-owned tech company in New Zealand. This project showcased the powerful combination of storytelling and technology in promoting cultural heritage while providing engaging digital experiences. Indigenous storytelling traditions provide insights into cultural worldviews, forming a basis for meaningful cultural exchange that respects origins while promoting mutual understanding among communities.

CROSS-CULTURAL EXCHANGE

In today's world, connections are not limited by physical boundaries, and shared learning experiences unite us all. With this idea in mind, Pontificia Universidad Católica de Perú (PUCP) and New York University (NYU) joined forces to create an art gallery, in WebVR using social VR, that reflects the wisdom passed down through generations. Professor Reginé Gilbert and Dr. Andres Leon-Geyer led this project.

Figure 3.3 Tumatauenga.

Source: Reproduced from russellstreet (2012). https://www.flickr.com/photos/27345927
@N07/7608849440. Licensed under a Creative Commons Attribution-ShareAlike 2.0
Generic (CC BY-SA 2.0).

This collaboration is unique because it combines language, culture, and innovation. The gallery was digitally *woven* in English and Spanish and hosted on the social VR platform. It allowed students from all over the world to connect and share their stories. The heart of the project lies in the exchange between PUCP and NYU students. The combination of diverse perspectives transcends borders and results in an intricately woven narrative. There were 18 groups, each consisting of three to four PUCP students and one NYU student.

The project is about exploring personal growth and cultural bridges. The journey begins with introspection. PUCP students created digital pieces that reflected their aspirations for their future selves. NYU students also created digital treasures that embody shared experiences and newfound wisdom. Each week, we had our 72 students engaged in an immersive and interactive experience, using the Slack tool as their primary means of communication to ask and answer questions, share reflections, and deepen their understanding of one another's perspectives. As the weeks progressed, the project evolved from personal introspection to collective artistic expression, gaining momentum and fostering meaningful cross-cultural exchanges.

Week 1: Letters to Their Future Selves

The project began with students writing individual letters addressed to their 18-year-old selves. These letters served as a form of self-reflection, where students shared personal insights, struggles, and advice based on their lived experiences. This exercise allowed students to examine their journeys and set the stage for empathy and connection as they read and discussed each other's letters.

Week 2: Art Piece Proposals and Cross-Cultural Inspiration

Building on the self-reflection from Week 1, students shifted their focus toward visual storytelling. They developed art piece proposals designed to reflect the richness of cross-cultural exchanges. These proposals encouraged students to explore identity, heritage, belonging, and shared experiences across cultures. Through Slack, they exchanged ideas, provided feedback, and collaborated on refining their artistic visions.

Weeks 3 and 4: Showcasing Digital Assets in the Social VR Gallery

In the final weeks, the students saw their creative visions come to life. They curated and showcased all digital assets in the Social VR Gallery, a virtual reality exhibition space where their works could be experienced in an immersive environment. The gallery displayed letters, artwork, and multimedia pieces, allowing students to interact with and respond to each other's creations in real time. This phase of the project reinforced the power of digital storytelling, demonstrating how technology can bridge distances and foster meaningful cultural dialogue.

By the end of the four weeks, the students had gained a deeper understanding of each other's backgrounds and created an archive of their reflections and artistic expressions. The project highlighted the importance of storytelling, digital collaboration, and cultural exchange, demonstrating how technology can be used to foster inclusive and meaningful connections across diverse communities. Unfortunately, at the time of this book's publication, the platform the students used was no longer in existence. This project was a fusion of language, technology, and human experience. It showcased the idea that connections are formed through shared knowledge. PUCP and NYU students came together to create an art gallery that resonates with past and future aspirations (Figure 3.4).

EXPANDING ACCESS TO SPATIAL COMPUTING THROUGH STORYTELLING

Storytelling a fundamental part of human existence, and stories are increasingly intertwined with technological development. There is a common saying in the West: Those who control the media significantly influence public perceptions. As we reflect on the stories we encounter daily, we should consider who has the power to shape the future of storytelling. To grasp the bigger picture, we need to be clear about who has access, who owns the narrative, and whether there is inclusion in the storytelling process. Creators can advocate for a technologically advanced, culturally diverse, and equitable immersive digital world.

Figure 3.4 Space by Andres Leon-Geyer.
Source: Reproduced with permission from Dr. Andres Leon Geyer.

To create this culturally diverse and equitable spatial computing environment, we must ask ourselves: How can we ensure that a select few
do not monopolize immersive storytelling? This begins with developing
inclusive content and spaces through education and training. A notable
example of this is OurWorlds.

OurWorlds is an organization dedicated to enhancing inclusivity as
the first Indigenous-built extended reality (XR) company. It preserves
and shares Indigenous storytelling through immersive, place-based
experiences. It provides a curriculum integrating Indigenous perspectives with STEM learning and geolocates experiences through mobile
apps, eliminating the need for expensive equipment. Additionally, it
offers educational resources designed for underserved communities.
Founded by Kilma Lattin, a recognized Native leader and Emmy Award
recipient, along with Catherine Eng, an award-winning app designer,
OurWorlds enables users to engage with authentic Indigenous narratives. This promotes cultural understanding and digital literacy through
mobile-accessible XR experiences. OurWorlds stands out in a landscape

dominated by large corporations that control most hardware and software technology.

Spatial computing involves significant costs, making it less accessible due to economic barriers related to headsets, AR smartphones, smart glasses, and the expenses of virtual production, including motion-capture studios and software licenses. In addition to these financial challenges, there are also infrastructural limitations. As of early 2025, around 5.56 billion people, which is about 67.9 percent of the global population, were using the Internet. However, most individuals without Internet access live in Southern and East Asia, as well as Africa. While spatial computing is primarily driven by Europe, China, and the US, there are opportunities for growth in other countries. The saying "it takes a village" is especially true when it comes to sharing diverse stories with the world.

Community-owned platforms may promote different kinds of narratives compared to profit-driven platforms. However, these barriers do not prevent individuals from creating content and seizing opportunities to share their stories and develop products through open-source networks like OpenXR, which is supported by the Khronos Group. This framework enables developers to create AR and VR applications that are compatible across various hardware platforms. It helps dismantle the barriers established by large tech companies, empowering individuals to thrive in a more open spatial computing ecosystem. In the gaming sector, Godot is an open-source game engine that is gaining traction for AR and VR development through its XR Tools. Open communities are committed to helping people share their stories.

In recent years, there has been an increase in the use of AI in storytelling. A significant resistance to this from writers emerged during the 2023 Writers' Strike, where the Writers Guild of America advocated for protections against AI in their contracts. The agreement mandates that writers be informed if they receive AI-generated material. Additionally, it prohibits AI from being credited as a writer, restricts AI from writing or rewriting content, and ensures that AI cannot undermine writers' credits. Writers can use AI with company consent, but companies cannot require them to do so (Coyle, 2023).

AI plays several critical roles in spatial computing, including recognizing gestures, generating objects and scenes, enabling conversational navigation, and guiding autonomous vehicles. This technology is set to transform our interactions, moving from screens to more natural, human-centered interactions within physical spaces. For businesses, adopting spatial computing is essential for digital transformation and maintaining competitiveness in an increasingly blended virtual and physical world.

While high-end spatial computing may require significant resources, democratized tools like AR filters on social media platforms have already made spatial storytelling capabilities accessible to millions. People without technical expertise regularly use these tools to create beautiful visual narratives, share cultural knowledge through location-based overlays, develop instructional content visualized in three-dimensional space, build practical applications for emergencies, and express their creativity through digital transformations.

Just as social media democratized content creation beyond traditional media gatekeepers, accessible spatial computing tools are enabling broader participation in this new medium. The ongoing challenge is to ensure that these technologies continue to evolve toward greater accessibility, incorporating diverse input into their development.

The future of spatial computing storytelling is still to be determined. Creators, developers, and communities have the ability to influence its direction through collaboration, staying informed, and exploring different methods of creating and distributing technology. However, to foster fairness and inclusivity, we must challenge the dominance of large companies and financial interests that currently control most of the industry. The main challenge is not the exclusivity of spatial storytelling, but rather ensuring that the development of these technologies prioritizes inclusion. It is crucial to incorporate diverse perspectives to ensure that these advancements address the needs of all communities.

"In Bloom" Acknowledgments

Estella Tse extends a heartfelt expression of gratitude and acknowledgment to the individuals who contributed their expertise, dedication, and passion to realize this exceptional project. Tse led the project as creative director, with Vicky McGuinness as project lead and TORCH head of public engagement, Rhiannon Jones as project manager, and Emma Jones as senior coordinator of the humanities cultural program. The team has steered this endeavor with remarkable leadership. Project officer Izabela Jaroslawska, and Tasha Patel, TORCH creative industries lead, have brought valuable insights into the project's success. The technical prowess of Brian Mitchell, Rachel Grenville-Hunt, and George Henfrey, along with the creative ingenuity of Byung Kim and Carl Hewlett, have shaped the immersive experience. Kieran Cox, Fusion Arts director, and the coordination of Carmen Rodriguez-Macias, Niveen Sukkar, and Feng Ho have been invaluable. Special thanks to each contributor, including Lori Nishikawa, Charlie Goelst, Patrick Replogle, and many others who have lent their expertise, ensuring that this endeavor truly shines.

QUESTIONS FOR REFLECTION

1. What positive stories are you sharing to promote empathy and compassion in your community?
2. How might you unintentionally be reinforcing harmful stereotypes or divisive messages through the stories you tell or share?
3. In what ways can storytelling be used to create inclusive environments where everyone feels valued, or environments where certain groups feel unwelcome?
4. What techniques can you use to authentically incorporate diverse cultural perspectives into immersive experiences while respecting and honoring their origins?

PROJECTS FOR CONSIDERATION

Storytelling and Spatial Computing Project

Participants will create an interactive story designed specifically for three-dimensional environments. Your project can take the form of a VR narrative where users physically move through the story, an AR experience that blends digital elements with real-world spaces, or a three-dimensional game world where the environment itself reveals the narrative. Your story should take full advantage of spatial computing's unique strengths, immersing users in three-dimensional spaces where they can interact with environments and objects from multiple perspectives. Example projects might include an immersive historical experience where users physically walk through different time periods, a mystery where clues are hidden throughout a three-dimensional environment for users to discover, or a narrative revealed through architectural spaces that change as the user progresses. This assignment challenges you to reimagine storytelling beyond traditional linear formats, creating experiences that could only exist within spatial computing.

Cross-Cultural Storytelling Workshop

Explore storytelling from a global perspective by learning about different cultures and their unique ways of telling stories. You can work alone or with others. Your task is to research a culture different from your own and create a story that accurately and respectfully reflects its traditions and storytelling techniques. Then, you will bring this story to life in a spatial computing environment, showing how culture influences both storytelling and design. As you work, think about how your own background and beliefs might shape your choices. This will help you create more inclusive and diverse stories.

Universal Design for Spatial Computing

When exploring the use of computer-assisted design in architecture, Juhani Pallasmaa declares:

> The computer is usually seen as a solely beneficial invention, which liberates human fantasy and facilitates efficient design work. I wish to express my serious concern in this respect, at least considering the current role of the computer in education and the design process. Computer imaging tends to flatten our magnificent, multi-sensory, simultaneous and synchronic capacities of imagination by turning the design process into a passive visual manipulation, a retinal journey.
>
> (Pallasmaa, 2005)

We already have magnificent capabilities for creating fantastical worlds, sharing stories, having sensual experiences, and forging deep connec tions with the world and each other. In our development of increasingly embodied technologies that occupy places of prominence in our homes, on and in our bodies, and in our environment, we run the risk of abandoning our current capacities and replacing them with augmenta-tions that may not live up to their promise of ascendance. Beyond this, we run the risk of developing technologies that create an even wider divide between those for whom the technologies are optimized, and those who are often forgotten in the development process. We use this

Human Spatial Computing. Reginé Gilbert and Doug North Cook, Oxford University Press.
© Reginé Gilbert and Doug North Cook (2026). DOI: 10.1093/9780191966477.003.0004

chapter to explore universal design (UD), a framework for approaching design problems that attempts to ensure access for as many people as possible.

The UD framework was initially developed by American architect Ronald Mace in the late 1990s in collaboration with a group of other designers and researchers. Mace and the team worked to reframe discussions around accessibility in architecture and product design. Accessibility frameworks often attempt to make a product or service work for someone with a *specific* restriction. UD instead seeks how to make a product or service work for *everyone*. The subtle difference here is that all people, given a long enough life, will at some point have a temporary or permanent disability. The UD framework has been adopted broadly by architects and interior designers as they examine the need for spaces that will continue to adapt to residents as they age and change. Asking how something might age alongside its user is often forgotten in the development stages of technology. We might lose access to technology as we age, as our eyesight, bodies, and our ability to adapt all change. UD is an attempt not just to design for others, but to design for our future selves by uncovering a design methodology that is "applicable to all ages, personal abilities and sizes, with an inclusive capability that transcends barrier-free and accessible design" (Watanuki, 2010).

PRINCIPLE 1: EQUITABLE USE

The design is useful and marketable to people with diverse abilities.

Guidelines:
1a. Provide the same means of use for all users: identical whenever possible; equivalent when not.
1b. Avoid segregating or stigmatizing any users.
1c. Provisions for privacy, security, and safety should be equally available to all users.
1d. Make the design appealing to all users (Center for Universal Design, 1997).

Providing equal access to an experience does not ensure equitable access to the full experience. Taking a UD approach to access means that we are working carefully to ensure full access to as many users as possible, while also understanding that users' abilities are not static and will change over time. Designing for equity means thinking of the application in development as a destination instead of a piece of software. When we design spatial applications that exist in three-dimensional space, we are inviting users to inhabit physical spaces, which can be either a virtual environment or an augmented physical environment. Our spaces should invite as many users as possible—and provide them all with the full experience of our application.

In the same way that an amphitheater in a well-designed public park will have wheelchair-accessible viewing platforms, adjacent seating to accessible viewing areas, accessible parking spaces, ramps, handrails, etc., our design should accommodate users who are entering our applications with a range of abilities. We should seek to provide the same experience to all users where possible—and where that is not possible, to provide an equivalent experience where needed that maintains the overall tone and feel. In some cases, there may even be a non-VR version of an experience that it makes sense to make accessible to users.

When we include a ramp in a public park (Figure 4.1), we allow wheelchair users to move more freely—but we also allow for equipment dollies, fatigued or injured visitors, small children, cleaning equipment, etc., to move more freely. In the same way, including equity-focused features in an experience allows for more users to feel invited into a space that encourages freedom of movement and expression.

Let us take as an example spatialized text—text that is placed into a three-dimensional environment as opposed to just a two-dimensional overlay. If we want our text to follow a universal and equitable approach, we should consider why we are using text in the first place. Are we communicating something essential to the audience? Is the text a form of feedback for another interaction, a subtitle for an audio track, or in a menu? Text is troublesome because of its associated variety of access issues, concerning the following:

Figure 4.1 Stairs and Ramps.

Source: Photo by Sujira Su (2019). Reproduced from https://www.pexels.com/photo/
stairs-and-ramps-11441014/. Licensed under Pexels Free Use License.

- Color and contrast
- Size and legibility
- Translation and localization
- Spatialization and location in the environment.

A robust text implementation accounts not only for variations in how users interact with text, but also for how text interacts with the environment. Static text placed in the environment runs the risk of not being in the user's field of vision, while overlaying text on the user's vision may block other content. We must solve for application-specific, contextually and environmentally aware, and high-contrast typography overlays. When we take the time carefully to consider a text implementation, we not only provide greater access for users with hearing and vision issues, but also make it easier to localize content for a variety of languages, users in loud environments, users with difficulty distinguishing multiple audio sources, users experiencing audio source or hardware issues, users interested in privacy in shared spaces, and others.

When we start to see the broad benefits of a universal approach, it becomes clear that it is about both creating equitable access for those who are often excluded and providing new opportunities for expanded access for all users.

Too easily we find ourselves alienating users without realizing it—when we don't onboard them properly, when we make poor assumptions, cause offense, or create discomfort. When we think about spatial applications as environments, we are again confronted with who will feel emboldened to engage with our experience with their full selves, and who will be more hesitant or feel held back. We are inviting users to engage in intimate behavior with us: to hand over their sensory input, to allow us to do three-dimensional scans of their homes, gather biometric data, and use their whole body as an input device. These are not trivial requests—permission is often only granted, with full awareness, to friends and family. We must both build trust and maintain it—with a variety of users.

Privacy, security, and safety should be available to all users. This chapter isn't the only place where we discuss these issues, but note that these are core equity concerns. Regarding safety, some users are more susceptible to harassment in online social environments, and the embodied and immersive nature of these technologies make the types of harassment perpetrated by aggressors potentially more invasive.

Security and privacy regarding user data and information is perhaps one of the greatest equity issues—one that demands a book all its own! As users are asked to give up increasing amounts of personal data in exchange for subsidized software and hardware, privacy is rapidly becoming a luxury of the wealthy. As we look to the future of spatially aware devices, embodied computing, and integrated wearables, we must ensure we do not solve for equity of access by eliminating equity of privacy.

All in all, equitable design should be *appealing* to a variety of users. Accessibility is valuable; inclusion is a noble goal, but equity exists on the far side of the spectrum where accessibility and inclusion fade from view—users from a variety of backgrounds feel not just welcomed, but as if they are the primary user, and an invited guest. The types of experiences that neglect a robust exploration of equity (not just accessibility and inclusion) lead us toward a perpetuation of cultural dominance by those who have great access. Spatial computing devices are already prohibitively expensive for many users, are only available in certain regions, and are currently designed with an orientation toward gaming and physical activity for nondisabled people.

Equity—designing for the enjoyment of all—is not just an invitation to a more idyllic world; it is an opportunity to expand the audience, forge deeper relationships with users, and encourage others to do the same. The more people feel invited into the spaces that we create, the greater the chance that those spaces will attract more users. When the ecosystem has a large variety of experiences and tools for users who require such inclusive content, there are more reasons for new waves of people to purchase spatial computing devices and grow the industry even further. Their voices in our communities will speed up the rate of improvements we can develop. Most impactfully, having users with disabilities become developers in this industry will help us reach the goal of making designs that appeal to everyone. We must design inclusively to welcome them to this space, too.

PRINCIPLE 2: FLEXIBILITY IN USE

The design accommodates a wide range of individual preferences and abilities.

Guidelines:
2a. Provide choice in methods of use.
2b. Accommodate right- or left-handed access and use.
2c. Facilitate the user's accuracy and precision.
2d. Provide adaptability to the user's pace (Center for Universal Design, 1997).

As mobile phones became the dominant browsing device for websites, we saw a massive shift away from static websites designed for desktop use and moved into the era of mobile version and responsive design. Mobile version indicates a secondary website designed only for viewing on mobile devices, while responsive design provides the same experience as desktop browsing but with each element designed to be scaled to a variety of screen resolutions.

In the design of spatial applications, we must take both of these approaches simultaneously as we filter our features into those that can be made responsive and those that need to be fundamentally changed in order to provide alternative user experiences. We split these into distinct categories as we investigate designing applications for flexibility.

Using three-dimensional object scaling as an example, let us explore how we might break down possible features that may be fixed or flexible, depending on the scenario. Allowing a user to scale the size of a three-dimensional object is a helpful example because it can be understood to apply (although with significant differences) to both virtual reality (VR) and augmented reality (AR) applications. For the purposes of this example, we attempt to keep it broad and applicable to both. Our example application has a function for manipulating the scale of three-dimensional models in an environment.

A fixed implementation allows the user to scale objects up and down on all three axes using a joystick, touchpad, or a series of two buttons. The scaling is locked to increasing and decreasing all values at once, and to a single control mechanism. This basic design allows for rapid and simple use by many users and is a common implementation currently integrated into many applications. However, an implementation like this may not be available for all users at all times, as it requires high dexterity, may cause fatigue (depending on use in the application), requires a reset mechanism, has minimal accuracy without additional input, and requires additional buttons for rotation and placement.

A flexible implementation should account for a range of individual user preferences and a spectrum of user abilities. It is important to conduct user experience interviews for every application with a variety of users in order to uncover their needs as they relate to what is being built.

Some options for flexible implementations could include:

- Voice control for reset of scaling to 100%.
- Left- and right-handed control options.
- The option to remap buttons to joystick input, or vice versa.
- A virtual control interface (slider, lever, virtual buttons, etc.) that puts control of the object into the environment itself.

- Hand-tracked or controller-based scaling using a pinch-to-zoom mechanism.
- Separate axis scaling split into virtual controllers or buttons.
- Visual, audio, and haptic feedback for scaling parameters when helpful and/or necessary for accuracy.

Flexible implementations embrace the need for a variety of possible input schemes when necessary, acknowledging that not all applications need to provide them for all tasks. When an application is able to provide various input methods, especially for precision tasks, it allows users to develop new intuitions for the best way to work, play, and interact. Something as simple as changing the size of an object can become quite complex when we take the environment, the user, other objects, and performance issues into account. Elegantly designed systems allow for a variety of users to easily find a method of interaction that works well for them, provides accuracy for the task, and allows for possible variation based on their current level of ability.

Many designers favor static systems because of their perceived elegance and ease of implementation, but when static systems leave out input methods, ignore user preferences, exclude users with a range of potential disabilities, or don't provide enough input for the task, all users are left wanting. When we provide more options for all users, we invite them to determine new, and often unexpected, ways of interacting with our applications. Smartphones have had to rely on a minimal number of possible input types and methods, but spatially aware systems that can leverage hand, eye, facial, voice, body, and other input are poised to demand more from both users and developers.

With the development of input devices increasingly capable of capturing brain activity (electroencephalogram (EEG) and other brain-machine interfaces), subtle muscle and hand movements (electromyography), and other inputs yet to be determined, it is important to begin exploration of how we might expose controlled parameters to a variety of input methods. It is easy to fall into previous assumptions for control, relying on perceived "best practices," but it is still too early in the days of spatial interfaces to standardize anything. The time for standardization may never come as we continue to increase the pace of technological development and our own evolution. While it may seem daunting to implement a multitude of input methods, we are far from a place where standardization, or the expected, is good enough.

Input method is just one of the many ways that we should be exploring flexible design for immersive applications. A few other examples worth considering include:

- Adjustments for user pace and allowing more time for certain tasks that may be arbitrarily timed.
- Adjustments for user height, sightlines, etc.
- Audio settings that allow clarity for dialogue and necessary feedback while diminishing background and environmental sounds.
- Variation for user movement in fully virtual environments.
- For games, having significant variation for difficulty and precision is essential—not just for user access but also for demos and shareability.
- Allowing alternatives to controllers or hand-tracked applications.

As with all these considerations, it is important to explore the unique aspects of the experience we are developing and our intended audience. While the underlying hope of UD is to invite everyone in, this goal will remain as elusive as the limitations of our teams, our project budgets, and our own creativity. Not everything *must* be for everyone, but if our experience does not have space for certain types of users or audience segments, then we should understand clearly why that is. It is easy to become trapped by our own interests, concerns, and passions and be beholden to static systems, where flexibility of design may be better suited not only to inviting in more users, but also to enhancing the experience for all users.

PRINCIPLE 3: SIMPLE AND INTUITIVE USE

Use of the design is easy to understand, regardless of the user's experience, knowledge, language skills, or current concentration level.

Guidelines:

3a. Eliminate unnecessary complexity.

3b. Be consistent with user expectations and intuition.

3c. Accommodate a wide range of literacy and language skills.

3d. Arrange information consistent with its importance.

3e. Provide effective prompting and feedback during and after task completion (Center for Universal Design, 1997).

Simplicity and flexibility often end up as opposing forces in the design of robust experiences. When considering them side by side, we have to be very careful to not turn up the complexity and weight of our experiences by adding too many features—even in the name of flexibility. Dieter Rams famously said, "Good design is as little design as possible" (Lovell, 2011). While Rams's work was mostly confined to product design, his minimalist approach to design has permeated much of application and software design—though often only at an aesthetic level.

The minimalist approach may not be quite appropriate for spatial computing. Skeuomorphic designs, made up of "elements that reflect ornamental references to previous (and potentially obsolete) analogs, are ubiquitous in current user interfaces. The uses of skeuomorphism in digital interfaces are typically aesthetic, such as realistic textures (leather and stitching)" (Stevens et al., 2013). Often this led to user interface designs that were trying replicate the visual language, aging of materials, and ornamentation of the real-world objects that they sought to replace. "This design technique relied heavily on the use of visual embellishments like beveled edges, gradients, shadows, and reflections in applications and interface design" (Curtis, 2015).

Apple and its founder Steve Jobs advocated for skeuomorphic design and implemented it across most of the company's products:

He and Scott Forstall (then, the head of Apple's Human Interface Team) believed that this was necessary in order to bridge the gap between designer and user. Jobs argued that this technique added sentiment to devices, which included comfort and familiarity. Others have used words like "gimmicky" and "patronizing" to describe the design technique.

(Curtis, 2015)

When Apple decided to bury its skeuomorphic design in the early 2000s, it buried the metaphor that had served as the gradual onboarding to digital ubiquity. As companies continue to move toward increasingly narrow visual brand guides that allow for little to no variation between disparate products (e.g., Google's 2020 redesign of its mobile app icons), we are discovering that our systems are not as intuitive as originally thought, and that when we threw out skeuomorphic design in the name of minimalism, we abandoned our ability to work in deep metaphors. This is a design perspective that we must revisit and put back to work—not skeuomorphism, but the skill of distilling complex actions and controls into quickly digestible interfaces. We need to recover our ability to internalize and adapt our conceptual models using our past experiences, metaphors, and intuitions.

Having lived through this sort of change with a system, already developing the intuitions, can make the metaphors and onboarding systems seem bloated and useless. The problem here is that abandoning these often means losing a depth of understanding of how the systems are meant to operate. We see this in the gradual distance from low-level computer interaction enjoyed by the majority of users who grew up with tablet and mobile devices instead of the personal computer—living life with the surface technology and with the actual computation almost entirely obscured.

Spatial computing goes beyond mobile interfaces where skeuomorphism was a layer over the experience. Here, it *is* the experience. This becomes problematic on a variety of levels when users rely too heavily on their experience of nondigital environments and bring their expectations with them. Making something *simple* to a user in a simulated or augmented environment means bridging the gap between what is possible with the hardware and what the user expects from the application.

It is in the breakdown of this attempt that users lose immersion or interest in the experience.

The reality of attempting to do simple design often means standing close to the side of basic design—where what looks simple is actually crude—before crossing the line to simplicity where the design is able to hide the complexity from the user and enable intricate actions with carefully designed and researched controls.

Let us explore this using the example of controlling a virtualized aerial drone in an AR head-mounted display with hand tracking enabled. Traditional drone controllers use a series of joystick and button presses to allow for control of the system. The most basic attempt to allow for control is to put the exact same type of controls into the environment and allow the user to manipulate them with their hands. Multiple joysticks, buttons, and the first-person view from the drone are all displayed around the user. This is a version of the experience that may prove useful for certain applications and relies on users with pre-existing drone piloting experience to immediately understand the control scheme. Porting over physical controls to virtual environments does not give us the chance to explore expanding our capabilities— encouraging users to develop new intuitions—and perhaps developing systems that cross the line from basic working implementation to simple design.

While we won't propose a final solution to the question of aerial vehicle control in AR, in an attempt to cross that line we should ask:

1. How can this problem be uniquely solved in three dimensions?
2. Are there parts of the control system that can be assisted by machine-controlled device handling? Does the device have object detection, error tolerance, and motion smoothing? Can we abstract one-to-one control and provide the user location control versus motion control?
3. How do users control other forms of movement in three-dimensional space?
4. Is it possible to distill all necessary controls into a single mechanism without losing the full capabilities required for the application?

When solving problems that are fundamentally three dimensional, we should avoid immediately relying on our traditional ways of solving them and explore solutions that are possible only in three-dimensional digital space. With the whole body as an input device, the simplest experience may not be simplest to design.

Our quest for simplicity does not stop at interface and control design—for spatial applications, it should extend through our entire experience. Take caution against embracing a basic approach that would leave users without the proper feedback, options, and parameters to create the most compelling experiences. It is important that we continue to explore what is necessary, what is meaningful, and what feels best for a variety of users. While the goal of simplicity is to make these tools and experiences easy to interact with by the largest variety of users, we should also be careful that we do not cross too far over the gap already widened by mobile devices—the obfuscation of computing. As we continue to move toward embodied and spatial computing, it is worth asking how far we wish to abstract away from ourselves the computing that so clearly defines us. How aware do we want the general user to be of how the technology actually works, how to build and reimagine it for themselves, and how to work with it in the most effective ways possible? A great concern is that companies may not be incentivized to allow this type of access and instead focus on merely creating magical experiences for users, instead of inviting them to become wizards themselves.

PRINCIPLE 4: PERCEPTIBLE INFORMATION

The design communicates necessary information effectively to the user, regardless of ambient conditions or the user's sensory abilities.

Guidelines:
4a. Use different modes (pictorial, verbal, tactile) for redundant presentation of essential information.
4b. Provide adequate contrast between essential information and its surroundings.

4c. Maximize "legibility" of essential information.
4d. Differentiate elements in ways that can be described (i.e., make it easy to give instructions or directions).
4e. Provide compatibility with a variety of techniques or devices used by people with sensory limitations (Center for Universal Design, 1997).

The ways in which we consume, understand, and process information are as varied as any other part of a person. Our senses are not standardized or static—we all experience each of our senses in a different way through the course of our life. Our ability to process certain types of information changes significantly as well—not just as individuals, but as a collective. Exploration of our body and our senses is important as we try to unpack the depth of experience and how we might create experiences that are meaningful and transformative for a variety of users. How we take in information in spatial applications can approach a level of richness like our experience of physical reality. Chapter 6 investigates how we can design for the senses in a way that embraces the unique opportunities of spatial computing. There we explore how to work with users who may not be able to engage with the critical information presented in our applications because of a variety of sensory and/or design issues.

Information perception and processing goes beyond the senses and approaches cognition, culture, and exposure. Perception connects back to equity as we seek to provide the same information to a wide range of users. We must be careful about the assumptions we make of users, their familiarity with similar systems, their cultural background, and the efficacy of our designs to match user expectations. Creating spatial interfaces often relies on a combination of text, three-dimensional objects, two-dimensional interfaces, colors, and symbols—all of which are subject to sensory issues, misinterpretation, and misuse. Our systems should rely on a variety of feedback types to ensure users receive critical information in more than one modality (e.g., providing text and audio feedback for completion of a task). When we increase the level of information clarity, we enable all users to move more quickly through applications, raise ease of use, and ensure a greater level of access.

For example, colors hold significant cultural meanings and associations that vary widely across societies. It is essential to understand the cultural connotations of colors when designing for spatial computing experiences to ensure that the chosen colors evoke the intended emotions and communicate appropriately. For instance, the color red is often associated with love, passion, and energy in Western culture, but in Asian cultures, it symbolizes luck, celebration, and prosperity. Meanwhile, in South African culture, it represents mourning and spiritual matters.

When designing spatial computing experiences that involve color, it is crucial to consider the cultural context of our audience. A color that evokes positive emotions in one culture might have different connotations in another. Being mindful of these cultural nuances can enhance the effectiveness of our design and help us create experiences that resonate with a diverse range of users.

PRINCIPLE 5: TOLERANCE FOR ERROR

The design minimizes hazards and the adverse consequences of accidental or unintended actions.

Guidelines:

5a. Arrange elements to minimize hazards and errors: most used elements, most accessible. Eliminate, isolate, or shield hazardous elements.

5b. Provide warnings of hazards and errors.

5c. Provide fail-safe features.

5d. Discourage unconscious action in tasks that require vigilance (Center for Universal Design, 1997).

Using the body as an input device creates many opportunities for mistaken input, unintended or unconscious actions, and potentially dangerous movements. While some experiences do not require assistive measures (e.g., where the goal is the development of precision skills), many do. A user's ability to perform precise actions with hand tracking or tracked controllers can be greatly affected by a variety of factors. Did the user have too much coffee before lunch? Can they hold a virtual object perfectly steady at shoulder height while performing a hand manipulation of that object? Where possible, we should solve for user intent based on the specific goals of our experience, provide guides and assistance, and minimize the need for precision when dealing with manipulating objects in three-dimensional space.

Allowing users deep control, manipulation, and interaction with our environment comes with the possibility of users breaking our experience. Did the user drag the menu into the floor? How do they get it back? Do they know how? Did the user throw a necessary object outside of the physical boundaries of your environment? Will that object respawn?

Solving for error tolerance is often an exercise in solving for all the ways in which a user might try to break our application and, in the process, break themselves. Even with exhaustive user testing, we can never test for all the ways users might try to push the limit, though we should test as much as we can with a variety of users. We must design carefully to ensure that critical functions and features do not have impassable fail states triggered either by the application or by user actions. An impassable fail state is when a user is no longer able to progress through an experience, perform a required action, or continue use of an application. This means considering all of the components discussed in this chapter as we examine fail states for our application that may be triggered by the user or by other factors outside of our control—for instance, when a user's limited physical mobility prohibits progression through an application.

Many perceived fail states are not actual. A perceived fail state for a user may appear when they are not able to progress to the next stage of an experience or they cannot discern how to progress. Though they are functionally the same, from the user's perspective a fail state that is triggered by a lack of perceptible information is a design issue, and not a software bug.

If a user closes an application—perceiving a fail state—the perception becomes actual. A perceived fail state could be solved with a simple audio and visual cue, a timed relocation of objects that leave a specific boundary, or guided narration with subtitles that takes the user through a step if they have not progressed. All of this must be held in balance as we seek to develop user intuitions by letting them explore, while also making sure that users have all the help they need to work and play with ease.

This is an even greater need when we address AR experiences that exist outside of the home environment, to ensure that users are receiving all the necessary information, cues, and warnings to secure their safety and the safety of those around them. Environmental triggers must be planned carefully, reducing the urge or eliminating the possibility of playing while driving or operating machinery, and carefully delineating the transition between safe and dangerous play spaces.

This work requires an incredible amount of careful design, exhaustive databases, and cultural understanding. Should users be able to play an AR role as a shooter on the grounds of a memorial? Even further, what if an application intentionally or unintentionally directs users to a dangerous or inappropriate environment for the use of the application? These are problems that we have already encountered with the rise of more location-based applications and games. When these applications extend beyond the boundaries of the home, more people than just the primary user become involved. From safety, privacy, and emotional perspectives, we must also consider nonusers in the user's environment. The potential for these technologies to become ubiquitous in public settings will have a profound effect on users and nonusers alike. While we may feel a greater affection for our users, we must also consider the unintended consequences that our application may have for nonusers.

PRINCIPLE 6: LOW PHYSICAL EFFORT

The design can be used efficiently and comfortably and with a minimum of fatigue.

Guidelines:

6a. Allow user to maintain a neutral body position.

6b. Use reasonable operating forces.

6c. Minimize repetitive actions.

6d. Minimize sustained physical effort (Center for Universal Design, 1997).

While high-intensity spatial applications, especially those targeted toward fitness, are an important part of development, we must be mindful of the difficulty of sustained physical effort and repetitive movement. For non-fitness applications, we should be considering how to accommodate users with limited mobility, stamina, range of motion, and physical fitness. Using our whole body as an input device can be exhausting. If we expect that spatial computing may overtake traditional forms of computing for daily tasks and sustained use, then we must design methods of use that not only meet the ergonomic standards of current forms of computing, but surpass them. We should be looking for ways to allow for comfort, ease of use, minimal risk of strain or injury, and the possibility of active use. We have the chance to imagine computing that is not sedentary and does not force us into a sustained posture that will cause long-term damage to our body.

Asking users to perform strenuous activities repeatedly—even in a fitness application—should be examined carefully, vetted properly, and tested rigorously. There are incredible opportunities to create positive impact on the way people use their bodies throughout the day by replacing sedentary passive activities with active and engaged activities, but in doing this we should work to optimize for health and safety.

This could mean adding a seated option for sustained activities so that users are not being made to stand for long periods of time and can adjust posture, or allowing users to switch a two-handed task to one-handed. Look for ways to encourage users to spend more time in our application without becoming fatigued or putting themselves at risk of injury due to overexertion, repetitive motion, or loss of balance.

PRINCIPLE 7: SIZE AND SPACE FOR APPROACH AND USE

Appropriate size and space are provided for approach, reach, manipulation, and use regardless of a user's body size, posture, or mobility.

Guidelines:

7a. Provide a clear line of sight to important elements for any seated or standing user.

7b. Make reach to all components comfortable for any seated or standing user.

7c. Accommodate variations in hand and grip size.

7d. Provide adequate space for the use of assistive devices or personal assistance (Center for Universal Design, 1997).

When designing or augmenting immersive environments, we are confronted with the difficulty of making that environment feel, operate, and function similarly across a range of users. Variations in user height, room size, and ceiling height alone provide a significant challenge that requires careful consideration. One way to take a flexible approach to design of spatial applications is to adapt to fluctuations in the user environment. For all spatial applications, we are limited by the size of the user's environment. For VR applications, this dictates how much space we can expect users to have for movement within our application without any joystick or other user-controlled movement system. For AR applications, we have the much more difficult task of not only adapting to the shape and size of the environment, but also adapting to the variety of objects and surfaces within that environment.

The general recommendations are for VR users to have at least a 9 × 9-foot area of object- and wall-free space with 6.5 × 6.5 feet reserved as the designated use space, to allow for some amount of overreach before collision outside of the marked area. To expect that all users are operating within these suggested guidelines assumes that all users have enough square footage in their home to devote to the use of these devices.

While many users may be able to meet these requirements, some may have designated spaces that far exceed these, while others users have spaces that fall below them, or choose to remain stationary during use. Further still, these requirements often do not account for user height in spaces with ceilings and obstructions that do not allow for full arm extension overhead without striking the ceiling.

When web design moved to a responsive model as user traffic shifted to mobile devices, it did so as a necessary reaction to changes in user behavior and device friction. The need for responsive design in spatial applications is apparent, as there are few standard spaces in which we can expect users to operate. We must investigate methods of adapting our critical features to fit and shift into a variety of user spaces to account for variation in the size and shape of the space and of the user themselves. Users of different sizes in environments of different sizes will have varied experiences with our applications, and there are opportunities to design systems now that can respond to those differences. If we start to think responsively now, we can save ourselves some of the heartache endured by those designers who have had to rebuild their product to operate on thousands of different device and browser specifications.

BUILDING EXPERIENCES FOR EVERYONE

When we can invite the broadest possible user base to engage with our applications, we increase our chance of successful adoption, long-term use, and shareability. The UD framework is not perfect, but it does give us a unique perspective from which to view our work as design applications and experiences that will exist in our environments with us. There are incredible opportunities for research and investigation in these areas, and there is so much more to learn from architects and designers who have long-standing experience solving complex spatial problems. In many ways, spatial computing is the convergence of architecture and software development. The considerations of UD are interrelated and require a simultaneous approach as we solve problems that demand multisensory and multifaceted solutions. We should not limit ourselves to theory and practice from the world of software as we hope to create experiences that embed themselves more deeply into the lives of users.

As we reimagine the ways that we will experience physical spaces, how we will approach computing, how we will play, and how we will work, let us make sure that we imagine those things for as many people as possible. Those currently with a disability should challenge themselves to consider the limitations of others whose disability may differ. We must consider designing for our future selves as well as for someone who will encounter disability in their own life, given enough time.

We must stay curious about how we can make experiences not just more accessible but more adaptable and flexible over the long term—and invite people from other backgrounds to engage in this thinking with us. UD is best done in diverse teams where we are able to push the limits of our designs against a variety of perspectives.

WHAT ARE WE MISSING?

As we move forward with spatial computing, what is it that we have missed along the way?

Accessibility in spatial computing:

- Spatial computing should prioritize accessibility to ensure inclusivity for users with disabilities.
- Designing for accessibility in spatial computing involves considering factors such as visual impairments, hearing impairments, mobility limitations, and cognitive disabilities.
- Providing alternative input methods, voice commands, captioning, and haptic feedback can enhance accessibility in spatial computing experiences.
- Developers and designers should follow accessibility guidelines and standards to create accessible interfaces and interactions in spatial computing.

Ableism:

- Ableism refers to discrimination or prejudice against individuals with disabilities, and it can manifest in spatial computing technologies and applications.

- Designers and developers must be mindful of ableism and, when designing spatial computing experiences, must actively work to avoid excluding or marginalizing individuals with disabilities.
- Promoting UD principles and considering diverse user needs can help combat ableism in spatial computing.
- Collaboration with individuals with disabilities, disability advocacy groups, and accessibility experts is crucial to ensure inclusive spatial computing solutions.

Culture in spatial computing:

- Culture plays a significant role in the design and adoption of spatial computing technologies.
- Different cultures may have unique perspectives, values, and preferences that influence the use and acceptance of spatial computing.
- Designers should consider cultural factors such as language, symbols, aesthetics, and social norms to create culturally inclusive spatial computing experiences.
- Localization efforts, involving adapting content and interfaces to specific cultural contexts, can enhance user engagement and acceptance of spatial computing technologies across different cultures.

Global perspective in spatial computing:

- Spatial computing has a global impact, and its development should consider diverse global perspectives.
- Different regions and countries may have varying technological infrastructures, economic conditions, and access to resources, all of which can affect the adoption and implementation of spatial computing.
- Inclusive global development of spatial computing should involve addressing infrastructure gaps, bridging the digital divide, and considering affordability and accessibility in different regions.

- Collaboration between international stakeholders, policymakers, and technology providers is crucial for a holistic and equitable global perspective in spatial computing.

Interconnection of human and nature in spatial computing:

- Spatial computing has the potential to facilitate a deeper connection between humans and the natural environment.
- AR experiences can overlay digital content onto the physical world, allowing users to interact with nature in new ways.
- Spatial computing can be used to create educational experiences, environmental simulations, and conservation efforts to promote environmental awareness and sustainability.
- Designing spatial computing experiences should encourage respect, appreciation, and preservation of nature to foster a harmonious interconnection between humans and the natural world.

QUESTIONS FOR REFLECTION

1. What feature of your application is accessible to the smallest number of users?
2. Does your application provide a variety of input and feedback methods that leverage a variety of sensory input? If not, why?
3. How are users invited into your experience? Is your onboarding or tutorial geared toward a range of users?
4. How can you build in flexible and responsive features to accommodate variation of users and hardware over the life cycle of your application?

PROJECT FOR CONSIDERATION

Identify a single VR or mixed-reality experience able to be played on a head-mounted display. If you do not own one, consider reaching out to a local library, university, entertainment facility, or other space that may have devices available for use.

Play the experience for several 5–10-minute sessions. For each session consider changing the parameters in one of the following ways:

- Play seated.
- Play using only a single controller.
- If the experience is compatible with hand tracking, play with no controllers.
- Play with the audio turned off (if subtitles or text assistance are available, toggle these on for a separate play-through).
- Play in a small room.
- Consider coming up with your own parameters that may alter your play experience.

For each session spend five minutes detailing your experience and then answer the below questions.

1. Were you limited in what you were able to accomplish during the experience in any way? If so, how?
2. How might the experience be redesigned to allow you to complete any actions you were unable to?
3. Did you feel uncomfortable or frustrated at any point? If so, why?
4. How might the experience be redesigned to make it more comfortable or ease your frustration?

This exercise is not a replacement for broad playtesting—especially for playtesting with those with disabilities. What it does do is provide you with an opportunity for hands-on reflection on how to consider experiences from a different perspective.

5
—

Merging Human Creativity with Technology

To be human in a world shaped by the silent architect of our times, technology, is to exist in a paradox. We are both creators and creations, shaping technology while being reshaped by it in return. As humans, we experience emotions, make decisions, and create tools that help us thrive and survive. Our lived experiences lead to innovations; imagine a world without hammers, knives, or axes. Humans would still be innovative, but in different ways. The earliest human technologies consisted of stone tools, which have now advanced to innovations like spatial computing. For over two million years, humans have continually innovated technology, and in the 21st century, these advancements are occurring faster than ever.

How do our technologies reflect and shape who we are? With our tools evolving from simple hammers to spatial computing, the question shifts from what these technologies accomplish to how they transform our understanding of ourselves, individually, socially, and as humans. The onset of the global COVID-19 pandemic in 2020 profoundly impacted our use of spatial computing, accelerating the way people used it to connect with others. Virtual meetings became a primary means for individuals to connect with colleagues, friends, and family. There were virtual funerals in social VR, and people set up cameras to allow those unable to attend in person to participate via Zoom.

Human Spatial Computing. Reginé Gilbert and Doug North Cook, Oxford University Press.
© Reginé Gilbert and Doug North Cook (2026). DOI: 10.1093/9780191966477.003.0005

In the past few years, students taking a user experience design course at New York University (NYU) have been asked to work in groups and answer questions related to design. The course aims to teach students how to create inclusive and accessible user experiences.

One of the first questions asked is: "What does it mean to be human?" The question prompts students to remember that they are designing with humans in mind, so they must consider what being human means. Although students are from various cultures and socio-economic backgrounds, a pattern has emerged in the word choices used in their responses over the years. The recurring words include: ability, choices, communication, compassion, creativity, curiosity, emotions, intelligence, language, and social. This chapter examines each of these human traits categorized by students through systems. Humans live within systems. Examining human traits through different lenses can help us create better designs in spatial computing.

By understanding how people perceive and interact with the world around them, we can create interfaces that are intuitive and easy to use, which can lead to more immersive and engaging experiences for users, as well as increased efficiency and productivity. Additionally, considering diverse perspectives can help us create designs that are inclusive and accessible to people of all abilities and backgrounds. Overall, examining human traits from different points of view (lenses) is an important part of creating successful designs in spatial computing.

The following list provides five ways to apply lenses to human traits, and these are considered at the end of each section on traits that follows.

1. **Systematic lens**: How do structural elements shape our experience?
2. **Cultural lens**: How do shared meanings and identities interact with technology?
3. **Societal lens**: What does spatial computing mean for our collective experience?
4. **Individual lens**: What does spatial computing mean for personal observations and behaviors?
5. **Internal lens**: What does spatial computing mean for our thoughts and feelings?

HUMAN TRAITS THAT INTERACT WITH SPATIAL COMPUTING TECHNOLOGIES

Ability

When asking five people to define the term "ability," it's likely that each will provide a different interpretation. In the design field, "ability" refers to the potential to physically or mentally perform tasks. Spatial computing, which involves various inputs and outputs, effectively utilizes and enhances our inherent abilities.

It is important to note that perspectives on ability are interconnected. Societal and systematic understandings of "ability" can significantly shape cultural, individual, and internalized views, and these perspectives can influence each other. Human abilities are fluid and diverse, differing from person to person. No two individuals have the same unique combination of strengths, and abilities may change over time due to factors such as age, experience, injury, or circumstances.

A disability is typically defined as a condition—physical, cognitive, sensory, or emotional—that may limit a person's ability to perform certain activities or engage with their environment in the same way as others. However, this definition is contextual; a disability is not solely about an individual's limitations but also about how society, infrastructure, and technology influence access and inclusion. Disabilities can differ significantly in their impact on a person's daily life, affecting physical, psychological, and social functioning.

Disabilities can influence an individual's ability to participate in work, education, leisure activities, self-care, and caregiving within their specific environment. Each person's experience with disability is unique and multi-dimensional. With the right supports and services, individuals can enhance their functioning and improve their ability to manage daily activities. Ultimately, disability is not just a personal limitation but an interaction between individual capabilities and external factors, such as access to healthcare, assistive technologies, and community support.

In 2022, one of the authors sponsored and provided advice for research conducted by Equal Entry involving blind participants using virtual reality (VR). Current VR systems are mostly inaccessible to blind users, but simple and practical solutions can enhance their navigation and interaction experiences. Equal Entry, in collaboration with XR Access, studied how blind users perceive virtual environments, identifying key challenges and potential solutions. The research focused on describing three-dimensional content and navigating within a virtual space. Through testing with blind participants, the researchers discovered that VR accessibility issues often arise from poor selection mechanics, a lack of audio feedback, and complex interaction methods. The study outlines 11 key lessons that can assist developers in creating more inclusive spatial computing experiences.

Virtual reality technology presents exciting possibilities, but also creates unique challenges for blind and visually impaired users. Researchers discovered several important insights when testing VR with blind participants (Equal Entry, 2022). Here are some of the key challenges and solutions from that study.

Object Interaction Issues

- **Small Object Selection Problem**: Hand controllers make targeting small objects difficult
- **Solution**: Expand selection areas dynamically to improve accuracy
- **Raycast Selection Challenges Problem**: Users struggle to hold controllers steady for precise pointing
- **Solution**: Offer two-hand grip options and head-based pointing alternatives
- **Controller Direction Confusion Problem**: Users couldn't tell where their controller was pointing
- **Solution**: Add physical markers (textured surfaces) to help users feel the controller's orientation
- **Lack of Grab Feedback Problem**: Users weren't sure if they successfully grabbed items
- **Solution**: Add sound cues for object pickup and release actions

Navigation Challenges

- **Insufficient Walking Sounds Problem**: Footsteps don't change in pitch, making distance judgment difficult
- **Solution**: Implement three-dimensional audio cues to help users orient in space
- **Missing Wall Collision Feedback Problem**: Users can't tell if they're walking into walls
- **Solution**: Stop footstep sounds when movement is blocked and play collision sounds

Information Access Issues

- **Unskippable Descriptions Problem**: Long product descriptions forced users to listen completely
- **Solution**: Add skip and fast-forward options for speech output
- **Fixed Speech Speed Problem**: Users had to listen at a set speed, slowing navigation
- **Solution**: Allow users to adjust speech output rate dynamically
- **Interfering Background Audio Problem**: Music or ambient noise made speech announcements hard to hear
- **Solution**: Provide options to mute background sounds when needed
- **Information Overload Problem**: Users received excessive details all at once
- **Solution**: Allow users to request additional details in stages
- **Need for Physical Guidance Problem**: Users struggled with orientation, requiring hands-on assistance
- **Solution**: Implement software-based controller assistance or direct teleportation options

Making VR accessible for blind users isn't just possible; it's necessary for creating truly inclusive digital experiences. Many solutions, such as improved audio cues, alternative selection methods, and customizable speech output, are straightforward but highly impactful. By prioritizing universal design principles, developers can ensure VR technology expands access rather than creating new barriers. This research demonstrates that thoughtful adjustments can create a more inclusive digital world for everyone.

One tool that helps people with disabilities access virtual reality is WalkinVR. WalkinVR is an assistive technology specifically designed to make VR experiences more accessible for individuals with physical disabilities. This software solution enables users with limited mobility to fully participate in VR.

The creators of WalkinVR have developed a way for people with various disabilities to engage in VR experiences. It allows individuals with mobility and neurological disabilities to play games through a plug-in on the digital video game service Steam, which adapts the experience to meet their needs.

WalkinVR offers different modes to accommodate players with disabilities. If a player requires assistance, they can invite a friend to join them in the game. Those with mobility issues can use controllers to navigate the virtual environment or utilize the space drag feature. Additionally, players can interact with the virtual world directly using their hands instead of relying on controllers (see Figure 5.1).

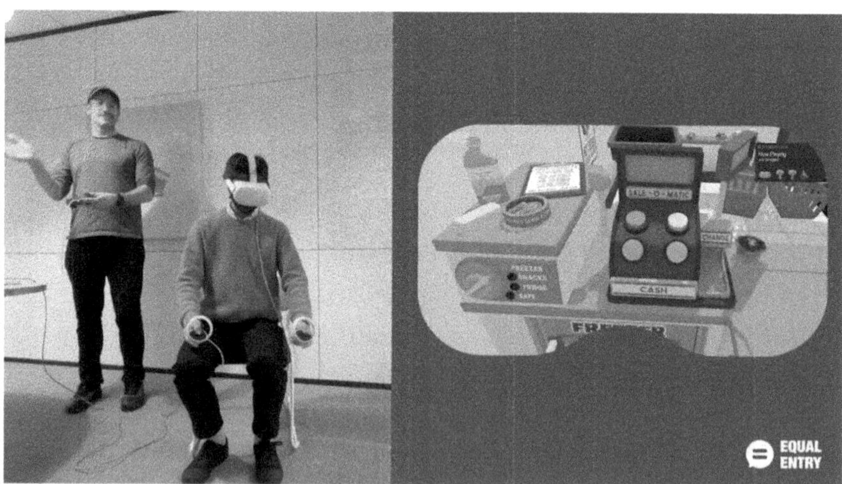

Figure 5.1 Thomas Logan and Kenji Yanagawa Showcasing WalkinVR Using the Experience, Job Simulator.

Source: Photo by Amanda Fujii. Reproduced with permission from Thomas Logan of Equal Entry. https://equalentry.com/virtual-reality-accessibility-walkinvr/.

How can we create a world where different abilities are valued, supported, and included? True inclusivity recognizes that ability is not defined by a single standard; rather, it embraces the diverse ways in which people experience, interact with, and contribute to the world.

The following questions explore ability through the five lenses:

1. **Systematic lens**: How does a person's capacity to perform specific tasks impact their experience within organizational systems?
2. **Cultural lens**: In what ways do societal norms influence our definition of ability across different cultural contexts?
3. **Societal lens**: How do varying definitions of ability shape broader social dynamics and structures?
4. **Individual lens**: What unique personal skills and talents might be overlooked when using standardized measures of ability?
5. **Internal lens**: How does one's perception of personal capabilities affect their willingness to engage with new experiences?

While ability describes what we can do, it is our choices that determine what we will do.

Choices

Humans are self-aware, and thus we have options when it comes to making decisions. These decisions turn into our choices. Although our abilities are limited, we have the power to choose our actions, beliefs, and values, which ultimately shape our lives. Through our choices, we express our humanity and define who we are as individuals.

All choices in spatial computing are designed—every object has its affordances programmed. Social VR and other experiences allow people to customize avatars allowing freedom of expression and choice. People are able to select hair color, eye color, skin tone, and accessories like earrings and clothing.

Customizing an avatar allows people to make an avatar reflective of themselves or the person they dream of being. However, most experiences lack options for people who use assistive technologies, for example, wheelchairs, canes, walkers, or hearing aids. If options are provided for creating an avatar to reflect each user, there needs to be more consideration of the different types of people who may use a product.

The following list shows how the five lenses apply to choices:

1. **Systematic lens**: How are actions and processes directed by established protocols within organizational frameworks?
2. **Cultural lens**: In what ways are behaviors shaped by the shared beliefs and values of particular cultural groups?
3. **Societal lens**: How do broader societal expectations influence individual and collective choices?
4. **Individual lens**: What role do expressions of personal autonomy play in shaping unique behaviors and decisions?
5. **Internal lens**: How are actions driven by an individual's self-awareness and personal desires?

By fostering choice and freedom of expression, spatial computing opens up possibilities for individuals to shape their realities and communicate their ideas in innovative and compelling ways.

Communication

When we interpret another person's words or actions, we communicate. Spatial computing enables us to share in diverse ways and immerse ourselves in alternate realities. However, our interactions are only sometimes easy to comprehend, and this depends on how and where we communicate with each other.

Billinghurst et al. (2003) examined how people communicate face to face using AR and projection screens, and concluded that different communication tools result in a greater number of communication styles. In their first experiment, they compared AR technology collaboration with unmediated and screen-based unions. In the second experiment, collaborations using three distinct AR displays were compared. The researchers found that users displayed similar collaborative behaviors in AR interfaces to those seen in in face-to-face unmediated collaboration. However, their communication behavior varied based on the type of AR display employed.

The following list shows how the five lenses apply to communication:

1. **Systematic lens**: How does communication enable and sustain coordinated functioning within complex systems?
2. **Cultural lens**: In what ways does communication serve as a medium for shared understanding across different cultural contexts?
3. **Societal lens**: How does communication shape and maintain societal structures and norms over time?
4. **Individual lens**: What role does personal expression through communication play in forming meaningful connections?
5. **Internal lens**: How does the process of internal dialogue influence our conscious awareness and decision-making?

   Effective communication opens channels of understanding, but compassion transforms those channels into bridges of genuine connection.

Compassion

What is the meaning of compassion? Can it be learned or is it inherent? Compassion is about being able to understand and help others when they need it. It involves both internal and external factors and can be affected by the circumstances. Empathy, fairness, kindness, selflessness, and a connection with others are some of its fundamental qualities. To teach people compassion, spatial computing simulations are used to create immersive experiences. Nondisabled people often lack compassion toward those with disabilities, and there are over 1 billion people with disabilities in the world. For example, autism is a disability that affects approximately 1% of the world's population.

According to the World Health Organization (WHO), approximately 1 in every 100 children has autism. The WHO defines autism spectrum disorders (ASD) as "a diverse group of conditions" that "are characterized by some degree of difficulty with social interaction and communication" (WHO, 2023). Spatial computing allows people to experience situations through narratives, simulations, and interactive scenarios.

Through various simulations, Autismity (a division of SPOSA, a Slovakian nongovernmental organization that brings family members who are autistic together with others) allows people to experience a day in the life of someone with autism. One scenario is a school setting where people experience various sounds (such as someone tapping their feet on the ground) and visuals (some stationary objects move for people on the spectrum) that someone with ASD might experience. Autism can cause people to feel sensory overload, and the simulation attempts to enhance people's compassion for others by putting them in someone else's shoes. We all see the world differently, and spatial computing does provide an opportunity for people to experience things they might not experience otherwise. There is controversy on whether a spatial computing experience can allow someone to feel for another, but the attempts continue. Professor of philosophy Erick Ramirez says spatial computing may not be the "empathy machine" we think it is because we need to consider "our biology, cultural concepts, past experiences, emotions, expectations and even features of the specific situations in which you find yourself" (Ramirez, 2018). He continues:

> Imagine if I came to the conclusion that homelessness wasn't that big a deal because I enjoyed the challenging puzzle elements in the VR experience *Becoming Homeless* [a VR experience created by Stanford University for people to experience homelessness]. Even worse, imagine if I believed I now had better insight into homelessness, and that my enjoyment left me with the impression that it wasn't as bad as I feared.

The following list shows how the five lenses apply to compassion:

1. **Systematic lens**: How does compassion foster cooperation and collective responsibility within organizational structures?
2. **Cultural lens**: In what ways does compassion embody shared values and ethical frameworks across different cultures?

3. **Societal lens**: How does compassion enhance social harmony and cohesion within communities?
4. **Individual lens**: How do expressions of compassion reflect personal emotional responses to others' suffering?
5. **Internal lens**: How does compassion toward oneself reveal deeper self-empathy and understanding?

Compassion connects us to the world as it is, but creativity empowers us to envision the world as it could be.

Creativity (Blending of Virtual and Real Worlds)

Creativity is defined as the tendency to generate or recognize ideas, alternatives, or possibilities that may be useful in solving problems, communicating with others, and entertaining ourselves (Franken, 1994). Spatial computing allows for an interactivity that is not as accessible through the typical ways people experience creative projects.

Patrick Hackett and Drew Skillman took creativity to another level when they launched Tilt Brush (acquired by Google in 2015). It allowed people to create art in a virtual environment using their controllers. Since the inception of Tilt Brush, it has had many users and allowed for people to create worlds, characters, and virtual environments for people to navigate. In 2021, Google decided to shutter Tilt Brush and made it open source, which led to the launch of Open Brush in 2021—an open-source project that has brought the magic of Tilt Brush to new platforms (see Figure 5.2).

Spatial computing has opened new avenues for creative expression as developers continue to explore how to build new ways of creating and reinventing mediums that benefit from spatial interfaces. There is already a range of three-dimensional modeling and asset-creation tools available—notably Adobe Substance 3D Modeler (formerly Oculus Medium prior to being sold by Meta to Adobe), Gravity Sketch, Masterpiece, and several others. Design teams working on early prototypes use tools like ShapesXR to rapidly prototype and collaborate on designs with multiple team members working together in VR to solve spatial design problems.

Figure 5.2 Google's Tilt Brush (Salon Viva Technology, Paris).

Source: Reproduced from Jean-Pierre Dalbéra (2016). https://www.flickr.com/photos/72746018@N00/28099682105. Licensed under a Creative Commons Attribution 2.0 Generic (CC BY 2.0).

Many major architecture firms now also use VR headsets to visualize early designs, share concepts with outside stakeholders, and rapidly ideate new forms using quick three-dimensional modeling tools in the headset. From sculpting and modeling to music creation and sneaker design, most creative disciplines can already find an application for exploring new possibilities in their discipline. Though most of this is in its very early stages and unexplored, it is ready for new companies, designers, and artists to push the boundaries of how we might enable and empower human creativity through spatial computing.

The following list shows how the five lenses apply to creativity:

1. **Systematic lens**: How does creativity drive innovation and problem-solving approaches within organized systems?
2. **Cultural lens**: In what ways does creativity serve as an expression of cultural diversity and collective identity?
3. **Societal lens**: How does creativity fuel broader societal progress and evolutionary development?

4. **Individual lens**: How does creative expression unleash personal potential and highlight individual uniqueness?
5. **Internal lens**: How does creativity ignite internal thought exploration and expand mental frameworks?

Creativity generates answers to questions we didn't know existed, while curiosity ensures we never stop asking new ones.

Curiosity

How curious are you? What makes us curious? In life, we constantly learn, explore, investigate, and naturally desire to know more about things.

Curiosity VR allows users to map their homes and turn them into interactive gaming spaces. With custom tools, multi-room layouts, and multiplayer features, players can enjoy a variety of games in their familiar surroundings. Spatial computing enhances this experience by providing new perspectives, making the same physical space feel different depending on the game being played.

Humans' curious nature has us seek out new things and with spatial computing the possibilities for curiosity and creativity are endless.

The following list shows how the five lenses apply to curiosity:

1. **Internal lens**: How does curiosity reveal deeper self-empathy and personal understanding?
2. **Systematic lens**: In what ways does curiosity drive inquiry and discovery within established systems?
3. **Cultural lens**: How does curiosity shape cultural learning and exploration across different communities?
4. **Societal lens**: How does collective curiosity fuel broader societal progress and innovation?
5. **Individual lens**: How does curiosity inspire personal learning and continuous growth?

Curiosity allows us to explore the world around us, yet it is our emotions that help us connect with that world on a deeper level.

Emotions

Situations happen throughout life that can bring an array of emotions. Each day we experience a range of emotions from sadness, anger, happiness, and more. Emotions are both physical, physiological, and complex. Emotions and affective factors, such as confusion, frustration, shame, and pride, are recognized as major influences in learning (Immordino-Yang & Damasio, 2007). Due to the immersive presence of spatial computing, people's emotions can be affected greatly in positive and negative ways.

Emotions are psychological states that are biologically based and arise from neurophysiological changes related to our thoughts, feelings, and behavioral responses, often accompanied by a sense of pleasure or displeasure. Currently, there is no scientific consensus on a definition of emotions. It is important to be cautious about the types of memories we create for users, as we must consider the potential to trigger trauma. Additionally, we should embrace the power of emotional connections.

The following list shows how the five lenses apply to emotions:

1. **Systematic lens**: How do emotions affect performance and decision-making processes within organizational systems?
2. **Cultural lens**: In what ways are emotional expressions guided by cultural norms and typical emotional patterns?
3. **Societal lens**: How do collective emotions influence broader societal moods and emerging trends?
4. **Individual lens**: How do emotional responses signify personal feelings and reactions to external stimuli?
5. **Internal lens**: How do emotions impact self-perception and overall mental health?

     Emotions alert us to what deserves our attention, but intelligence helps us determine what to do with that awareness.

Intelligence

AI and AR have seen increased use in the retail industry, from allowing users to "try on" clothes to seeing how furniture might look in their home. There is a wide range of use cases for using AI and AR for customer service and navigation.

In general, intelligence allows humans to learn and apply what they know. Over time, human intelligence has been incorporated into the digital world through AI, a form of computer science that uses inputs that allow machines to think and learn like humans. Bias in AI, a critical issue, is the research focus of many computer scientists.

AI enhances AR and VR by enabling real-time object recognition and tracking, responsive computer vision, natural language processing for voice commands, predictive analytics for personalized experiences, and usage analytics for optimization and customer satisfaction, ultimately delivering immersive and tailored VR experiences.

The following list shows how the five lenses apply to intelligence:

1. **Systematic lens**: How does intelligence improve efficiency and effectiveness within organized systems?
2. **Cultural lens**: In what ways is intelligence valued differently across various cultural contexts?
3. **Societal lens**: How does intelligence influence societal progress and social stratification?
4. **Individual lens**: How do measures of intelligence mark or define personal cognitive abilities?
5. **Internal lens**: How does perceived intelligence influence self-perception and overall self-confidence?

Here are five ways to reexamine intelligence used in spatial computing:

1. Creatives can ensure that AI algorithms designed with empathy and ethical considerations can be achieved through careful planning and implementation of ethical guidelines and standards.
2. To prevent AI from perpetuating discrimination and bias in society, we can ensure diverse representation in the development of AI systems and create accountability measures to address instances of bias.

3. Balancing the benefits of AI automation with the potential loss of jobs and economic disruption is a complex issue that requires careful consideration and planning. However, strategies such as retraining programs and support for impacted communities can help mitigate these challenges.

4. Implementing measures to safeguard against the misuse of AI-powered technologies, such as deepfakes and disinformation campaigns, can involve combining technological solutions and regulatory frameworks to limit their harmful effects.

5. Promoting greater transparency and accountability in developing and deploying AI systems can be achieved through measures like open data sharing, independent auditing, and ethical review boards. These strategies ensure that AI systems are developed and used responsibly and ethically.

Intelligence describes our capacity to reason and learn, but language describes our ability to transmit that reasoning across time and space.

Language

There are over 7,117 languages spoken in the world; English is the most widely spoken, followed by Mandarin Chinese and French (Ethnologue, n.d.). When thinking about languages, most people forget that "language" also includes sign language. Included in the 7,000-plus languages spoken are 300 forms of sign language used primarily by deaf and hard-of-hearing communities around the world. The use of spatial computing is being used to help people learn and understand how people use spoken language and sign language.

Deb et al. (2018) sought to use AR to assist the deaf community. The objective of the study was to create an AR application that displays three-dimensional animated sign gestures on a mobile system when the camera focuses on a media card with a marked letter. A quasi-experimental design was used to assess the system's efficacy and learning outcomes. The experimental outcomes showed a substantial improvement in the students' sign-language learning abilities when using the AR application.

AR has opened new possibilities for individuals with physical disabilities to access and interpret information, which helps improve their interactions with others. This technology combines real-world and virtual elements in a dynamic, interactive environment. Educational specialists are excited about the potential for AR to provide innovative methods for teaching individuals with disabilities. It has the potential to help them better understand complex spatial situations and abstract concepts that can be difficult to grasp in the physical world. Additionally, it may enable new and practical approaches to learning that are not possible with other technology-based teaching methods.

The following list shows how the five lenses apply to language:

1. **Systematic lens**: How does language function as a communication tool with structured rules and patterns?
2. **Cultural lens**: In what ways does language serve as a shared symbolic representation within cultural groups?
3. **Societal lens**: How does language act as social glue and contribute to identity building across communities?
4. **Individual lens**: How does language enable personal expression and the creation of individual meaning?
5. **Internal lens**: How do mental representations of language influence cognitive processing and thought patterns?

   Language without social interaction becomes monologue; social interaction without language loses precision—we need both to build relationships and communities.

Social Interaction

Social interaction plays a crucial role in designing and implementing spatial computing systems. Integrating social interaction into spatial computing can significantly enhance the user experience by fostering collaboration and social engagement among users. Ethical considerations must be considered when designing socially interactive spatial computing systems to ensure user safety and privacy.

Spatial computing can be leveraged to encourage social interaction and collaboration among users across various industries. The adoption and use of spatial computing in different sectors are directly impacted by the level of social interaction facilitated by the system. Due to our evolution and biological nature, humans are social. Engaging with other people is what most of us do daily—whether for work, school, or play, we socialize with others. We seek out others in different ways. Spatial computing allows people to be social and interact worldwide through games, events, and experiences.

Social VR is a transformative or transformational technology that enables VR users to connect, engage, and participate in a wide range of activities together, including watching movies, playing games, attending concerts, or collaborating at work. With its vast potential and numerous benefits, Social VR has emerged as one of the most significant applications of VR technology.

Zheng et al. (2022) examined safety in social VR. For their study, they looked at 14 different commercially available social VR applications. They narrowed their selection by considering the number of downloads across various VR app stores, including Oculus Store, Steam VR, and Sidequest. From this analysis, they chose four social VR apps for further investigation:

1. Rec Room: This app allows users to interact with various objects and participate in mini games alongside other users.
2. VRChat: Known for its nontraditional social interactions and the creation of performative memes, VRChat provides a unique social VR experience.
3. Horizon Worlds: This app allows users to explore virtual worlds and consume and create content within those environments.

4. AltspaceVR: This app is another social VR platform that enables users to connect with others and engage in various activities within shared virtual spaces.

The research team suggested that:

A key concern mentioned by multiple users across platforms was the existence of minors in these VR environments. Although users seemed to be split on whether to blame parents or developers for negligence, users unanimously expressed that minors did not belong on the platform, as their safety could not be guaranteed.

(Zheng et al., 2022)

The key findings of the research were that further investigation is required regarding child safety, user trust, prevention of abusive language, and other safety concerns. People seek safe places, whether they are online or off. The individual and organization are responsible for creating and using Social VR to make it a welcoming environment.

The following list shows how the five lenses apply to social interaction:

1. **Systematic lens**: How do structured and organized social interactions influence group dynamics within formal systems?
2. **Cultural lens**: How are social customs defined and perpetuated by specific cultural contexts?
3. **Societal lens**: In what ways is social behavior shaped by broader societal expectations and norms?
4. **Individual lens**: How does personalized social engagement reflect unique interaction preferences and styles?
5. **Internal lens**: How do subconscious social behaviors and internalized norms affect interpersonal relationships?

    Social interaction reveals what makes us fundamentally human—and these insights must inform how we design the technologies that will shape our future, particularly in immersive environments.

DESIGN CONSIDERATIONS

Critical Design, Speculative Design, and Humans

Critical design brings the future into the present to elicit a response. Kei-ichi Matsuda's 2016 short film *Hyper-Reality* provides a glimpse of the future where spatial computing merges the physical and virtual worlds. The story follows a person's daily routine, beginning with them sitting on a bus and using their digital device. In this AR world, they are constantly bombarded with advertisements and information. While on the bus, the main character types two questions into Google on their digital device: "Who am I?" and "Where am I going?" As a result, a hologram-like image of the person appears in front of them, and an AR map displays their destination. These questions are crucial as technology becomes more advanced and intertwined with our lives.

The film depicts a future where technology effortlessly integrates into our daily lives, blurring the lines between reality and virtuality. It highlights the potential impact that AR and spatial computing could have on our identities and experiences. In many ways, this film explores the possibilities of a world where people are constantly connected to their devices and ranked based on their interactions with them. As with all things, there are both positives and negatives to this scenario. The film highlights the risks associated with advancements in technology, such as hand recognition systems failing after an accident, which can result in users being denied access to essential services. Considering a future where we may rely more heavily on technological systems for every-day functions, it raises the issue of a "dual vulnerability." If someone is physically injured and simultaneously disconnected from the digital services they depend on, they may struggle to obtain the necessary care and assistance.

Speculative Design 100 Years into the Future

Speculative design is a form of creative and critical design that delves into potential futures through provocative and imaginative design concepts. It involves envisioning and designing artifacts, experiences, or scenarios that challenge assumptions, question norms, and stimulate discussions about possible societal, technological, or cultural changes. Anthony Dunne and Fiona Raby introduced the concept of speculative design as a subset of critical design, which uses design to provoke thought and reflection on social, cultural, and ethical issues. Their work has been influential in pushing design beyond functional and aesthetic considerations and encouraging engagement with complex and abstract concepts that shape the future.

Speculative design often involves creating thought-provoking prototypes, installations, narratives, or scenarios that challenge present assumptions and explore potential future possibilities. It encourages people to consider the broader implications and consequences of emerging technologies, societal changes, and cultural shifts. By presenting alternative futures, speculative design prompts discussions and debates that can lead to a deeper understanding of our current choices and their potential consequences.

In 2022, the Human Spatial Computing course at NYU included a speculative design project that utilized augmented reality (AR). This initiative encouraged students to explore speculative design within the realm of spatial computing, focusing on key topics such as human–computer interaction, ethics and privacy, storytelling, human identity, ecosystems, accessibility, and bias.

The students' work was organized around five central themes: generational healing, listening to communities, food deserts, productivity culture, and mental health access. These themes were derived from the study by Bray et al. (n.d.), which examined power imbalances in design and research interactions, particularly in marginalized communities. Bray et al.'s research, conducted with community design practitioners using the Building Utopia toolkit, which highlights the importance of employing design tools that consider race and identity, especially when collaborating with Black and Indigenous communities. The findings from this study helped shape the course, guiding students to adopt ethical and inclusive design practices in their speculative AR projects.

The four-week timeline included research, ideation, poster concepts, and final presentations. Participants utilized augmented reality (AR) technologies and visualization platforms to create immersive experiences that explored key aspects of their proposed solutions. The audience, comprised of the Human Spatial Computing class, examined the intersection of speculative design and critical thought.

During the project, participants analyzed the current state of their chosen themes, identified factors that could drive positive change, developed augmented reality scenarios, and explored the impact of spatial computing. They also presented a comprehensive SWOT (strengths, weaknesses, opportunities, and threats) analysis. The final presentations combined AR assets and dashboard-style visualizations to illustrate potential futures for humanity's relationship with technology and societal advancement.

This project successfully integrated lessons on ethics, human–computer interaction, universal design, accessibility, inclusion, and the mind–body connection. By utilizing spatial computing technology, the project aimed to address various issues, communicate narratives, and deliver practical benefits to individuals, which will enhance its long-term effectiveness and usefulness.

By the end of the course, students gained a deeper understanding of the importance of storytelling and community engagement in designing spatial computing experiences. Overall, applying spatial computing technology to tackle different challenges, convey stories, and provide meaningful advantages will ultimately increase its sustained effectiveness and relevance.

Designing With Intention and Impact

Designing with intention refers to the conscious consideration of the desired outcomes and goals during the design process. It involves purposefully incorporating inclusive and ethical principles into the design decisions. However, the impact of design is evaluated based on how it is actually experienced by users. The intention behind a design may not always align with its actual impact, and it is crucial to assess and address any unintended negative consequences or exclusionary effects.

To achieve positive impact, designers in spatial computing should actively engage with diverse communities, seek feedback, and iterate on their designs. They should aim to understand the needs, values, and perspectives of the users to create experiences that are inclusive, accessible, and respectful. By involving communities in the design process, designers can better align their intentions with the impact of their creations, resulting in more thoughtful and beneficial spatial computing experiences.

QUESTIONS FOR REFLECTION

1. How can spatial computing technology be leveraged to enhance specific aspects of the human experience, such as ability, choices, communication, compassion, and creativity?
2. How can co-design and participatory design principles be applied to ensure that the product or service being designed is sensitive to aspects like accessibility and ableism?
3. Can you critically analyze past designs from a human-centered perspective and identify areas where they could have been improved? Discuss how a more human-centered approach could have positively impacted those designs.
4. How can you employ critical and speculative design principles to envision a future scenario and design products, services, or systems that challenge the status quo? How would you design "with" the future self or community, considering long-term consequences and questioning your intentions versus impacts?

PROJECTS FOR CONSIDERATION

Design Workshop with Focus on Human Experience

1. Hold a design workshop exploring different aspects of human experiences mentioned in the literature, such as ability, choices, communication, compassion, creativity, and more.
2. Design a product or service using spatial computing technology, considering the different aspects of the human experience.
3. Use methods like codesign and participatory design, ensuring their techniques are sensitive to aspects like accessibility and ableism and balancing the intention and impact.
4. The workshop would also include activities where they critically analyze past designs and discuss how those designs could have been improved with a more human-centered approach.

Critical and Speculative Design Project

1. Based on the ideas of critical design and speculative design mentioned in the literature, participants can engage in a design project where they envision a future scenario and design products, services, or systems for that scenario. The aim here would be to challenge the status quo and speculate on the kind of future we might have if we keep designing with the same mindsets and assumptions.
2. The challenge for participants would be to design with the future self or community in mind rather than for themselves. The focus should be on their intentions versus their design's impacts, and methods should promote understanding of the long-term consequences.
3. Designing for future scenarios—what would happen if certain technologies advance, if specific resources are depleted, etc.? The participants should present their designs, assumptions, and the imagined future scenario for which they are designed.

The Body

Every person experiences the world differently—through their body with their senses. Spatial computing systems allow for varying levels of override of those senses to create experiences that induce presence, create a sense of digital embodiment, and provide the opportunity to transcend our body entirely and enter a new (albeit digital) body. Virtual reality (VR) head-mounted displays (HMD), paired with hand controllers, allow for real-time audio, visual, and haptic feedback capable of generating experiences with a range of sensory possibilities. High-end flight simulators allow pilots to test experimental controls for aircraft that have yet to be built while hearing audio feedback and radio tower guidance.

Tyler Hurd's 2017 VR music video "Chocolate" allows users to embody a robotic god being worshiped by a herd of cats in an experience described by the creator as "shiny and glimmering, smooth and sexy, cute and strange, overwhelming and astonishing." As we consider designing for these experiences it is important to explore how presence and embodiment are achieved, how to design for all the senses, and to consider the implications, opportunities, and dangers of playing with embodiment.

Spatial computing systems offer us the opportunity to bring our bodies into the digital realm—and to explore possibilities for embodying new forms that deviate from our own. The sensation of bodily presence that can be granted in a VR experience can often be as powerful as the experiences we have unaided by these systems. In their research

Human Spatial Computing. Reginé Gilbert and Doug North Cook, Oxford University Press.
© Reginé Gilbert and Doug North Cook (2026). DOI: 10.1093/9780191966477.003.0006

on the efficacy of embodiment in VR, Cebolla and colleagues describe VR as having a similar cognitive effect to reality: "VR can be considered an advanced imagery system and an experiential form of imagery that is as effective as reality in inducing cognitive, emotional, and behavioral responses" (Cebolla et al., 2019). The experiences that we have are uniquely ours, filtered through our minds and the stored conceptual model of our own bodies.

Using these technologies, we can begin to affect our perception of our own bodies. According to Matamala-Gomez et al. (2019), "VR systems allow the replacement of a person's real body with a virtual body representation, allowing the subject to feel embodied in a virtual body."

We now explore how our senses are engaged in spatial computing environments, the difference between embodiment and presence, and the importance of and understanding how we relate to each other, and ourselves, as digital bodies in virtual environments.

THE SENSES

Spatial computing systems are an invitation to recover our full range of senses in our relationship with computing. It is when we engage all the senses that we start to create deep, rich, and lasting memories, which may become indistinguishable from memories generated outside of the use of computing devices. For our purposes here, we examine seven senses and explore how each of these can change our experience, the information we receive, and what we are able to do with that information. It is also important to acknowledge that sensory input is deeply personal, highly subjective, and varies greatly between individuals.

Note that our senses change as we age—and so does our ability to interpret that sensory information. In a study about age-related changes in sensory processing, the authors noted that "sensory function declines with advancing age, especially for hearing and vision [. . .] Likewise, there has been a long awareness of cognitive deficits with advancing age in otherwise healthy adults" (Humes et al., 2013).

Vision

We perceive a massive array of information visually—from text, to how we interpret emotions, to our experience of grandeur and scale. The way that we lean on visual information for spatial computing systems is different from most other forms of computing because the experience itself should exist in full three-dimensional space. Our vision, however, is limited to a single perspective within that space, meaning that the information we receive is also limited. Remember that vision operates differently for many users with variations in the forms of degrees of vision on a spectrum toward blindness, and variations in perception of color, focal ability, distance, and other aspects. However, we must also account for variation in user hardware affecting vision, like display resolution, field of view, and environmental factors (especially for augmented reality (AR) experiences).

Visual information can feel like it supersedes our other sensory input for spatial computing because it currently has higher fidelity than most others (other than hearing). However, if we rely too heavily on sight for information transfer, we run the risk of having the experience feel hollow compared to our multisensory reality. We also run the risk of users not receiving all the information they need if they are not looking at the right place. We should work diligently to ensure that our visual information is as legible as possible for a variety of users. Below are just a few examples of how we might consider this:

- Incorporate best practices for color-blind users to perccive important information, including proper color variation and the use of symbols where previously color was the only signifier.
- Information that is essential but is only available visually—can it be perceived in another way? How much of that information can be perceived by a blind or low-vision user? Could the same information be made accessible using different sensory information?
- Ensure all text is high-contrast, large, and adjustable in size. Do not assume that methods used for text clarity in

two-dimensional applications will work in all three-dimensional applications—test and get feedback from users at a variety of points along the vision spectrum.
- Do not rely only on visual information for critical feedback to users—use audio and haptics where applicable as well.
- Ensure that user height is considered so that seated users and users of various heights do not have a disadvantage due to line of sight.
- Be aware of visual noise and clutter that may obscure objectives or goals in a crowded environmental scene.
- Look for opportunities to augment the existing control scheme with gaze-based input that allows users to employ vision as a primary or secondary control method.

Hearing

Spatial audio (audio that has its source placed in three-dimensional space) allows the user a deep sense of presence and creates unique opportunities to provide feedback, enrich experiences, and create connection. Spatial audio encounters hurdles as we navigate variations in user hearing ability, significant hardware variation, user customization of audio output devices, and the difficulty of capturing and implementing spatial audio that feels genuine in each experience.

Audio must account for noise from the user's environment for both VR and AR experiences. Neither the developer nor the user can control noise from heating, ventilation, and air conditioning (HVAC), nearby roads, other people in the environment, other audio outputs, and a variety of other sources. All of this makes audio difficult to navigate for spatial devices. Like visual information, we should attempt to give all critical information as many sensory cues as possible—giving users visual, audio, and haptic feedback (device permitting).

Accounting for audio difficulties allows for ease of demoing experiences, which often takes place in loud environments, while also providing greater access to users with hearing issues, users with broken or poorly functioning audio output, and users who do not process auditory information with as much clarity as visual information. This is where we get a clear understanding of how all users benefit from the development of features that may at first seem to be catered toward a small group—as most users will encounter either hearing loss or a device audio issue during their lifetime. While a device audio issue may be temporary, accounting for audio-reliant components of an experience allows for continued use by all users and expanded use by those with a range of hearing ability. This will become increasingly important as we confront (and become part of) an aging population globally that relies increasingly on assistive devices, technology, and interfaces.

When we combine multiple forms of sensory information we create greater legibility while also generating a richer environment. For spatial applications, it is essential that the audio experience matches the visual experience in style and esthetic to generate an authentic experience. Audio does not necessarily need to be realistic or follow the rules of the real world (this is true for all the senses). It may be worth foregoing realism for clarity. In certain instances, for example, it may be helpful not to spatialize audio and instead rely on mono or stereo output to enhance clarity and ensure user reception, regardless of their position in the environment.

To guarantee that the primary audio cuts through any environmental audio, music, or other sounds present in a scene requires creating a clear hierarchy of audio that adjusts dynamically based on user position. This ensures that the user can hear the primary audio, which may include critical information. Allowing users to easily adjust the hierarchy can also be helpful for those who may have trouble distinguishing one level of hierarchy and may wish to adjust the volume for each independently.

Smell and Taste

While we currently lack the hardware capabilities to provide robust simulation of olfactory and gustatory input, it is worth considering how these senses may be present in the future, and how we interact with them currently. If I ask you to imagine your favorite salty or spicy food right now, can you? Close your eyes for 10 seconds and think about it.

Did your mouth water? Did you have any sensation of taste? Did the texture of your mouth change? Could you get a hint of it in the air?

Many (but not all) of us have these sorts of responses to memories, suggestions, or other sensory stimulation. It is possible to trigger some of these sensations without simulating them or by simulating a different sense that triggers a sense response. This serves as an opportunity not to consider what our spatial application smells like, but rather to ask the user what this experience smells like, and if they are able to summon a response. Are the visual and audio experiences rich enough that they provoke enough of a sense of presence to leave a user with an imagined olfactory response?

Consider that experiences that achieve this level of sensory response are those that have stumbled into the surreal world of inviting user imagination to augment an already rich experience. Not all experiences can, or even should, attempt to reach this space, but it is worth exploring how we might create experiences that connect with users on such a deep level—until we have the ability to provide that type of output directly.

Touch

The sensation of touch is very difficult to manage in VR and AR and is where users are often frustrated with the current state of spatial applications. Users are often so mesmerized by the other sensory input they receive that they will attempt to sit in virtual chairs, or lean against virtual walls, only to be quickly met with the harsh reality that those objects do not, in fact, exist. Currently objects are interacted with through tracked motion controllers using button presses, or through manipulation with hand tracking and gestures. Neither of these provides a one-to-one tactile experience that relies on our existing mental model of object interaction; however, that does not mean that it is not tactile. A button press is tactile—a hand gesture is tactile—and controllers can (though maybe not for the mass market user base for some time) provide increasingly sophisticated haptic feedback.

It is unlikely that we will have the ability to meaningfully simulate tactile experiences from the physical world into digital space without extreme leaps in the technology we currently have. Instead, we must focus on how to make the tactile experiences we do have (interactions between the user and their physical environment and interactions with the device) as powerful as we can. It is worth considering, when we imagine the whole body as an input device, how we might invite users to touch more than just the controllers or their own hands. While exploring this tactility we should also be asking how users who may have limited hand function can accomplish critical tasks through other sensory input (like gaze or voice).

What other surfaces or objects can we invite into our experience that have a tactile component? The user is standing or sitting on a surface. Can we invite the user to engage with that surface or object as a part of the experience instead of ignoring it? For example, could we ask the user to lie on the floor during part of an experience, sit on the ground, put their hands on the ground, touch their hands to their knees, rub their thumbs into their index fingers, etc.? We should attempt to invite the user to bring their physical selves, and their physical surroundings, into the digital space that we are creating. When we ignore these possibilities we ignore a deep well of sensory possibilities that may awaken new sensations and feelings in our users.

Vestibular

The vestibular sense, most closely connected with the fluid in our inner ear, is our sense of movement and balance, which gives us information about where our head and body are in space. The vestibular system pairs with our vision to understand, interpret, and react to movement. This is what triggers feelings of motion sickness or nausea while riding in vehicles; it is also what triggers feelings of discomfort experienced by users in virtual environments when they experience simulated movement. This issue will persist, creating uncomfortable situations for a variety of users, until we discover a direct manipulation of the vestibular system that eliminates these responses. Until such a time, it is important that those developing experiences are mindful of the type of discomfort experienced by users with vestibular sensitivity, how to mitigate it, and how to imagine natural-feeling movement systems that lean into how our senses work together to create movement that uses our whole body.

While many VR experiences leverage joystick-controlled locomotion systems—where a user uses a single joystick to move their vision in an environment—this approach is often associated with reports of discomfort, nausea, and disorientation. While many users do not experience these effects, it can become a barrier to continued engagement not just with the experience in question, but with all spatial applications. If an application promised a delightful experience, but instead the user felt nauseous and ill, they might be unlikely to try another similar experience soon after. When we ignore vestibular issues we do a disservice not just to our users, but to users of all related applications.

Proprioception

Proprioception—the sense of our body in space—is how we know where each body part is relative to the other and to the environment. We experience this sense mostly through our muscular and skeletal system. We use our proprioception when we reach for an object out of view, when we climb stairs without looking at our feet, and it communicates with our vestibular sense when we stand on one foot to adjust our body to keep us balanced. Proprioception in virtual environments becomes interesting because we can alter the body, change how we experience proprioception, and do so dynamically. We engage with an expanded form of proprioception when we drive a car. We develop a mental model for our body operating a much larger machine, becoming aware of it at a level where we can execute complex calculations of speed and distance while maintaining a safe distance between other objects. Our senses expand to incorporate information from the dashboard, the view of the windows, the sound of the motor, the feeling of the brakes, and the movement of the steering wheel. We transfer some amount of our sense of self into the vehicle to operate it effectively. We are not the car, but in some ways we are able to embody the vehicle, to varying degrees of success. Spatial computing offers a unique opportunity to extend our existing sense of self and body in ways previously unimaginable.

We can ask "What if arms were cooked spaghetti?" The user's arms appear as a series of intertwined noodles that lack the rigid control of a skeletal system and instead rely on their ability to manipulate noodle-specific physics to interact with their environment.

While this question might seem silly, it's a question we have a few other ways of asking without disastrous consequences. We can ask significant questions about the nature of the body, how the body interacts in space, and how the body relates to itself. When we take this question beyond spaghetti and instead ask, "How could we comfortably control flight with our body? How do we use arm position to control an interface? When we touch a specific part of the arm, can we call it a complex function?"

Proprioception is where our ability resides to instill new intuitions in users. We can create impossible experiences, simulate dangerous environments, and provide complex tools that rely on the development of new skills. It is easy to lean too heavily on user expectations of how things should work when sometimes it may be necessary, or just good fun, to allow users to develop new intuitions and actions that can feel like an extension of the body.

Cybersickness and Vection

One of the more significant issues facing adoption, and retention, of users for spatial computing interfaces is the high potential, especially for first-time users, for them to experience some form of cybersickness. Lawson & Stanney (2021) provide the following description of this:

> Cybersickness is a form of motion sickness that occurs as a result of exposure to immersive eXtended Reality (XR) environments, such as virtual reality (VR) and augmented reality (AR) applications. Depending on the immersive content, 20%–95% of users

typically experience some form of cybersickness, ranging from a slight headache to an emetic response. The most common symptoms include general discomfort, headache, eyestrain, stomach awareness, nausea, sweating, sopite syndrome (a.k.a. drowsiness), and disorientation; on very rare occasion (~1%) an emetic response is experienced. Symptoms can last from minutes to days post exposure, with aftereffects manifesting as postural ataxia, visual displacements (e.g., altered vestibulo-ocular reflex), altered hand-eye coordination, among other ailments. Cybersickness has been referred to as the "elephant in the room," due to its potential to drastically limit the proliferation of XR technology.

A 2022 study into the causes of cybersickness in VR experiences points to unexpected vection and loss of control as their root cause. Teixeira et al. (2022) found that "visually induced illusions of self-motion (vection) are thought to cause cybersickness during head-mounted display based virtual reality [and] unexpected vection and a perceived loss of control increase the likelihood and severity of cybersickness."

While designers have discovered a variety of measures that seem to have some mitigating effect on vestibular discomfort (narrowing field of view during movement, adding user interface or guides during movement, and a huge range of others) no current intervention seems to be able to reduce reported vestibular issues to satisfactory levels.

Other approaches, such as teleportation or blink movement (where the user does not move using a joystick but instead their vision fades in and out as they are moved to another part of the environment) have very low vestibular incident rates but do not create a natural sense of movement that fully engages with how our vestibular system, vision, and hearing work together to interpret and feel movement.

This is not a solved problem, nor has it experienced the depth of exploration needed to solve it. We must continue to explore new ideas that embrace a multisensory approach while developing experiences that use our natural body movement in physical space as the core form of movement, using teleportation, joystick-based movement, or other artificial forms of locomotion only when necessary. There are exceptions to this—specifically in the adaptation of traditional forms of video games into spatial computing.

Di Luca et al. (2021) published a collection of findings (shared publicly on GitHub) related to over 100 different solutions, interventions, and systems for implementing locomotion in VR experiences. They provide a comprehensive look at the current approaches to solving for a meaningful, accessible, and comfortable solution to artificial locomotion in virtual environments. These explorations are still in their early stages, and we expect further novel approaches as developers continue to chase excitement, intensity, and ease of travel in virtual worlds.

Not all applications have to be all for users. Not all users will find it comfortable to do barrel rolls in a simulated spaceship—but that doesn't mean it isn't an experience worth creating. However, we must consider how we market, present, warn, and onboard users into experiences that may create mild (or extreme!) discomfort. Users and developers alike underestimate the effect of these issues, and we must work carefully to manage user expectations to ensure a comfortable experience.

PRESENCE VERSUS EMBODIMENT

Before we dive into an examination of how we understand and engage with our bodies through immersive technology, it is important to draw a clear distinction between embodiment and presence. The sense of presence that may be experienced in a virtual environment may be just that—a sense of my body being present in that virtual place. This is one way in which we embody virtual environments: that we take our bodies with us into these environments. We say, "I am here with my body." When we take it a step further from presence and arrive at a sense of full embodiment, we move to the feeling of "I am here and *this* is my body," this being the body that is presented to us in the virtual environment, and which deviates from our understanding of our own physical body (Figure 6.1). This distinction is important from a design perspective as we work to understand what type of embodiment we are aiming for: the presence of a physical body or the embodiment of a virtual body.

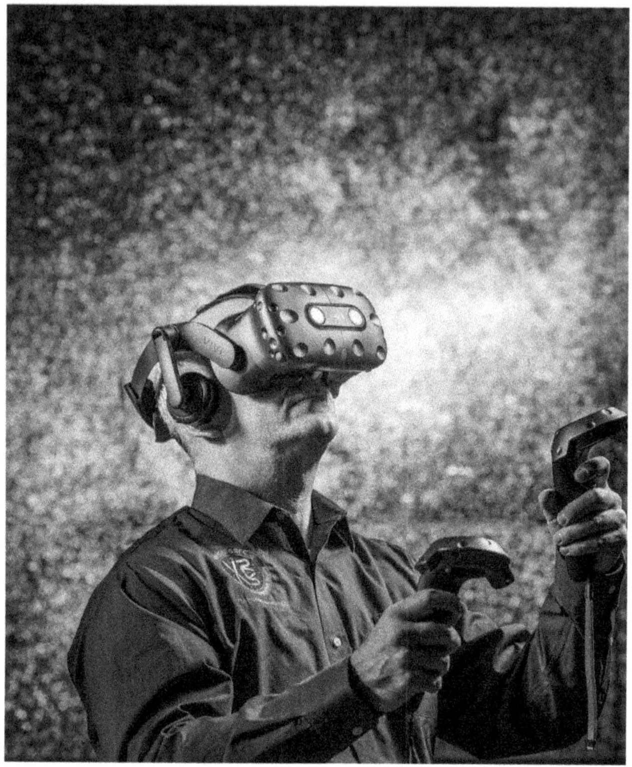

Figure 6.1 Exploring the Universe in Virtual Reality.

Source: Reproduced from NASA Goddard Photo and Video (2019). https://www. flickr.com/photos/24662369@N07/4946 7767318. Licensed under a Creative Commons Attribution 2.0 Generic (CC BY 2.0).

MAINTAINING REAL-WORLD PRESENCE

It is important to determine exactly where we want to ground the user in reality. If we provide a clear view in or through a device into the real world, via mixed or AR, then we already place the user physically in their current environment. As we start to layer additional information on top of the real world, we interrupt their full sense of presence and their sensory data. When determining the type of presence our experience should facilitate, we should understand the limitations of the medium, possible disruptions, and how to solve for unintended actions.

PRESENCE

Presence in a spatial computing application exists on a continuum; it starts with us grounded in reality and moving to be occupied in reality, occupied in VR, and then grounded in VR. Note that a variety of factors may contribute to establishing or prohibiting a user from arriving at the intended point on the spectrum of presence. When understanding the relationship between presence and embodiment, consider that full embodiment of a virtual body is one step on the spectrum beyond a full groundedness of presence, and that the two relate to each other very closely. It will be much more difficult to induce a feeling of embodiment of a virtual body if we have not first established a grounded sense of presence in a virtual environment.

Grounded in Reality

Example: An AR heads-up display (HUD) for road directions while cycling.

In this case, we have a user in movement, potentially at speeds up to 30 mph, outdoors, in a rapidly changing environment, and encountering other people and vehicles. This application must keep the user as focused on the real world as possible. We should design for clarity, simplicity, and transparency. Clarity for the real world must be the top priority with all information provided by the application existing on a secondary layer. Only information that is necessary will be provided to the user and provided in as few ways as possible—limiting use of visual and audio information. All information should be transparent to ensure that no information in view is fully obscured.

It is easy in the design of applications like this to get lured into the possibilities of the technology and create experiences that exploit user attention and indulge expectations. When presenting users with information during activities where lack of presence, obscuring of real-world information, or distractions become dangerous, we must be mindful of every component and edit our applications to provide only critical information and encourage users to maintain active perception.

An area for careful exploration here is when it may be appropriate to provide users safety-related data in a variety of environments. Current VR systems provide users with visual feedback to show when they are putting their head or hand outside of their predefined safe play space—some systems will even pass through a camera feed from the front of the headset to give the user a view and perspective mimicking their vision. These pass-through systems are currently limited in their ability to provide one-to-one visual information and, while helpful for grounding the user in situations where safety is a concern, note that there exist the lack of full field of view, inaccurate representation of depth, and limited fidelity.

The following factors contribute to groundedness in reality:

- Transparency of multiple sensory inputs allowing for sensory connection to the physical environment. This could mean a transparent display, limited audio output, etc.
- Limited overlay information.
- Lightweight hardware.
- Minimal physical activity or cognitive load required for user input.

Occupied in Reality

There are scenarios where we may wish to provide the user with access to view their physical environment but not for the purpose of grounding them—either because of the capabilities of the hardware or because the experience we are designing necessitates it.

For business applications, this may be for a training experience in a physical environment where we wish to enable the user to see the environment while being occupied by a training task viewed through a transparent AR HMD. An early example of commercially available games using this is Thomas Van Bouwel's 2021 VR game *Cubism*.

The game allows the user to play a three-dimensional puzzle game in a VR headset with a camera pass-through feed enabled to view the physical environment from within the display. This type of experience is often referred to as "mixed reality," where the user sees virtual three-dimensional objects overlaid on a video feed of their environment displayed inside of an HMD.

When we start to imagine creating more complex experiences where we add large amounts of opaque content to AR scenes, the line between maintaining grounding and occupation becomes less clear. As we start to alter user interactions with real-world objects, we change how they perceive their own bodies in space, what they are capable of, and their relationships with the environment around them. For instance, if we add an opaque three-dimensional wall overlaid onto the user's physical environment in front of a large glass door, we create an opportunity for the user to believe in the reality of our false wall, instead of the glass door. When we start to embody the virtual world we lose our connectedness to our physical environment—potentially treating a glass door as a solid wall.

It is important to determine exactly what we want the user to be present to: the environment or the preoccupation. In the example of an AR training application in a real-world environment, we want the user to be grounded in the environment while also treating the training tasks shown to them as if they are part of that environment—observing all safety protocols of the environment and learning the operation for which they are being trained. This is a delicate balance that is hard to achieve and should be carefully determined early in the design process to ensure the right mixture of real-world presence and digital occupation.

The following factors contribute to occupation in reality:

- User interactions designed to be undertaken in the user's physical environment.
- Varied level of environmental clarity that corresponds to the intended level of presence versus occupation.
- Multisensory information related to occupation—audio feedback, narration, visual cues, haptic feedback, etc.

Occupied in VR

When we enter a VR experience using an HMD we immediately forfeit some of our sensory input. This varies with the device—for example, its level of light leak, its audio output, its input and control method used, etc. Relinquishing control over how we receive some sensory input does not mean we are immersed or that we have moved our sense of embodiment (SoE) from the physical world to the digital—this is highly user- and experience-dependent. When designing VR experiences we must be very clear about what level of presence and embodiment we are hoping to achieve, either partial or full.

For the use of applications with some amount of pass-through video feed into the physical environment we already move more toward that connection to the physical environment. This can also be true in full virtual environments that are limited in their presentation of a compelling reality or feel more like a piece of software, such as applications overly reliant on two-dimensional menus and interfaces, or those that have a poorly conceived style.

Grounded in VR

In their 1997 article, Theresa Ditton and Matthew Lombard provide a powerful framing for immersion:

> [I]n the most compelling virtual reality experiences, the senses are immersed in the virtual world; the body is entrusted to a reality engine. The eyes are covered by a head-mounted display; the real world is invisible. The ears are covered by headphones; ambient sound is muffled. The hands are covered by gloves or props: "touch only the virtual bodies." Virtual reality may share common elements with reading a book in a quiet corner, but this book has stretched in all directions and wrapped itself around the senses of the reader—the reader is swallowed by the story.
>
> (Lombard & Ditton, 1997)

This sense of presence, induced by a multisensory approach (discussed later in this chapter) where the user becomes fully present in the virtual environment, is a difficult state to achieve and is generally approached in one of two ways: creating a realistic environment or creating a believable environment. Depending on the intention of the experience we may be developing, it is important to understand which components of what we are building need to remain true to reality and which can deviate significantly. For example, for VR training mandated for dangerous professions, it may be important to retain as much truth in the simulation as possible: "A compelling virtual world needs to be believable, authentic, and visually appealing in addition to capturing attention. This is especially true for professional VR applications that rely on maximal comparability to the real world, such as training environments for surgeons, firefighters, or pilots" (Weber et al., 2021).

EMBODIMENT, REALISM, AND THE TRUTH

It is when we start to examine the spectrum of presence, leading to embodiment, that we are aided by an understanding of the possibilities of verisimilitude. Verisimilitude is when something appears or feels real but is clearly not so—it is what allows us to suspend our disbelief at the theater and the cinema. Verisimilitude is also sometimes called "truth-likeness"; it is the approach to designing experiences that are unrealistic but maintain believability. They are not true, but they *feel* true. This is the goal for any experience that deviates from our conceptual models for physics, time, our own bodies and limitations, environmental fidelity, and a variety of other factors. In their powerful 2020 article, Slater and colleagues lay out a strong proposal for approaching design from the perspective of possible verisimilitude:

> To the extent that a VR system supports natural sensorimotor contingencies (being able to use the body to perceive in a manner similar enough to perception in everyday reality) it will typically lead to participants experiencing "place illusion," the illusion of

being in the place depicted by the virtual reality. A VR system may support (i) credible responses to the actions of the participant, (ii) contingent events that are directed specifically and personally toward the participant (for example a virtual human character smiles at the participant), and (iii) scenarios that are faithful to expectations when they simulate events that could occur in reality in a domain in which the participant has expertise.

(Slater et al., 2020)

SENSE OF EMBODIMENT (SOE)

In examining how to design for, and understand, embodiment in immersive experiences, the SoE framework presented by researchers who looked at the ethics of realism in AR and VR provides helpful insight. SoE refers to "the ensemble of sensations that arise in conjunction with being inside, having, and controlling a body especially in relation to VR applications" (Slater et al., 2020). The researchers propose that SoE is determined by three primary drivers: sense of self-location, sense of agency, and sense of body ownership.

Self-location

Slater et al. (2020) use the term "self-location" to mean "one's spatial experience of being inside a body and it does not refer to the spatial experience of being inside a world (with or without a body)." We can also see self-location as clearly related to proprioception and our ability to sense our body in space—even if that body is a digital representation and the environment is virtual.

Sense of Agency

Sense of agency, meanwhile, is one's "global motor control, including the subjective experience of action, control, intention, motor selection and the conscious experience of will" (Slater et al., 2020). As users engage in acts of discovery, object interactions, and physics-based locomotion—as they accept the unique physics of the virtual environment—they will start to become more grounded.

Body Ownership

In the pursuit of embodiment, it is important to explore a holistic approach that incorporates bottom-up (sensory information) and top-down (the processing of that information) methods:

> Here, bottom-up information refers to the afferent sensory information that arrives to our brain from our sensory organs; for example, visual, tactile, and proprioceptive input, whereas top-down information consists of the cognitive processes that may modulate the processing of sensory stimuli; for example, the existence of sufficient human likeness to presume that an artificial body can be one's body.
>
> (Cinque & Vincent (eds), 2022)

In a compelling enough virtual experience, the need for "human likeness" may even be unnecessary as we continue to explore the boundaries of how malleable our sense of body ownership is. Each one of our senses helps us tune into our virtual body, calibrate ourselves to the virtual environment, unlock the capacity to learn new skills that conform to our digital body, and open us up to intimate experiences with other users.

Social Presence (Our Bodies Together)

Immersive technology provides the possibility to create experiences that are socially impactful, intimate, and may mirror experiences we have in physical space with each other more than they mirror other mediated social encounters, such as videoconferencing. Lombard and Ditton capture what is possible when we start to move more of our physical self-expression into digital spaces:

> Interactants vary physical proximity, eye-contact, intimacy of conversation topic, amount of smiling, and other behaviors to establish an equilibrium between conflicting approach and avoidance forces and thereby optimize an overall level of intimacy. Other scholars have expanded the list of intimacy behaviors to include posture and arm position, trunk and body orientation, gestures, facial expressions, body relaxation, touching, laughter, speech duration, voice quality, laughter, olfactory cues, and others [. . .] A medium high in presence as social richness allows interactants to adjust more of these variables and therefore more precisely adjust the overall level of intimacy.
>
> (Lombard & Ditton, 1997)

Cultural variation in expression of intimacy, the appropriateness of certain behaviors for people of different genders in different cultures, and the ways body language and nonverbal communication differ across cultures are all worth exploring as the audience for spatial applications becomes increasingly global. Users from certain backgrounds may feel uncomfortable with certain levels of embodied proximity to other users, the representation of their digital avatar, the ability of other users to touch their avatar, and other potentially invasive behaviors.

With increased potential for intimate expression and feelings come morally and legally complicated issues for user safety, privacy, and care. As more and more users spend time in immersive, embodied, spatial social environments (e.g., VRchat, Rec Room, Horizon Worlds) there is a massive responsibility on these platforms to provide user protections to ensure that vulnerable users, especially those under 18 years of age, are protected from potential harm, harassment, grooming, and sexual abuse.

IMMERSIVE SEXUAL EXPERIENCES

It is impossible to ignore the current and future expansion of the use of spatial computing for sexual exploration, pornography, consensual sexual experiences between users, and the potential for minors to experience sexual harassment, trauma, and consumption of increasingly immersive sexual content. Dekker et al. (2021) suggest that users of VR pornography "felt more desired, more flirted with, more looked into the eyes. They were also more likely to feel connected with the actresses and more likely to feel the urge to interact with them." If spatial computing systems allow for greater feelings of connection and intimacy than traditional two-dimensional media, then pornography and sexual content are no exceptions. With relatively little research, and even less accurate data on usage, it is an area worth significant study as users spend more and more time seeking pleasure through 360-degree video experiences, simulated encounters, and encounters with other users.

Sexual encounters in spatial social applications between consenting adults are one thing—but the possibility of underage users engaging in embodied sexual encounters with adults online is a risk behavior that all platform designers must take seriously. In fact, 32% of teens "report having been contacted online by someone with no connection to them or their friends" (Noll et al., 2013). As online interactions graduate from text, images, and video to embodied virtual environments where users interact in real time, we can expect that for many adolescent users some of their earliest sexual experiences may take place in these environments.

A 2018 survey in collaboration with PlutoVR found "a high prevalence of multiple kinds of harassment within social VR spaces [and that] 49% of women reported having experienced at least one instance of sexual harassment [and] 30% of male respondents reported racist or homophobic comments" (Outlaw, 2018). If our potential level of intimacy and connection in these virtual environments can exceed that of our digital mediums, even approaching the levels experienced in the real world, then the potential for harassment and harm is also increased. Since 49%

of women are experiencing at least one instance of self-defined sexual harassment in social VR spaces, it is crucial that those managing these platforms understand the dangers of leaving platforms unregulated, un-moderated, and without proper safety mechanisms (e.g., user reporting, removal of repeat offenders) which are paramount to creating a safe space for a variety of users.

SETTLING INTO OUR BODIES

We can redefine our bodies, inhabit new ones, connect with others, and unlock completely new experiences through spatial computing. We have only just begun to see the potential of these technologies, the effects on our bodies, and how they may change our relationships with others. These are not trivial experiences and will require constant collaboration, substantive research, new approaches, and an openness in the community to work toward implementations of these technologies that positively enhance our experience of what it means to be human. As we continue to explore how to design for meaningful embodiment, we must remember that our experience of our body isn't the experience of others. Further, these technologies often privilege certain groups who have greater financial freedom, and for whose bodies these systems were optimized.

Your body will change. It's changing right now—aging, adapting, conforming—and that won't stop. This means that our approach to design must continue to change as well. Our societal relationship with our own bodies, and others', is also changing. During the rise of the global COVID-19 pandemic in 2020, the whole world had to confront something that many of us have known through personal trauma—that other people's bodies can be a danger to our own. The need during the pandemic for richer digital experiences, better long-distance communication methods, and active at-home entertainment has helped to accelerate the adoption of these technologies. As the world continues to navigate the compounding complexity of our shared global crises, let us not lose sight of our need to connect with each other, find new ways to understand each other, and find empathy for each other. If these technologies are going to enhance the human experience, we must carefully consider the potential harms, the limited accessibility to a global user base, and the need for deeper studies into the long-term effects of their use.

QUESTIONS FOR REFLECTION

1. What is the most overwhelming sensory experience you have ever had? Which senses were engaged, at what level, and what if any overlap was there between them?
2. What is a spatial computing interaction that could be better adapted to engage more senses? What is an interaction that could engage less?
3. In what ways might an experience you are designing (or one that you have tried) be physically, emotionally, or socially unsafe for a user?
4. Are there ways that current spatial computing systems could be improved to be better suited to your specific body, sensory inputs, and abilities?

PROJECT FOR CONSIDERATION

1. Identify a strong memory of yours—something fun and exciting.
   - Make a section for each of the seven senses and label them 1–7.
     i. Under each section, list parts of that memory that correlate to that sense (the smell of something cooking, the view through a window, the way your hand felt holding a book, the sound of water, etc.).
     ii. Make these entries as detailed as possible.
     iii. Look for items you have listed that overlap between multiple senses (e.g., the touch, taste, sound, smell of a drink) and mark those items with the additional numbers (1–7) for the other senses that overlap.

- On a separate page start with items that have the fewest senses associated with them and write down one way that you might translate this sensory experience into a spatial computing application.
- Work through your whole list.
- Once you complete this, write a step-by-step walkthrough of what playing through this memory in a spatial computing experience might feel like from the perspective of a user.

Affordances of Immersive Technology and the Future of Computing

How we relate to objects and environments in spatial computing experiences relies heavily on the history of similar interactions we bring from the physical world. We look at how these relationships are defined, how we can change those relationships, and the challenges presented by replicating real-world objects in virtual environments.

WHAT IS AN AFFORDANCE?

Affordances are how we can interact with the world around us—they are the relationships that we perceive between us, our environment, and all that is contained within it. They are the open possibilities of interaction, reaction, activity, and action. The term, as commonly used by designers and technologists, originates from psychologist James J. Gibson in his 1979 book *The Ecological Approach to Visual Perception*. Gibson highlights the relationships that exist between an animal (often, but not always, referring to humans) and its environment:

> The affordances of the environment are what it offers the animal, what it provides or furnishes, either for good or ill. The verb to afford is found in the dictionary, but the noun affordance is not.

Human Spatial Computing. Reginé Gilbert and Doug North Cook, Oxford University Press.
© Reginé Gilbert and Doug North Cook (2026). DOI: 10.1093/9780191966477.003.0007

I have made it up. I mean by it something that refers to both the environment and the animal in a way that no existing term does. It implies the complementarity of the animal and the environment.

(Gibson, 1979)

Gibson expands his definition later in his book to include objects contained within the environment, other animals, displays, and more. He presents a very expansive view of the term that encompasses a wide array of potential relationships. The term has been used, and reimagined, by a variety of researchers, designers, psychologists, and others. None has found as much traction as designer Don Norman in his book *The Design of Everyday Things*, which has become one of the most influential texts on the subject.

The term affordance refers to the relationship between a physical object and a person (or for that matter, any interacting agent, whether animal or human, or even machines and robots). An affordance is a relationship between the properties of an object and the capabilities of the agent that determine just how the object could possibly be used. A chair affords ("is for") support and, therefore, affords sitting. Most chairs can also be carried by a single person (they afford lifting), but some can only be lifted by a strong person or by a team of people.

(Norman, 2013)

It is essential to have a deep understanding of how these relationships work to be able to consider translating the affordances of the physical world into the virtual, or to develop entirely new relationships that were not possible in the physical world.

Spatial computing experiences have an incredibly unique opportunity to reimagine the affordances of real-world objects and environments by augmenting our perception of them in augmented reality (AR) and can create entirely new ways of interacting with invented or imagined objects in virtual reality (VR).

A plastic water bottle affords being filled with liquid, drinking, being thrown to the ground, being filled with pebbles, being filled with gasoline and lit on fire, being cut into tiny pieces with a saw, being melted, having a secret map placed in it and thrown out to sea . . . the list of affordances for a single object can stretch as far as our imaginations and the constraints of the object can reach. Real-world objects are incredibly complex, with nearly endless affordances, and our ability to act on them creatively is a deeply connected part of the human experience. Bringing the richness of possibility contained in real-world objects and environmental interactions into spatial computing experiences is an impossible task.

Gibson also reminds us that affordances are inherent in the environment itself, not just present in the objects:

A path affords pedestrian locomotion from one place to another, between the terrain features that prevent locomotion. The preventers of locomotion consist of obstacles, barriers, water margins, and brinks (the edges of cliffs). A path must afford footing; it must be relatively free of rigid foot-sized obstacles.

(Gibson, 2015)

With limited sensory input and often cumbersome hardware, it is already incredibly difficult to compete with the richness of the real world when designing interactions for digital experiences. The real limitation, however, lies in the fact that every affordance for a spatial application must be programmed into the experience, ensuring that the depth of interaction is limited by the time, dedication, precision, and skill of the designer. This can severely limit the open-ended creativity in virtual objects that we have come to expect from their real-world equivalents.

In his critique of both Gibson's and Norman's approach to the term, Martin Oliver offers a helpful critique of the overall value of their approach:

Researchers and designers persist in using the term affordance because of the desire to speak about technology in a general enough way that it can be theorized in its own right. It also promises an appealing control over users—if affordances permit some actions and constrain others, users are more likely to behave as expected. There is thus a tension between recognising the complexity of the concept and having a language simple enough to be useful.

(Oliver, 2005)

What has become evident in the development of new technologies is how difficult it is to determine emergent affordances that are designed into a product with the intent of the designer. Most designers do not set out to design harmful experiences, but many fall prey to the illusion that they can control the affordances available to the user to encourage specific action patterns and play methods. While Oliver would have us abandon the term altogether because of its imperfections and rampant misuse, we should instead work toward commonly held definitions and careful usage. One common mistake is conflating affordances with signifiers, which we clearly differentiate in the following section.

AFFORDANCES AND SIGNIFIERS

Norman helpfully suggests the concept of signifiers as differentiated from affordances. Designers, researchers, and writers commonly conflate signifiers and affordances—something Norman references in his revised edition of *The Design of Everyday Things*. If an affordance is the possible relationship between a user and something in their environment, a signifier is something that explicitly highlights and encourages a specific relationship. "Affordances determine what actions are possible," he writes. "Signifiers communicate where the action should take place. We need both" (Norman, 2013).

Signifiers allow designers to communicate specific intent to the user. For example, picture a user in a VR environment, wearing a head-mounted display and holding controllers, who sees a table with a book and a candlestick on it. They reach their hand toward both objects. When their hand approaches the book, there is haptic feedback triggered through the haptic motor in the controller. The book is highlighted with a thin white outline, and the user is shown a digital representation of the physical controller with one of the buttons blinking. If the user presses that button, the book attaches to the controller position and opens. The user can hold the book and examine the open pages. Upon releasing the button, the book returns to its place on the table. If the user moves their hand toward the candlestick they see no outline, have no view of the controller or button, and feel no haptic feedback. In this example, the book affords grabbing and holding and the candlestick does not, but both are objects that a user could perceive as affording similar interactions. The signifiers are the haptic feedback, the white outline, and the view of the controller highlighting the button. All these signifiers work together to encourage the user to interact with the book, and the lack of them in relation to the candlestick discourages the user from attempting to interact with it.

While signifiers can be helpful to guide users toward specific actions, they can also create significant noise in the environment. This can reduce sense of presence, or overemphasize specific interactions while undermining others. In an interview with GameDeveloper.com, Paul van der Meer was asked about how to create a comfortable and flexible VR user interface. For him and his team, it came down to answering three questions: "Which info do we need when?, What is the most direct way to present that info?, and What is the most comfortable way to get that info?" (Game Developer Staff, 2018). When designing interactions and interfaces for immersive experiences, van der Meer provides incredibly important encouragement to edit down to necessities and to be mindful of the experience of the user. Clarifying affordances using signifiers is a delicate process that requires careful consideration, especially in VR environments, where disruptions "may cause severe breaks in presence for VR users, which may disrupt their place and plausibility illusions, but may also affect their virtual activities or task performance" (Gottsacker et al., 2021). Having a user use a two-dimensional interface as a menu that isn't a part of the virtual environment can cause this sort of disruption. For certain types of experiences, such as those that require large amounts of text displayed, manipulation of values, or other complex data or control methods, it may be difficult to find methods of displaying and interacting with information in a way that is natural without disrupting a user's sense of presence. This is where the diegesis becomes a helpful counterpart to signifier design.

DIEGETIC DESIGN AND SIGNIFIERS

"Diegesis is defined as the internal consistency of an experience or story/narration, including the appearance and behavior of entities/objects and their environment" (Gottsacker et al., 2021).

Unlike skeuomorphic design, which relies on preexisting analogs to communicate to the user what is possible, diegetic design relies on the ability of the user to embody the rules, realities, and restrictions shown to them to learn what is possible in the world being presented. We can differentiate diegetic from nondiegetic interactions by how they interact with the virtual environment and the user. Anil Çamci provides a clear outline of the difference between diagetic and non-diagetic objects in virtual environments:

> Diegetic visual objects are often affected by the physical forces implemented in the virtual environment, and interact with other objects accordingly. The lighting and other occlusion effects can alter the visibility of these objects. On the other hand, nondiegetic visual objects are most commonly presented in the form of visual overlays. These can be head-up displays that relay relevant information about the VR, or user interface (UI) elements such as menus and buttons. Non-diegetic visual elements persist over the user's field of view and are commonly positioned relative to the user rather than the world-space of the VR. These objects are usually unaffected by lighting and occlusion. Some non-diegetic UI elements can be spatially mapped into the virtual environment while remaining external to the implied universe of the VR.
>
> (Çamci, 2019)

Depending on the immersion goals of the experience, it is important to know how (and when) to use non-diegetic objects and interfaces, and when to avoid them so as not to have a negative effect on the user's immersion level in the virtual environment. Just because something is diegetic does not mean it is meaningful, creates deeper immersion, or is even the right approach. The use of this approach should directly correspond to the goals of the application.

Many VR experiences have deeply explored how far diegetic design can be pushed to create worlds where the user is free of external distraction and is able to build an internal model of how the world works with minimal guidance from the application itself. *Gorilla Tag*, the breakaway VR title released in February 2021 and the most popular VR experience in the world as of January 2023, is almost entirely diegetic in its approach to world-building. In *Gorilla Tag*, the user cannot use a button to access a two-dimensional menu. Instead, they must physically navigate to the menu in the game world using their hands to push themselves across the ground, like a gorilla. In the press release announcing the game's full release in late 2022 the studio, Another Axiom, describes its approach to diegetic design:

> Our passion is building Diegetic Virtual Realities. Instead of treating our world like a video game, we are building *Gorilla Tag* to make it feel like it's a plausible, alternate space that could exist if the rules of reality were just a little bit different. People come away from our world with real dreams and memories of having been there with their friends.
>
> (Game Press, 2022)

With millions of users and one of the highest product ratings for a VR game, there are clear lessons to be learned from a game that explicitly seeks to abandon non-diegetic interfaces and go all-in on building a new world.

Let us use another example to explore this idea. We want the user in a VR environment to be able to separately adjust the volume levels for music, environmental audio, and player voice chat. A non-diegetic approach would allow the user to click a button to bring up a two-dimensional menu not anchored in three-dimensional space, visible in front of them, and navigable using another button press or joystick movement. The menu would have three options with visual indicators of volume levels for each of the three settings.

A diegetic approach to this could be to create a grabbable tool that is held at the player's waist. The tool may have three signifiers, such as knobs, labeled to denote each volume type: a note symbol for music, a small landscape for environmental audio, and a face for player voice chat. As each knob is turned, the player would hear sample audio for each of the audio types and could quickly adjust the level as it is heard in the three-dimensional environment.

PERCEIVED AND ACTUAL AFFORDANCES

Not all the affordances that we perceive are possible; for example, a door that has a push panel but is locked, a speaker cabinet that has no speaker inside, a cup in a VR coffee shop that cannot be picked up. It is easy for an affordance to be misidentified because of cultural context, expectation, personal history, misalignment of user expectation by the designer, or a state change that is not communicated with a signifier. We call these false affordances—an action is perceived to be possible but is not. Often, as in the case of a locked door, the user has an object that, by design, changes its properties to allow or limit an affordance. This is a great example of when signifiers are extremely important—for the communication of when an affordance is actual and not just perceived. The deadbolt on a door is itself able to be turned, and it also communicates the state of the object. Once the locked and unlocked positions of the deadbolt are learned, we can understand that state of the object by merely observing it. For doors with internal locks, this can be shown through a rotating label, marker, or color panel that communicates the state of the door.

Let us inspect the door:

- **True affordance**: A door that affords opening and can be opened.
- **False affordance**: A wall that looks like a door but does not open.

- **Blocked affordance**: A locked door with no signifier indicating it is locked cannot be opened. It could be opened, but not right now.
- **Hidden affordance**: A door disguised as a bookshelf affords opening, but only if I know that it is a door and not a bookshelf.
- **Discouraged affordance**: An unlocked door that says "do not enter" affords opening but has a signifier discouraging me from opening it.
- **Adaptable affordance**: A door in a VR environment that can be opened with a button press, by pulling the handle, or by gazing at the handle for more than two seconds. In VR, there is an opportunity to make certain actions easier and more accessible to users, and to unlock new potential interactions. Adaptable objects and environments are difficult to design not only because they require careful design consideration, but also because we must introduce the user to each variation in the interaction.

When designing interactions and environments for spatial computing experiences, we should be thinking about how each interaction in our application might be perceived by the user, how we communicate the state of the object, and whether or not we are guiding the user toward the best experience and use. A persistent complaint across many VR experiences is the overall lack of interactivity in a given environment where a large percentage of the perceivable objects and environmental features are not able to be acted upon in any way. This is the difficult balance—creating an environment with enough rich detail to induce a feeling of presence and excitement, while also enabling the user to feel like they have agency in that environment. Significant thought should be given to the objects and surfaces in a virtual environment that have no interactivity programmed into them. How can we encourage the user not to interact with them, and if they try to, how do we communicate that that object does not in fact afford the action they are attempting?

REPRESENTATIVE AFFORDANCES

Gibson, in examining the relationship between humans and displays, touches on why uncovering the affordances that reside in virtual environments can be quite difficult:

> A surface of clay is only clay, but it may be molded in the shape of a cow or scratched or painted with the profile of a cow or incised with the cuneiform characters that stand for a cow, and then it is more than just a surface of clay.
>
> (Gibson, 2015)

The display is more than just what it is; rather, it communicates a deeper reality to the user that summons their understanding, via culture and experience, of what is being shown to them. Their perception of what is possible in a virtual environment relies on how clear the representation of the perceived affordances is to them. Does the user see a cow, or a *representation* of a cow? Or are they knowingly *pretending* to see a cow? The perceptual relationship between the user, the display, and the content being displayed is the primary concern of the designer. This relates to this book's exploration of embodiment and presence, where we understand that the user's type of embodiment has a direct correlation to the robustness of the perceived affordance in the virtual environment.

The affordances of the virtual environment are not the same as those of the real-world physical objects that they represent. All correct affordances in a virtual environment rely on the perceived affordances of the user lining up exactly with the programmed affordances implemented by the creator. A piece of paper in a virtual environment may afford reading, dropping, and throwing, but it may not afford crumpling or tearing unless the creator has designed a system to manage this interaction. It is also important to remember that the user is never actually holding a piece of paper. We can encourage the user to believe they are holding it, but they are holding down a button on a controller to "grab" the piece of paper, or perhaps using hand tracking to mime holding it. The paper does not exist, but the affordances do. If the virtual paper has a perceivable tear and bends at the tear when it is picked up, there is a reasonable expectation that it affords tearing, and so it should. Every time we mismatch perceived and actual affordances in a virtual environment, we risk frustrating the user, lowering their sense of embodiment, and discouraging them from exploring other interactions in the environment.

DEVELOPING NEW AFFORDANCES

If the designer can make the virtual environment compelling enough, there is the possibility of generating new affordances that are unique to that environment and do not rely on the user's understanding of the physical world and its expected affordances. The possibility for the development of new affordances in a virtual environment hinges on the designer influencing the perception of the user to bridge the gap between representation of an object and believability of an object. In the virtual environment, we can alter, modify and alter the user's perception of the world. This manipulation allows for the introduction of new potential relationships between the user and everything in their perceived environment in ways that transcend the possibility space in the physical world that is limited by time, physical laws, etc.

The development of new affordances is facilitated through a variety of means. First, we must introduce the user to a new interaction. For example, let us use telekinesis, that is, the ability to move objects at a distance without physically touching them. Telekinesis would be incredibly useful in a variety of situations but is not an ability that any user possesses. Therefore, they do not have a mental model for manipulating objects at a distance. When introducing this new ability to a user, initial guidance would be needed to teach the user the laws that govern how objects are manipulated by telekinesis. For example, imagine the user is using a hand-tracking-enabled device and is shown an outline of a hand in front of them with the palm opened. When they place their hand where the outline of the hand is, an object in front of that outline begins to glow. The user is then shown the same hand outline making a closed fist, moving to the left, and returning to an open palm. The user repeats this action and sees the object that was glowing move at equal radial distance to the movement of their hand until they open their palm and see the object drop. The user now has a basic model for the use of telekinesis in a virtual environment that allows them to move objects at a distance. By using their open palm, the user can quickly scan an environment for objects that glow—signifying to them that this object can be manipulated using this new ability. Using additional visual signifiers (e.g., changes in color of glow, intensity of glow, other visual and audio cues), we can introduce additional possibilities for manipulation: pinch an object to scale its size; rotate fist to rotate object; raise fist to raise object; and thumbs up to lock object in place. While this may not be the ideal means of implementing telekinesis, it shows how one might train a user quickly on a set of relationships and interactions that have no real-world equivalent.

Through careful attention to the designed affordances of virtual environments, we can unlock new human potential and develop new intuitions. Designers can explore developing new tools for users to play, create, and alter their surroundings. This space is still relatively unexplored and the possibilities for interaction design are ripe for constant reinvention as we work to uncover the true potential of embodied spatial computing. The few interaction methods that are used most often in the current generation of spatial computing application methods remain quite primitive, often clumsy, and demand to be redesigned. Many applications rely on turning a controller into a laser pointer used to interact with a two-dimensional menu floating in three-dimensional space. While this is simple and easy to implement, it makes us consider in what ways we can reconceptualize two-dimensional interactions as made-for-three-dimensions interactions? There are many depictions of advanced versions of this in films—for example, *Minority Report* and *Iron Man*—where we see characters interacting with complex data in three-dimensional space, though often using outrageously strenuous physical movements to execute simple commands.

As the spatial awareness of spatial computing systems continues to advance, so should the software on which they run. It doesn't help to have more advanced sensors and higher-resolution displays if many of the tasks done are easily replicated on traditional two-dimensional displays. This means approaching problems from their root and not the stem—starting over by asking, "What must be done?" and working from there, instead of starting from "What has been done?"

HOW AFFORDANCES DIFFER IN SPATIAL COMPUTING, IN TRADITIONAL COMPUTING, AND IN PHYSICAL OBJECTS AND ENVIRONMENTS

When designing a digital immersive experience, we must clarify the distinct ways that affordances differ from how we understand them in relation to physical objects. Natural physical objects, like a stone or a tree branch, have affordances that are discovered through the nature of the object and the intent of the person interacting with it. Designed objects also carry the intent of the designer, the limitations of the design, and any signifiers that clarify intended use. Virtual objects and environments have all of this and are unbound by the restrictions of reality and physics, but often do not meet user expectations, either intentionally or because of a limited range of potential interactions programmed by the designer.

MAPPING AFFORDANCES FOR SPATIAL COMPUTING DEVICES

The virtual environment can be seen as a connection between the physical and digital world, where the user brings their physical body, grounded in their physical environment, into digital space. This makes mapping affordances complex as they must extend from the physical environment into the digital in a way that feels natural and intuitive. When making a map of affordances, it can be helpful to differentiate and correlate how they connect through physical and digital space.

Here we must be aware of three layers of affordances:

1. **The affordances in the user's physical environment.**

   The user sits, stands, lies down, walks, runs, swings their arms, and interacts with physical surfaces. How the user perceives the physical environment is greatly affected by the type of application and device being used. In an AR or mixed-reality environment, the user can still perceive the parts of the environment not occluded by digital content—creating an expectation for the user to be able to continue interacting with their physical environment without hindering the function of the digital experience. In a VR experience, the user may only be aware of the physical environment as a boundary line exposed to them for safety purposes in the headset, creating a lack of a perceived interaction with anything contained in their physical environment.

2. **The affordances of the device through which they are using to access the virtual environment.**

   The user may be using a head-mounted display that has buttons on it, controllers with buttons and sensors, and other forms of potential interactions, like hand and eye tracking. The Quest Pro, a VR headset with mixed-reality capabilities released by Meta in late 2022, includes a variety of features:

   • Face and eye tracking that allows for capture of users' facial expressions and eye movement.

   • Multiple buttons on the headset itself for controlling volume and power.

   • Two hand controllers with a series of buttons and touch surfaces that can be programmed to accommodate a variety of interactions and whose movement can be tracked in three-dimensional space independently of view of the headset due to their own dedicated tracking system. That is, that the controller can be separated from direct line of sight in a physical environment from the user—differentiating it

from most other controller types available at the time, which
require direct line of sight to tracking cameras or external
sensors.

- Full-color video pass-through allowing the user to see a
  video feed of their physical environment while in the
  headset—this feed being of limited resolution, quality, and
  field of view.
- An overall product weight of 722 g, significantly heavier than
  its predecessor, the Quest 2, at 503 g. This can affect the
  relationship between the device and users, who may find it
  less comfortable to wear for prolonged periods of time.

This is just a high-level example of some of the affordances of a single
device used for spatial computing. As companies keep advancing these
technologies, we can expect to see even more possible input methods,
tracking capabilities, and increased fidelity—all of which will significantly impact the ways that users interact with the devices and their
environments.

3. **The affordances that reside solely in the perceived virtual
   environment displayed by the device.**
   The affordances present in the virtual environment are directly
   influenced by the affordances present in the user's physical
   environment and those of the device itself. When determining
   the design of an immersive experience, we must consider the
   relationship of these three levels and the possible variations.
   Here we highlight a simple interaction and some questions to
   consider as we look for the interrelatedness of each.

Context

The user is in a physical environment wearing a standalone VR HMD.
Inside-out tracking leverages cameras on the device to track the device

in the room. Full-color video passthrough is enabled and the user is holding two controllers. User is attempting to move a virtual object from a virtual surface to a physical one.

Physical

The user is in a physical environment wearing a standalone VR HMD. Inside-out tracking leverages cameras on the device to track the device in the room. Full-color video passthrough is enabled, and the user is holding two controllers.

- Is the user sitting or standing? User posture directly alters sightlines, user reach, body movement, and potentially placement of user interface elements.
- Is the room brightly lit from an exterior window? If so, this may cause the user to lose some tracking of the device or controllers when facing directly toward the window, meaning that if the experience requires full 360-degree physical movement, it is possible the relationship between the device and environment can create issues here.

Device

The device is a mixed reality capable HMD and includes two controllers with multiple buttons.

- Is the user holding the controllers in the intended position with access to all input methods?
- Is the HMD correctly adjusted to provide a comfortable experience to the user for an extended play session?
- Does the passthrough video have enough clarity?

Virtual

User sees their physical environment with digital three-dimensional objects that can be moved by positioning their controller to overlap with the virtual object, pressing a button to attach the virtual object to the placement of the controller, then releasing the button to let the object drop from where it is virtually held.

- HMD affords being worn.
- Controllers afford being held.
- Button affords being pressed.
- Virtual object affords being moved by the user.

A Method for Understanding Affordances

This exercise originates from the workshop "The Hidden Nature of Objects: Diagrammatic Drawing," run by Doug North Cook at the Immersive Design Summit in early 2019. It has since been adapted into a workshop that is part of the Immersive Design Residency at Fallingwater. It is meant to help hone the identification of affordances and help participants see the subjective nature of them through the sharing of one individual's perceived affordances with another.

For an Individual

Using paper and something to write with or a digital drawing tablet, identify a single object and create a series of drawings from different angles, perspectives, views, and abstractions. The goal is not to draw something beautiful, exact, or even accurate—it is to capture as many ideas of the object as possible. Different objects can be better understood with different types of drawings: exploded axonometric drawings for objects that are made up of multiple components; assembly and disassembly plans for objects that can be taken apart; or multiple perspective views for objects that vary significantly on each side. Once complete, start diagramming onto the drawings every perceived relationship between the user and that object. Indicate where the user might grab, swing, lift, hold, poke, bite, pull, or any other possible action. Separately, make a list of any relationship that doesn't easily map to a specific part of the object. Lastly, draw a quick series of storyboards where a stick-figure person is using the object in a variety of ways that are better captured with a human form in relation to it—try to get at least five of these.

Once these are all completed, go back to the drawings and to the list of affordances and work to expand the list and the drawings in an exhaustive way. Spend at least 30 minutes here—if not stuck or some-what bored at some point, the exercise may require more time spent on it. Write until unable to write any more and then sit, think, and continue to write. If an idea seems strange, wrong, absurd, dangerous, unexpected, or silly, write it down.

Do two final drawings by selecting two of the most outlandish rela-tionships identified and draw a reimagining of that object that optimizes that object for that specific relationship and has a clear signifier to encourage anyone interacting with it to perceive that same relationship.

Once this task is complete, go through all the work and on a fresh page make notes that correspond to what has been learned about this object from each drawing that perhaps has not been noticed before. Make special note of any perceived relationships identified that per-haps a different person might not have noticed and explain why. It is through this sort of direct, personal, and exhaustive inquiry that we can hone our ability to see, design, and articulate the affordances of an object.

For Groups

This exercise can be very helpful in a group setting, especially where we have significant deviation in perspective, background, and analyti-cal methods. Have everyone pair up with a partner—ideally the person whom they know the least, but this also works with just two partic-ipants. Have the partners collaborate on identifying an object in the room to draw. They both do the above series of drawings and writing prompts but without discussing or showing each other any of their in-progress work. Once both partners have finished, they then swap papers with each other. Have each partner make a new list of items they dis-cover in their partner's papers that they did not draw or write on their own. If we do this in a larger group, have each pair share their work with the group by having each person share the list of relationships that their partner identified that they did not, and any associated realiza-tions of learnings. Doing this in a group has the added benefit of being able to see how a variety of people's perceived affordances differ—even when they have identified seemingly mundane objects for the exercise.

In each repetition of this exercise, we may find new insight into objects, discover new ways of observing, unlock new categories of affordances, and deepen our ability to perceive affordances with expanded breadth and depth. This can easily be done asynchronously with another person if both have access to the same object.

This exercise is partially inspired by Gibson:

> A hollow object such as a pot can be used to contain water or wine or grain and to store these substances. An object with a level surface knee-high from the ground can be used to sit on. An elongated object, a stick, if the substance is elastic and flexible, affords bending and thus can be made into a bow for launching arrows. A rigid, straight stick, not bent or curved, can be rotated on its long axis without wobbling; it can be used as a fire drill or as an axle for a wheel. The list of examples could go on without end.
>
> (Gibson, 2015)

Something that Gibson highlights here is the way that we not only interact with objects, but act upon them to make them into something else entirely—a stick becomes an arrow launcher, etc. What is also clear here is how deeply personal affordances are: An object knee-high for one user is ankle- or shin-high for another; an object may only be able to be bent into a certain shape by someone with long enough arms or enough strength; and only people with the knowledge of how certain objects are constructed would perceive that an object affords becoming something else. This list is endless. What something affords depends on who is perceiving and attempting to act upon it. Physical ability or disability, cultural background, what is deemed permissible, social status, insecurities, the clothes someone wears—all these things impact what a user perceives to be possible. This is why it is so important to think deeply about ways of providing positive interactions to a variety of users, but it is also one of the great opportunities with spatial computing—the ability to craft experiences that can accommodate more types of users than a similar experience with a physical environment or object can, because the constraints of the physical world are lifted away if we allow them to be.

Definitional Relationships

How we interact with the world is a big part of what defines who we are—
nothing more so than how we interact with other people. Theologian
John Zizioulas (2010) suggests that "Personhood is not self-defining;
rather, it is other-defined." Our relationships define us—a concept called
relational ontology. Rooted in philosophy and theology, relational ontology provides a way for us to think about the effect of affordances;
how our relationships with objects, each other, and technology define
the very nature of who we are.

Note the importance of designing systems for interacting with others in digital spaces. The way that users can interact with and act on
other users, what those other users afford based on the context, and
how designers provide the context for those interactions define the
nature of those relationships and, over time, the nature of users themselves. How users interact with each other in virtual environments not
only defines their experience, but also, as spatial computing platforms
become more ubiquitous, may begin to define how society interacts.
It is important to remember the long-term effects of designing systems, social interaction modalities, and technologies that may become
woven into the very fabric of society. This is not work to be taken
lightly.

QUESTIONS FOR REFLECTION

1. What component of user experience present in current spatial
   computing devices do you find the most frustrating? Make a list
   of five potential new user experience solutions for it and detail
   all the affordances.
2. Who is a person in your life that has helped define who you are?
   Can you also identify an object? List the ways that the impact of
   both would be different if they were experienced entirely with a
   spatial computing device.

3. What is a way of interacting with an object you have in your
    home that you think other people might not consider? If you
    saw that object in a virtual environment would you interact with
    it the same way?

PROJECT FOR CONSIDERATION

Identify an object in your home, at a cafe, your office, anywhere—ideally
an object that is not overly complex.

1. Get two large blank sheets of paper.
2. On the first sheet draw the object from three to four different
    perspectives. The goal is not to draw it well, or beautifully; the
    goal is to capture details and possible points of interaction.
3. Make a list of every possible relationship between you and the
    object. Spend a minimum of 30 minutes. If your list has not
    passed 50 items, spend another 30 minutes on it. Keep going
    until you get bored, or until your ideas start to feel too silly or
    strange. Write down the silly and strange ideas, too.
4. Then go about diagramming those relationships onto your
    drawings. Put those relationships that have no clear interaction
    point—or are more abstract—on a separate list.
5. If possible, do this with another person. Draw the same object
    and make your own lists without sharing anything with each
    other until you have finished, then swap and look for differences.
6. Once you have finished, put an asterisk next to any relationship
    that would be difficult to replicate in a virtual environment and
    then make notes on how a similar feeling might be replicated
    through a different virtual affordance.

Spatial Computing and the Brain

A US history teacher introduces virtual reality (VR) reenactments of the Civil War but soon realizes that students' emotional responses are influenced by their personal biases. Despite experiencing the same virtual scenario, students form dramatically different interpretations based on their backgrounds and prior beliefs. Some focus on the revolutionary ideals, others on the hypocrisy of slaveholders proclaiming freedom, and still others on the absence of women from the political process. This observation reveals how personal biases profoundly shape our experiences in immersive environments, even when the presented content is identical. A visiting neuroscientist explains how these biases impact memory and learning, leading to developing a new curriculum tailored to individual cognitive profiles.

This intersection of neuroscience and spatial computing offers both challenges and opportunities. On one hand, technologies like VR show remarkable promise as therapeutic tools for memory loss and dementia. Research indicates that VR's immersive environments can enhance memory function through hippocampal-stimulating spatial navigation, multisensory engagement, and emotional connections that strengthen neural encoding (Voise Foundation, 2024). Brain–computer interfaces extend these possibilities, potentially allowing direct neural interaction with virtual environments without physical controllers, adapting content based on detected cognitive states, or providing access for those with limited mobility (Värbu et al., 2022).

The significant psychological effects of these technologies necessitate careful consideration of cognitive biases. Our brains frequently rely on mental shortcuts to efficiently process vast amounts of information, which can result in unconscious biases that influence our perceptions and experiences in spatial computing environments. These biases not only affect how users interpret content; they also fundamentally alter what information is recognized, stored in memory, and integrated into learning. As spatial computing continues to advance immersive experiences, researchers are exploring direct interfaces with the brain using electroencephalograms (EEGs) and brain–computer interfaces (BCIs). This work aims to enable real-time interactions between neural activity and digital environments.

EEGS, BCI, AND SPATIAL COMPUTING

Imagine a world where artists or designers could manipulate three-dimensional objects or content in AR/VR using their mind. According to Värbu et al. (2022), BCIs establish connections between the brain and external devices by interpreting neural signals, primarily through electroencephalography (EEG). Initially developed for medical purposes to assist people with disabilities in communicating and controlling assistive devices, BCIs operate through four key processes: recording brain activity, extracting relevant features, gathering necessary information, and integrating this information for practical applications. These technologies are particularly beneficial for individuals with disabilities or neurological disorders, and those using robotic prosthetic limbs. Ongoing research aims to enable control of objects through thought, detect emotions, and facilitate interaction with computers (Shih et al., 2012). While medical applications primarily focus on assistance, rehabilitation, and monitoring, non-medical applications have expanded significantly to include emotion recognition, attention monitoring, entertainment, smart home control, and user authentication.

The field faces several challenges, including signal reliability in noisy environments, individual differences between users, and the complexity of accurately interpreting neural signals. Current EEG devices vary widely in cost and capability, with Emotiv EPOC, Neuroscan Quik-Cap, and NeuroSky MindWave being the most commonly used. Researchers employ various techniques to obtain EEG data, including motor imagery (imagining body movements), visual evoked potential (responding to visual stimuli), and spectral analysis to monitor states like drowsiness or emotions. Signal processing typically involves power spectral density, Fourier transform, and common spatial pattern analysis for feature extraction, with linear discriminant analysis and support vector machine algorithms for classification (Värbu et al., 2022).

In the medical domain, applications for controlling robotic devices and VR rehabilitation show promise, while non-medical applications are expanding into cognitive load monitoring, authentication, and entertainment. Ethical considerations regarding privacy, security, and the potential to influence users' emotions or decisions remain significant concerns as BCI technology becomes more widespread.

THE BRAIN

The year 1848 was a pivotal time for studying traumatic brain injury (TBI). Phineas Gage, a 25-year-old railroad construction worker, suffered an accident that has significantly impacted the study of the brain from the 19th century to today. Gage was working on building a railroad in Vermont using long steel rods and explosives. An accidental explosion sent a steel rod through his cheek and the left frontal lobe of his brain. The blast was so powerful that the rod went entirely through his skull and landed a few feet away.

He was initially a well-liked and successful construction foreman for the Rutland & Burlington Railroad in Cavendish, Vermont, during the late 1840s. However, after he suffered the traumatic brain injury on September 13, 1848, his career took a dramatic turn. Although Gage survived the accident, those who knew him reported significant changes in his personality. John Martyn Harlow, Gage's doctor, treated him months after the accident and observed alterations in his behavior. He noted that Gage had difficulty focusing, used vulgar language, and often treated people as if they were insignificant. As a result of these changes, Gage was never rehired by his previous employers and could not work as a foreman again.

Following the accident, Gage held a number of odd jobs. He exhibited himself at Barnum's American Museum in New York, worked at the livery stable of the Dartmouth Inn in Hanover, New Hampshire, and drove coaches in Chile. In 1859, as his health continued to deteriorate, he moved to San Francisco to live with his mother, where he remained until his death in May 1860, following a series of epileptic seizures (Lapinski, 2022).

Gage's trauma posed questions about the correlation between personality changes and brain injury. The damage he incurred happened at the front part of the brain. Although he could walk, talk, and remember things, it was clear that specific brain functions had disappeared because of damage to the frontal lobe.

Ongoing research on the brain affirms that our personality and behaviors are largely influenced by the frontal lobe. This region of the brain controls decision-making, problem-solving, emotions, and reactions to the environment. It is also responsible for our social behavior, planning, organizing, and memory.

The frontal lobe is the part of the brain involved in higher-level thinking and the production of emotions. Therefore, damage to this area of the brain can result in significant changes to a person's behavior, including changes in their personality. Research into the frontal lobe has also revealed that it plays a role in our ability to develop relationships, as well as in our ability to express empathy. Research has also suggested that the frontal lobe develops our morality or sense of right and wrong.

If Gage had lived in the 21st century, a brain scan could reveal which parts of his brain did and did not have neural and physical connections. The frontal lobes are important for various functions as they connect nerve pathways to other areas of the brain. In case of damage to these lobes, other parts of the brain may also be affected. Note that the frontal lobes are the last part of the brain to mature.

For most people, experiencing the world involves multiple senses working together. Sight, sound, touch, taste, and smell combine to create a comprehensive understanding of our surroundings, which helps us react to our environment. Humans think differently, plan, use language, and make complex decisions. We have the ability to create, learn, and remember. These cognitive abilities enable us to understand and navigate our environments while transforming them through creativity and innovation.

Humans can imagine possibilities that do not yet exist, develop complex cultural and social systems, and build on knowledge across generations. We are also capable of problem-solving and recognizing cause and effect. As mentioned in Chapter 6, our senses of vision, hearing, vestibular awareness, proprioception, and presence significantly impact how we interact with spatial computing.

In immersive environments, your eyes perceive detailed images, even when they are stationary, and your brain processes these signals similarly to how it does in the real world. It integrates visual, auditory, and tactile sensations. The inputs in these environments can be realistic enough for your brain to suspend disbelief, making you feel as though you are genuinely in a simulated space, even if only temporarily.

When you accept that you are in an immersive environment, you may believe in your surroundings and feel emotionally and physically engaged. Your senses work together to convince your brain, creating a cohesive and immersive experience that makes you feel present in a digital world.

Distinguishing between reality and the worlds created using spatial computing involves complex systems of our brain. The brain has two lobes connected by a structure called the corpus callosum. It is a common myth that the two lobes have distinct and separate functions, with the left side responsible for logical and analytical tasks and the right side responsible for creative and artistic studies.

The reality is that both sides work together and are responsible for various functions. While it is true that some areas of the brain are specialized for specific functions, such as language processing or spatial awareness, these functions rely on the integration and coordination of activity in multiple areas of the brain. Most brain functions involve the interaction and integration of training in numerous brain regions rather than being localized to a specific part or side of the brain. We still have much to learn about the brain, despite the last 150 years of research.

Spatial computing can assist individuals who have suffered a traumatic brain injury (TBI), which is a significant cause of health loss and disability across the globe, with an estimated annual incidence of 27 to 69 million cases (Dewan et al., 2018). These injuries can result in permanent disabilities that affect an individual's psychological, financial, and social well-being. However, the use of spatial computing and VR is beginning to impact the treatment of TBI positively.

Researchers are exploring the use of virtual kitchens to better understand how VR can assist in the treatment of TBI. They utilized VR to assess and rehabilitate cognitive functions related to daily living activities. Calderone et al. (2023) systematically examined how VR aids in the rehabilitation of TBI. Their findings revealed that VR activates a network of cortical regions, including the parietal cortex, ventral premotor cortex, primary motor cortex, dorsal premotor cortex, inferior frontal gyrus, and supplementary motor areas, through visual feedback.

In addition to virtual kitchens, the study incorporated virtual supermarkets and malls to facilitate multitasking cognitive rehabilitation. As VR engages the network of cortical regions it promotes reactive synaptogenesis, a process in which damaged areas of the brain that have lost contact forge new neural connections (synapses) from remaining inputs. The multisensory stimulation provided by VR environments directly engages neural pathways, enhancing neuroplasticity and regeneration processes beyond what conventional therapy can achieve.

The study found that women exhibited more significant cognitive improvements than men following VR training (Bruschetta et al., 2022). Moreover, VR was shown to enhance cognitive flexibility, selective attention, and memory processes while also reducing symptoms of depression and anxiety. Given the safety concerns associated with reinjury in TBI patients, VR offers a secure environment for practicing real-world tasks without physical limitations. Additionally, gradual adjustments in task difficulty tailored to patients' specific needs proved beneficial for learning. In conclusion, the study suggests that VR is increasingly becoming a standard practice in clinical rehabilitation for TBI patients, effectively addressing cognitive, motor, and psychological aspects of recovery.

In particular, virtual reality allows a level of engagement and cognitive involvement higher than the one provided by memory and imagination but is more controlled and can be more easily measured than that offered by direct, "real" experience. Its multisensory stimulation means VR can be considered an enriched environment that can offer functional and ecological real-world demands (e.g., finding objects, assembling things, and buying stuff) that may improve brain plasticity and regenerative processes.

(Zanier et al., 2018)

VR can provide several benefits for patients with TBI, including enhancing their mindfulness (paying attention to the present moment without judgment), hand coordination, and eye coordination. Patients can engage in activities that promote experiencing nature or performing daily tasks. Additionally, patients may feel more secure in a controlled, virtual environment than in a natural setting.

Individuals who have experienced a TBI can greatly benefit from physical and cognitive rehabilitation to aid in their recovery. Spatial computing presents numerous opportunities to further improve their healing process and assist with daily tasks, ultimately leading to an overall improvement in their quality of life.

In a 2024 study titled "Virtual Reality Immerses You in Your Mind: The Experience and Stress-Reduction Benefits of VR Mindfulness Modules in Persons with TBI," Murray and Shmidheiser examined the feasibility and effectiveness of a single-session virtual reality mindfulness module (VRMM) for individuals with mild to moderate TBI. The study involved 38 participants, who reported their stress levels before and after the VRMM session and also took part in brief qualitative interviews.

The results showed that approximately two-thirds of the participants experienced a significant reduction in stress levels following the intervention. Qualitative feedback revealed that the immersive and realistic nature of the VR environment helped compensate for the cognitive deficits associated with TBI, enhancing focus and minimizing distractions. Importantly, no adverse side effects were reported, indicating that well-designed VRMMs are generally well tolerated in this population (Murray & Shmidheiser, 2024).

The study's authors concluded that VR-based mindfulness interventions are promising for reducing stress and providing cognitive support in TBI rehabilitation, emphasizing the necessity for further research in this area. No single part of the brain works in isolation; instead, different regions collaborate to support functions such as memory retention, emotional regulation, and motor coordination.

Brain Functions

Phineas Gage serves as an example that certain brain parts are accountable for distinct functions. Our understanding of diverse brain functions is derived from the usage of magnetic resonance imaging (MRI), which uses a magnetic field and computer-generated radio waves to produce detailed images of different body parts, including the brain. Another technique used to evaluate brain functionality is an electroencephalogram (EEG), which measures the brain's electrical activity by placing electrodes directly on the scalp (Figure 8.1).

Our brains control our behavior and cognition. Through our senses, our brain integrates our surroundings by way of visuals, sounds, perception, attention, and memory (among other factors). The brain is complex, and there are many things about it that neuroscientists still don't know. Neurons are the cells that are the basic unit of the nervous system. They are responsible for receiving and transmitting information throughout the body. Neurons receive input from other neurons or sensory receptors and share that input with other neurons or effector cells (e.g., muscles or glands) in the form of an electrical impulse called an action potential. Neurons are essential for the nervous system's function and communication between different body parts.

Our nervous system acts like a highway with many overpasses and connections. Neurons innervate other neurons, muscles, and organs. When a neuron innervates, it sends an electrical signal to the target cell, which can then cause a reaction (e.g., muscle contraction or secretion of hormones). The neuron forms a synapse with the target cell; a synapse

Figure 8.1 EEG Cap.

Source: Reproduced from Ryan Somma (2009). https://openverse.org/image/73a4a7e6-5bf5-4bae-9f42-43e73e2b586e?q=eeg%20cap. Licensed under a Creative Commons Attribution-ShareAlike 2.0 Generic (CC BY-SA 2.0).

is a connection between two neurons or a neuron and a muscle or organ. The signal passes across the synapse, allowing the neuron to communicate with its target.

Immersive spatial computing experiences engage different neural networks in the brain, and the effects can vary greatly depending on the type of activity involved. Understanding the brain's specialized regions and their functions is essential for immersive creators, as it allows them to design experiences that purposefully target specific cognitive processes. This neurological perspective helps clarify why different users react differently to the same virtual environments—their brains process and interpret spatial information based on their unique neural structures and past experiences.

Although human brains share a similar basic structure, they function uniquely from person to person. Our brains process and interpret sensory information in ways that lead to distinct subjective experiences of the same events. Most people, referred to as "neurotypical," process sensory information through predictable patterns that align with societal expectations. In contrast, neurodivergent individuals experience fundamentally different patterns in sensory processing, attention, and information integration. These differences are not just variations of degree; they often represent different kinds of processing, which can create both challenges and strengths.

For example, an environment that feels appropriately stimulating to neurotypical individuals might be overwhelmingly intense for someone with sensory processing differences, or it may be insufficiently engaging for others. These neurological differences influence perception, communication styles, learning approaches, and social interactions. As a result, neurodivergent individuals often have to navigate a world primarily designed for neurotypical processing patterns.

Neurodiversity is a concept that acknowledges and appreciates the natural variation in how individuals process information neurologically. This framework includes a range of conditions such as autism, ADHD, dyslexia, and others. It emphasizes that neurological differences are a normal part of human diversity, similar to variations in race, gender, or culture.

The neurodiversity paradigm shifts away from viewing these neurological differences as inherently problematic or as deficits that need to be corrected. Instead, it recognizes that neurodivergent individuals have unique cognitive styles that come with both strengths and challenges. This perspective encourages acceptance and accommodation rather than focusing on "normalizing" or eliminating neurological differences.

Additionally, the framework highlights that society benefits from neurological diversity, noting that many innovations throughout history have emerged from individuals who process information differently than the statistical norm.

Neurodiversity significantly influences how we interact with and perceive the world. Individuals with neurodivergent traits often possess unique strengths and perspectives that can enhance creative problem-solving, drive innovation, and introduce diverse ways of thinking. These individuals may experience heightened sensitivities or exhibit different patterns of attention and perception when compared to neurotypical individuals.

For example, someone on the autism spectrum might have an increased focus on details and patterns, allowing them to notice subtle aspects of an event that others might overlook. Conversely, individuals with ADHD may become more easily distracted, which can lead them to observe and interpret different facets of an event compared to those without ADHD.

Neurodiversity as a concept does challenge the notion of a single "typical" way of experiencing the world and promotes inclusivity of different neurological profiles. When creating spatial computing experiences, VR designers should recognize and embrace neurodiversity to foster inclusivity. This connects directly to how neuroscience and VR technologies are increasingly collaborating to develop therapeutic applications for various neurodivergent conditions.

The field is increasingly focused on "precision rehabilitation"—using the flexibility of spatial computing to tailor experiences to each individual's unique neurological profile rather than applying one-size-fits-all approaches (French et al., 2022). This promising convergence of neuroscience and VR technology suggests spatial computing may eventually become a key modality for supporting neurodivergent individuals across various conditions.

THE NERVOUS SYSTEM

Our nervous system controls our bodies and encompasses our brain, nerves, and spinal cord. When using AR or VR, we provide inputs such as using a controller, hand tracking, or touchscreen, which cause a reaction and create an output. For this to happen, millions of neurons go into action. Certain experiences require visual perception, attention, problem-solving, object recognition, motivation/rewards, and spatial awareness.

For example, *Pokémon GO*, a top-rated mobile application game made by Niantic and released in 2016, uses a phone's GPS to find a person's location and uses AR to make the character appear and lead players to catch them. The player's location determines the characters they encounter. The game requires people to move through streets, parks, and other areas. Playing the game activates various parts of the player's brain, including the optic nerve and vestibular system. There are various systems to consider when building and experiencing spatial computing. In the following text some, but not all, of the nervous system is examined (and see Figure 8.2). Researchers at Stanford University discovered that adults who played Pokémon video games extensively as children developed a specific region in their brain's visual cortex that responds preferentially to Pokémon characters. This region, located in the occipitotemporal sulcus, demonstrates how early visual experiences can create dedicated neural pathways. The study supports theories about brain plasticity and "eccentricity bias," which predicts that objects viewed in

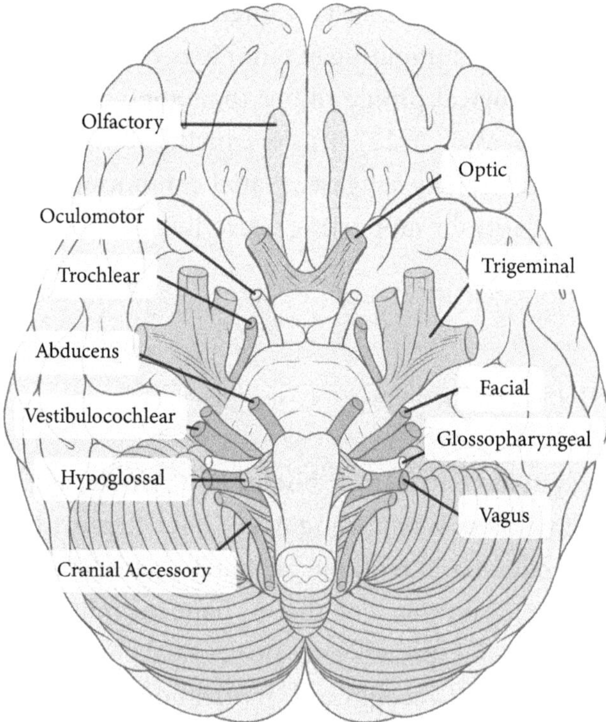

Figure 8.2 Human Brain, Normal Inferior View.

central vision (like Pokémon on small Game Boy screens) develop representations in specific brain areas (Gomez et al., 2019). Next we turn our attention to the olfactory nerve.

Olfactory Nerve

The olfactory system consists of the nose and nasal cavities. The olfactory nerve (also known as cranial nerve I, CN I) starts in the brain and ends in the upper part of the inside of the nose. Olfaction is a critical dimension to consider when creating an immersed facsimile of the natural world. In addition to being a key component of lived experience, odors are exceptionally emotional and visceral stimuli.

The use of VR technology that can stimulate the sense of smell has been found to help treat post-traumatic stress disorder (PTSD). This mental health condition is known for causing intense distressing thoughts and traumatic memories that can disrupt a person's daily life. It is also common for individuals with PTSD to experience depression, substance abuse, sleep disturbances, and anxiety. Certain scents can be particularly triggering and debilitating for people with PTSD.

Researchers at Wayne State University have developed an innovative treatment for PTSD that combines augmented reality (AR) with artificial intelligence (AI). This cutting-edge approach, led by Dr. Arash Javanbakht and his team at the Stress, Trauma, and Anxiety Research Clinic (STARC), allows therapists to manipulate virtual elements overlaid onto a patient's real-world environment. For example, therapists can create simulations of scenarios like grocery stores or restaurants to help patients gradually rebuild their confidence in social and occupational settings (Javanbakht et al., 2024).

This technology builds on earlier AR applications used to treat phobias and has shown promising clinical results. Initial feedback from first responders and other patients indicates its potential for broad application in mental health care (Javanbakht, 2024). While different regions of the brain operate independently, they also collaborate as part of an integrated nervous system. Next, we will discuss the trochlear nerve.

Trochlear Nerve

The trochlear nerve, also known as CN IV, is one of the ocular motor nerves that aids in controlling eye movement. As the smallest cranial nerve, it has the longest intracranial course and is the only nerve that exits dorsally from the brainstem. Originating from the midbrain, it connects to the superior oblique muscle, which is responsible for the rotational movement of the eyeball (Kim et al., 2022). When a person enters a new environment, they often observe their surroundings by looking around or, if they have visual impairments, by feeling their way about. They may use the trochlear nerve to rotate their eyes and take in their surroundings.

In VR or AR, it's essential to consider how people would react in the real world. Navigation is a crucial aspect to consider when focusing on the trochlear nerve. When someone enters a room, they often take a moment to assess their surroundings for potential risks or dangers, such as uneven flooring or bright lights. They may also notice interesting objects and features in the room while observing the people present to gauge the atmosphere. Additionally, they might look for possible escape routes in case of an emergency.

When designing a space, it is vital to consider that an individual naturally evaluates their environment. Addressing potential risks and ensuring users' comfort and safety is crucial. In expansive virtual environments, users can easily become disoriented. A well-designed user interface is essential for accessibility, allowing people of all abilities to navigate effectively. For those with visual impairments, there may be additional challenges. Researchers at NYU's Tandon School of Engineering are working to improve navigation for individuals who are blind or have low vision. They have developed a wearable belt, equipped with vibration motors and audio feedback capabilities, which helps users detect and avoid obstacles in their path. During testing, participants wearing Meta Quest 2 VR headsets navigated a virtual subway station while impaired vision was simulated. The results showed that haptic feedback significantly reduced collisions, and audio cues improved movement smoothness. This innovation aims to overcome the limitations of traditional mobility aids like white canes and guide dogs, potentially offering a more accessible and effective solution for independent navigation (Ricci et al., 2024).

Unlike the trochlear nerve, which helps the eyes look down and inward, the abducens nerve moves the eyes side to side.

Abducens Nerve

The abducens nerve (CN VI) controls the lateral rectus muscle, which enables individuals to see objects at different angles and distances, even when their eye is moving away from the midline of the body. This nerve provides depth perception, allowing individuals to distinguish between things closer or farther away.

The brain processes information from both eyes to create a three-dimensional image that provides a sense of depth. The abducens nerve (the sixth cranial nerve, CN VI), is responsible for eye movement. However, it only has motor functions; it does not have sensory functions. When the abducens nerve is dysfunctional, it can cause double vision, also known as diplopia. According to Dellwo (2020), the abducens nerve originates in the brainstem and extends to the orbit of the eye.

Currently, there are ongoing studies related to ocular nerves, including research investigating the use of head-cancelled virtual reality for individuals with ocular cranial nerve palsies, such as abducens palsy. This research aims to determine whether eye exercises performed in a VR environment can enhance the range of motion of the eyes. The application of VR technology could potentially benefit patients with abducens nerve palsy, a condition that impairs the ability to turn the eye outward (Houston, 2025).

Both the abducens and vestibular nerves originate from the brainstem, playing key roles in movement—one in controlling eye motion and the other in maintaining equilibrium.

Vestibular Neurons

Vestibular neurons are crucial to our body's balance and spatial orientation. They transmit information about acceleration, head movement, and gravity, all of which is used to control eye and body movements to keep us balanced, from our inner ear to the brain. The vestibulocochlear nerve (CN VIII) comprises the vestibular and cochlear nerves, each with distinct nuclei within the brainstem (Yoo & Mihaila, 2022). These neurons are also involved in learning, memory, and emotion.

For patients experiencing dizziness, vestibular rehabilitation is a type of physical therapy that can provide significant relief. Hefferman et al. (2021) found that VR and AR technologies effectively reduce symptoms such as dizziness, vertigo, and postural imbalance. Additionally, they showed that VR and AR can improve balance and coordination, assist with daily activities, reduce the fear of falling, and enhance patient satisfaction. While further research is needed to establish the long-term effectiveness of VR and AR in vestibular rehabilitation, the study concluded that these technologies could be valuable for improving the quality of life for patients.

When developing VR and AR applications for vestibular rehabilitation, the study suggests that designers should prioritize short-term symptom reduction. They should employ gradual exposure techniques, including adjustable fields of view, low-latency tracking, and customizable difficulty levels, to minimize motion sickness, which typically decreases by the fourth week. To enhance engagement and effectiveness, applications should incorporate gamification, adaptive therapy models, and objective measurement tools such as balance tests and eye tracking to complement patient self-reports.

For adults with unilateral vestibular dysfunction, exercises should primarily focus on gaze stabilization, balance training, and retraining spatial orientation. It is crucial for developers to establish meaningful collaborations with medical professionals and researchers to ensure their interventions are clinically validated and evidence-based. This commitment aligns with the higher research quality standards emphasized in the study by Hefferman et al. (2021).

Maintaining balance and spatial awareness relies on the vestibular nerve, while clear speech and swallowing are dependent on the hypoglossal nerve, highlighting the complex coordination of the nervous system.

Hypoglossal Nerve

The hypoglossal nerve (CN XII) plays a crucial role in the body by controlling the movement of the tongue. It works with other components to manage blood vessels and minor glands in the oral cavity, ensuring proper functioning. It regulates the tongue muscles for speech, swallowing, and other functions. It originates from the medulla oblongata and exits the skull through the hypoglossal canal (Kim & Naqvi, 2022).

When using AR or VR, individuals have the option to use their tongues as a means of controlling or receiving movements in a spatial computing experience. The hypoglossal nerve can detect these tongue movements and translate them into specific commands within the experience. For instance, moving the tongue to the left can cause an object to move in the virtual world, while moving the tongue up can trigger a particular command.

Shen et al. (2022) investigated the use of mouth haptics in virtual reality (VR) by incorporating ultrasonic transducers into a VR headset. This setup allowed participants to experience haptic feedback through their mouths. The study concluded that participants found mouth haptics to be more immersive than the limited haptic feedback provided by traditional controllers. The research team developed a thin, integrated ultrasound phased array that attaches to the VR headset, enabling users to feel non-contact sensations on their lips, teeth, and tongue. This technology aims to enhance immersion and realism in VR experiences. Although the primary focus of the study was not on disability, there are future opportunities for this technology to promote inclusion.

Just as the hypoglossal nerve is responsible for coordinating tongue motion for speaking and eating, the accessory spinal nerve plays a crucial role in head rotation and shoulder elevation, which are essential for posture and movement.

Accessory Spinal Nerve

The accessory spinal nerve (CN XI) is responsible for neck and shoulder movement. In AR or VR experiences, players must move their necks and shoulders. VR technology is also helping trainee surgeons practice complex procedures in a simulated setting, reducing the need for learning skills from actual patients. Neurosurgery is being demystified through VR, allowing medical students and patients to virtually enter and experience a neurosurgical operating theater (Nicholls, 2018).

Multiple technologies, including spatial computing, can assist with VR or AR worlds in treating injuries. Patients are placed in a situation where they are asked to complete tasks in a simulation. They can interact with these simulations using input devices, such as keyboards, mice, and controllers. Simulations can also create interactive experiences accompanying physical objects, such as robots, toys, and games.

The accessory spinal nerve governs motion in the upper body, but transitioning upward in the nervous system, the optic nerve plays a crucial role in sensory perception by transmitting visual signals to the brain.

Optic Nerve

Our vision heavily relies on the optic nerve, which connects our eyes to the central nervous system, comprising the brain and spinal cord. This nerve transmits electrical signals from the eye to the brain, which translates them into the images we see. Photoreceptor cells in the retina convert light into electrical signals. These signals then travel to the brain for interpretation, through the more than 1 million nerve fibers that comprise the optic nerve (National Eye Institute, n.d.).

The oculomotor nerve controls eye position during movement. Several muscles help control the eyes. The oculomotor nerve helps to adjust and coordinate eye position during movement. It is responsible for controlling several muscles in the eye, including the superior rectus, inferior rectus, medial rectus, and inferior oblique. The oculomotor nerve also helps to control pupil constriction and the eyelids. It is the third of the twelve pairs of cranial nerves and controls most eye movement.

The optic nerve allows us to perceive the world, but its function is closely supported by the trigeminal nerve, which provides sensation to the cornea and plays a role in reflexes like blinking to protect the eye.

> Eye tracking involves measuring the distance between the pupil's center and the cornea's reflection, which changes with the eye's movement. The measurement uses infrared light to reflect while cameras record and track the eye's movements.
>
> (Farnsworth, 2022)

Trigeminal Nerve

As surgery on nerves is complex, AR is used in the assistance of planning surgeries for the trigeminal nerve. Three-dimensional reconstruction and AR allow surgeons to explore the regions without working directly on a human body. AR is also used to assist in the navigation of the trigeminal nerve while surgeries are in progress. To conduct the use of AR, professionals use navigation markers, landmarks, and medical images to give surgeons a real-time three-dimensional image of the patient's anatomy, making it easier to identify the nerve and make precise decisions. In addition, this technology helps reduce the risk of damage to the nerve during surgery.

The trigeminal nerve (CN V) forms one of the twelve pairs of cranial nerves. It is responsible for the sense of touch, temperature, pain, and pressure in the face. This nerve is the largest of the cranial nerves and primarily serves as a messenger that sends sensory information from the face to the brain. The trigeminal nerve splits into three branches: the ophthalmic nerve, the maxillary nerve, and the mandibular nerve. Each branch is responsible for different areas of sensation in the face (NINDS, 2024). For example, the ophthalmic nerve is responsible for sensations on the forehead and scalp, the maxillary nerve for sensations on the cheek and upper jaw, and the mandibular nerve for sensations on the lower jaw and chin.

While the trigeminal nerve processes facial sensation and controls chewing, the vagus nerve extends far beyond the head, playing a vital role in autonomic functions like heart rate, digestion, and vocalization.

Vagus Nerve

The vagus nerve (CN X) enables the communication between the brain and the body's different systems within the body. The vagus nerve is a vast network within the body that contains two types of fibers. These fibers serve different functions, one for movement and senses and the other for managing internal functions. Starting from the head, the nerve travels through the neck and chest before ending in the abdomen, connecting various body parts. It plays a critical role in bodily sensations and regulates organ functions. The vagus nerve is a unique and essential nerve that facilitates vital bodily processes (Tewfik, 2017).

For those struggling with traditional meditation techniques, VR technology can be helpful. By providing a calming scenario, VR can promote relaxation and focus. When someone meditates in a VR environment, the vagus nerve is stimulated, which reduces stress and promotes tranquility. As a result, the heart rate decreases, and a sense of deep relaxation can be achieved. The vagus nerve's relaxation response can be triggered by calming visual scenes and soothing sounds in VR meditation. As the user engages with the virtual environment, their body's stress response is reduced, and they can experience greater mindfulness and peace. This connection between the mind and body through the vagus nerve can improve physical and mental well-being.

VR technology provides an immersive environment that fosters relaxation and mindfulness, allowing users to achieve the same benefits from meditation as traditional methods. The vagus nerve and its reactions are a critical component of this process. Additionally, the visuals and audio in VR can make the experience more immersive and engaging, helping users become more comfortable with meditation.

Having considered the nervous system, we now look at how spatial computing is revolutionizing training by creating adaptive, immersive environments that respond to users in real time.

NEW WAYS OF LEARNING

One of the most promising applications of spatial computing is for training. For decades, militaries, healthcare educators, heavy equipment companies, and many others have seen significant benefits from advanced simulation systems, in some early cases these systems used head-mounted-displays, prior to the past decade of consumer-facing devices. Muhling et al. (2023) reviewed a variety of VR training programs specifically in the medical field and concluded that "VR-enhanced learning environments with high representational fidelity—and thus a high degree of perceived presence, can increase learner motivation, enhance spatial knowledge representation, and improve contextualization of learning."

With the release of standalone mobile devices with robust tracking built in (e.g., the Oculus Quest in 2019), groups looking to train their teams in simulated immersive environments no longer have to purchase devices costing potentially tens of thousands of dollars—they can spend three hundred. The difficult part of this process that has not changed is the struggle of developing compelling, meaningful, and impactful training simulation software that has significant training outcomes. The magic that lives here is the ability to create a sophisticated VR training program and be able to ship it to anyone on a device that costs $300.

In 2017 Walmart announced a partnership with VR training company Strivr to roll out company-wide worker training using VR. Results showed that workers who used these programs not only had greater retention of the information, but also spent less time in training. In an age when workplace training is often either a webpage you try to click through as fast as possible, or a slide presentation in a big meeting room (where many participants are on their phones), VR and AR training programs offer a unique opportunity to place the user in a hands-on, immersive, and focused training environment free from any other distractions. Fully immersive training programs also provide interesting possibilities for tracking trainee progress and feedback.

As our minds are connected to our bodies, many of us learn better through physical movement. Training and educational applications that leverage spatial computing allow users to benefit not only from the feeling of embodiment they gain in a simulated environment, but also from their ability to experience training in three dimensions (rather than watching a training video or looking through a manual). Many complicated subjects that require training benefit from having core concepts, environments, step-by-step walkthroughs, and more displayed in a way that a user can explore in three dimensions.

By using VR, firefighters can don their gear and train in highly dangerous scenarios, allowing them to encounter complex situations that require strong decision-making skills. This immersive training helps them build greater confidence in the field. Similarly, heavy equipment operators can learn all the functions of a machine and become proficient in its operation before ever stepping behind the wheel. Students can also study astronomy while experiencing a fully immersive simulation of various physics concepts, observing the forces of the universe in action.

While spatial computing does offer transformative new learning methods, it is important to remain aware of how inherent biases can influence our perspectives and decisions, and we move on to consider this now.

BIASES

The teams creating spatial computing experiences may unconsciously embed their own biases into virtual environments. This can manifest in representation issues (who appears in virtual worlds), interaction mechanics (how systems respond to different user behaviors), and accessibility considerations (who can effectively use these technologies). Development teams lacking diversity may create experiences that work well for some populations but present barriers for others. For example, VR systems initially calibrated for male body dimensions and movement patterns created discomfort for many female users.

When presented with a journey while feeling rushed, most people will opt for a shortcut rather than take the long way around. Cognitive bias works in a similar manner. It is a shortcut that allows us to make decisions and judgments quickly by relying on familiar patterns instead of considering all the available information. Of course, cognitive biases can lead to wrong decisions and judgments, but for many people, relying on these biases is often a quicker and easier option than taking the time to analyze all the data.

Some biases are inherently good—bias can help us make decisions and improve efficiency for our day-to-day decisions. However, lack of awareness and understanding of individual bias can lead to flawed decisions and discriminatory practices, including stereotyping, unconscious bias, and a limited perspective. For example, if a company relies too heavily on data to make decisions, it could make biased decisions that do not reflect the actual situation (Gino & Coffman, 2021).

Different Types of Bias

Regarding decision-making and how we perceive life experiences and relationships, bias can play a significant role. It is essential to consider various types of bias when creating spatial computing experiences, as doing so can foster mutual respect between different cultures, assist with time management, and address environmental concerns. More than 180 different types of bias can impact our decision-making, perception, and judgment. Biases can influence how we interpret information and make choices. Below is a list of biases that people commonly experience, with examples of how each applies to design and development of spatial computing experiences.

Anchoring bias: The tendency to rely heavily on the first piece of information received when making decisions. For example, people may become fixated on a particular idea or approach early on, which limits the exploration of other possibilities.

Attribution bias: Attributing someone's behavior to their own personal traits instead of external factors, such as the environment or circumstances. For instance, some people may solely blame user error for negative feedback, rather than acknowledging potential design flaws.

Availability bias: A tendency to make decisions based on easily accessible information, even if it is incomplete. For instance, people may prefer to use technology or features they are familiar with, even if there are better options available.

Halo effect: Forming a complete opinion about someone based on just one characteristic. For instance, it is inaccurate to assume that all aspects of a product are of excellent quality because of a single positive feature.

Outgroup bias: Preference toward one's group over others can lead to potential oversights of valuable input from team members who come from different backgrounds or possess different areas of expertise. For instance, when teams favor their members' ideas, they may overlook valuable insights from others.

Overconfidence bias: When someone is overly confident in their abilities and moral judgments without relying on facts. This bias may result in applications that do not meet user expectations. Personal factors are seen as the cause of success, while external factors are blamed for failures.

Representativeness bias: Assumes that similarities between objects or events increase the likelihood of a specific outcome. For example, people may assume that a successful experience in one context will also succeed in a different context without considering potential differences that could impact the outcome.

Selection bias: Choosing information that aligns with a person's perspective while disregarding opposing information. For instance, selecting biased data may occur if researchers only opt for participants who are already knowledgeable about the technology, resulting in a partial comprehension of user requirements.

Self-serving bias: Occurs when individuals attribute their successes to their skill and talent while blaming external factors for their failures.

Social desirability bias: When people conform to social norms and give answers that are viewed positively, even if it is not their honest opinion, this can skew the development process.

Status-quo bias: A tendency to stick with what people are used to and resist change, and it can cause people to avoid implementing new approaches or technologies in favor of those that are familiar.

Stereotyping bias: Categorizing individuals and judging them based on their shared traits. For instance, stereotyping can result in the marginalization or inaccurate representation of specific user groups.

It is crucial to minimize the impact of these biases to create inclusive, innovative, and effective spatial computing experiences.

Interview Insights: Understanding Culture Bias

In a recent interview with Tanasha Brown, MSP, MSIO, CDP, one of the authors explored the complex relationship between culture and bias.

"There is a significant impact of culture on how individuals approach bias," Brown explained during our conversation. "However, comprehending bias requires self-awareness and comprehension of our own beliefs, regardless of culture."

Brown, a psychology scholar, suggests that accepting the existence of bias as a natural brain function is a crucial first step in recognizing how it affects belief systems.

"Thus, we must reflect on our experiences and beliefs and understand the reasons behind our biases," she emphasized. Brown recommends several practical approaches: "We can also seek diverse perspectives through conversations, reading, and listening to others' viewpoints.

Lastly, we can challenge our biases and beliefs by posing inquiries and expanding our knowledge of various cultures and perspectives."

This interview provides valuable insights into how we might better approach the complex intersection of culture, cognition, and bias in our increasingly diverse world.

What Specific Cognitive Biases May Influence Perception in AR and VR Experiences?

Using an innovative AR platform, Slowiński et al. (2022) investigated rational thinking and cognitive bias mitigation. They developed an "odd-one-out" (OOO) game to assess confirmatory biases, with 40 students both participating in the AR task and completing a comprehensive assessment of rational thinking (CART). Their findings revealed significant behavioral patterns. More rational thinkers demonstrated slower head and hand movements but faster eye movements during ambiguous tasks. These participants maintained more consistent hand–eye–head coordination patterns across different task conditions and were less likely to change their initial decisions when challenged.

The research demonstrates that multimodal behavioral markers can identify rational thinking tendencies beyond what eye tracking alone can reveal. This suggests more rational individuals employ more coordinated information-gathering and decision-making processes, supporting previous research on top-down attention in coordinated movements (Słowiński et al., 2022).

For successful AR/VR experiences, designers must consider thoughtful user interface and experience design; creating meaningful interactions; ensuring inclusivity and accessibility; maintaining user safety, security, and privacy; and addressing ethical implications to prevent potential harm. The study highlights the value of comprehensive behavioral analysis in understanding cognitive processing in augmented environments, which has implications for developing more effective immersive technologies.

Bias Questions

Asking questions throughout the design process can be helpful to designers at all levels, from students to managers, as they help to foster an understanding of the brain, culture, and bias and how these can impact the user experience. Kolko (2015) suggests some examples of the questions designers ask themselves, including:

- Who are the people who will use this product or service?
- How do they think, feel, and behave?
- What are their needs and goals?
- How do their cultural backgrounds influence their perceptions and behaviors?
- How might our own biases influence the design?

Asking these questions and considering the answers can help designers create products and services that are more inclusive, effective, and user centered. Additionally, many other sources of information, like academic journals, can help the creators better understand how the brain and culture can impact the design. In addition, testing, user research, and feedback are also essential to validate the design decisions and improve the user experience.

We must understand how our brains process information, how our cognitive biases influence our perception, and how our cultural backgrounds influence our interpretations. We must also consider how our brains and bodies respond to AR and VR experiences.

QUESTIONS FOR REFLECTION

Bias-awareness reflection questions:

1. **Personal Influence Assessment**
   - How do my lived experiences, background, and identity shape how I perceive users different from myself?

- What assumptions am I making based on my professional training rather than user evidence?
- In what ways might my organizational culture be influencing my design decisions?

2. **Systemic Understanding**
   - How do market pressures and profit motives shape which user needs receive priority in my work?
   - What biases are embedded in my industry's standard practices and methodologies?
   - How might my need to meet deadlines or satisfy stakeholders conflict with creating truly inclusive design?

3. **Impact Recognition**
   - How might design choices made under time/budget constraints disproportionately affect marginalized users?
   - In what ways am I balancing business requirements against the needs of underrepresented groups?
   - How can I advocate for inclusive practices while working within organizational constraints?

4. **Practical Application**
   - What small changes can I implement even within tight project parameters?
   - How might I document bias concerns that I don't have authority to address?
   - What allies or resources exist within my organization to support more inclusive approaches?

PROJECTS FOR CONSIDERATION

Conduct comprehensive user research around your chosen spatial computing concept, guided by these essential questions:

1. **User Identification**
   - Who specifically will use this product or service?

- What demographic, geographic, and psychographic factors should you consider?
- Who might be excluded from your initial user definition?

2. **User Psychology**
   - How do your target users think, feel, and behave in contexts relevant to your application?
   - What mental models do they bring to spatial interactions?
   - What emotional responses might different design elements trigger?

3. **Needs Assessment**
   - What are your users' explicit and implicit needs?
   - What goals are they trying to accomplish?
   - What barriers currently prevent them from achieving these goals?

4. **Cultural Contextualization**
   - How do cultural backgrounds influence perceptions and behaviors relevant to your application?
   - What cultural assumptions might be embedded in standard spatial computing paradigms?
   - How can your design accommodate cultural differences in spatial understanding?

5. **Bias Examination**
   - What personal or team biases might influence your design decisions?
   - How might your life experiences create gaps in your understanding?
   - What assumptions are you making about "normal" or "typical" users?

Where Do We Go From Here?

Most of this book focuses on personal spatial computing—the devices that humans will use to interact with computing systems in three-dimensional space. If we think of spatial computing as computing that directly interacts with our physical environment and has awareness of that environment, then it is important to at least speculate about how, in the future, AI and robotic systems may interact with our personal spatial computing systems. Future pairs of AR glasses, VR head-mounted displays (HMDs), mixed-reality HMDs, and other devices in our homes and offices will have advanced sensor technology. As these sensors, and the machine learning software that they feed into, become more advanced, we will be constantly providing directly into these systems massive amounts of contextual data about us, our environment, and others in that environment. At its developers' conference keynote in 2021, Meta showcased a vision for a headset that has enough awareness to know where your car keys are and then remind you if it sees them on the table while you are walking out of your home and most likely driving to a meeting. This simple use case demonstrates a system that has environmental awareness, object awareness, but most importantly it has contextual awareness of the environment, and the objects contained in the context of the life of the user.

How will we choose to design the way that we interact with these systems? Will we follow the path of current smartphone and smart home assistants (e.g., Siri, Google Home, and Alexa) that we interact with in very formal, cold, and removed ways (and receive equally cold and formal responses)? Or will we start to make these interfaces look more like us? As we look ahead to the type of systems that ChatGPT and its inevitable rivals will evolve into and imagine providing it with all our personal information, emails, text messages, photos, and live sensor data from a spatial computing device, how will we want to interact with that system?

Spike Jonze's 2013 film *Her* (Warner Bros. Pictures) shows us the life of Theodore Twombly, played by Joaquin Phoenix, who develops a relationship with his AI virtual assistant named Samantha, played by Scarlett Johansson. The film effectively depicts how we may begin to feel increasingly connected with systems that we design, especially as they start to show more human characteristics. At one point, Twombly begins using the camera on his phone to provide a live video feed to Samantha to give even more context to his life and so they can go on outings "together." It is this view (i.e., computers as companions) that we should be mindful of as we look at the inevitable convergence of deeply capable AI and more powerful, connected, comfortable, and lightweight spatial computing devices.

As AI systems continue to become more capable and contextually aware, we will interact with them through a variety of devices and interfaces. In the way that spatial computing allows us to bring our bodies into the computer, they could also provide a way for AI agents to take on an embodied form that interacts with us spatially. What sort of relationship might we begin to develop with intelligent systems if they are able to embody a friendly avatar that makes natural eye contact, walks around our living room, sits in a chair, talks about our day with us, and is connected to the Internet and to our personal data? With the capabilities currently available, it is already possible to see how these technologies could come together to create digital agents with which we can build meaningful relationships.

As we consider how AI systems may become embodied in a digital form, it is also worth considering how spatial computing systems may serve as secondary sensor inputs for robotic systems as well. Robotic systems can incorporate any amount of sensor data to build a usable model for their environment. We can imagine a group of users wearing spatial computing devices providing the data from their devices directly to a robot in the same environment so that that robot has significantly more sensor data from a variety of vantage points to build a more accurate model of the environment. This would improve accuracy and awareness, and provide greater context to that system of the users in the environment.

THE FUTURE OF SPATIAL COMPUTING

As we look ahead to where spatial computing will take us, the number of open questions is astounding. How will the technology continue to develop? What unforeseen consequences will emerge? How will spatial computing converge with other technologies like artificial intelligence (AI), advanced sensors, etc.? This final chapter explores how we might anticipate spatial computing to integrate with other technologies, how spatial computing might define who we become, what lessons we can learn from the advancement of other technologies, and what positive visions for the future we might imagine—a future powered by a human-focused path for spatial computing. This is an opportunity to explore possibilities and assess risks as technology advances.

Augmented Reality, Digital Twins, and the New Information Layer

In his short film *Hyper-Reality*, Keiichi Matsuda (2016) presents a dystopian vision of what personal spatial computing devices could become. The film depicts a day in the life of a user of an augmented reality (AR) headset as they move through an urban environment, the physical world depicted as having a persistent digital layer that facilitates work, social interaction, healthcare, and personal identity. Matsuda highlights the dangers of over-reliance on a digital layer once AR devices have gained mass adoption—showing what happens when user data is compromised and the user has to navigate the world without their augmentations; how the physical world becomes more difficult to navigate without them because the world has been built to be interacted with only through these augmentations, and interaction becomes limited in physical environments when users are focused on the digital layer more than the physical one.

The world that Matsuda shows may seem outlandish, but as [the world's largest and wealthiest] companies look for new ways to monopolize human attention and activity for profit we may find ourselves on a similar path to the one he portrays—even if it doesn't appear quite as sinister as Matsuda's vision.

In an interview with writer Greg Smith relating to his early explorations of this, Matsuda provides additional warnings about how AR systems may control users:

> Is there a dark side? Yes, and it's huge. Corporate AR could turn every worker into a drone. Predictive systems (including Amazon's suggestions and Google's personalized search results) may cause people to increasingly become narrowcast stereotypes, and there is a potential for sinister behavioural control based on suggestion. Oppressive governments may use it to mask social problems and spread propaganda. We must tread carefully.
>
> (Smith, 2011)

In that same interview, Matsuda discusses the ways that AR will change the way we interact with our physical environment:

> This increasing overlap between architecture and interaction is just the beginning of a massive period of change in our environment, which is the digitization of space. We already have many ways of extending physical space into the virtual realm, and these will continue to develop and be used to augment our world.
>
> (Smith, 2011)

As the architecture of the physical world becomes captured by a variety of devices, we witness what John Vickers, in his 2010 Roadmap Report for NASA, calls "digital twins" (NASA, 2010). However, the concept has much earlier beginnings in the science community and finds roots in the speculative work of David Gelernter's 1991 book *Mirror Worlds*.

Digital twins are simulations of real-world objects and environments informed by historical data, schematics and design documents, and real-time sensor data in cases where the digital twin is mapped to its real-world equivalent (Allen, 2021).

Several companies, including Meta and Google, have outlined plans to create digital twins of their own (consider the current state of Google Maps), with a clear pathway for additional sensor modules and user data from spatial computing devices left to fill in the gaps. This would give a few companies more complete models and real-time data of the world than any government—with much consideration required as to how government agencies will be able to access this data.

Artificial Intelligence

The public release of a variety of new tools and systems in 2022 show-cased the rapid development of artificial intelligence (AI). Midjourney, DALL-E, and Stable Diffusion gave users the chance to use text prompts to generate images—showing an incredible aptitude to create images in the style of any artist to whose work it has access. These deep learning-enabled models can interact with us through natural language processing. Tools powered by these types of models are only becoming more sophisticated and capable, and are rapidly moving into more and more domains.

The public beta release of OpenAI's ChatGPT system in November 2022 heralded a new wave of public perception about how we interact with AI—it gave users the opportunity to provide text prompts to the system and receive text in return. ChatGPT is built on the same type of deep learning systems that its image-generation counterparts are. It learns from the data that is fed into the model and then is additionally capable of learning, remembering, and reacting to previous prompts from individual users. What is displayed in ChatGPT is a designed and specific intelligence—it is not human, but we can interact with it in some of the ways in which interact with each other. We write to it, and it writes to us—often with compelling (if not accurate) answers.

AI systems like these force us to recognize dramatic and rapid transformations. Tools like Gravity Sketch, a VR design platform used by major automotive manufacturers to create vehicle prototypes in immersive three-dimensional environments, perfectly illustrate how AI is following the automobile's transformative path. Just as the automobile revolutionized physical mobility, AI systems are transforming cognitive and creative tasks. Car designers once worked exclusively with clay models and two-dimensional drawings; now they sculpt virtual vehicles in collaborative VR spaces enhanced by AI tools that suggest design optimizations, analyze aerodynamics in real time, and even generate novel aesthetic elements based on historical design language. We are on the cusp of a new technology-driven era, akin to the development of the automobile industry. Much as the automobile redefined transportation, urban planning, and even social patterns within decades of the Model T, we're witnessing AI rapidly redefine knowledge work, creative processes, and decision-making systems. Both technologies began as luxury innovations accessible to few, then systematically transformed entire economic sectors through iterative improvements and scaling efficiencies.

In the 2020s, several significant advancements have reshaped the landscape of spatial computing. A major breakthrough occurred with improvements in hardware, wearables, and the integration of artificial intelligence (AI). In 2024, Apple launched the Vision Pro, which established a new standard for mixed-reality experiences due to its high-resolution display and seamless blending of digital and physical environments (XR Today, 2024). Furthermore, the incorporation of AI into spatial computing has enhanced spatial awareness and positional tracking, leading to improved applications in AR and MR (Tilt Labs, 2024). Another important development is the emergence of geospatial AI models, such as Nvidia's Earth-2 project, which combines AI with physics simulations for applications like climate modeling (Barron, 2024).

Technological advancements are influenced not only by innovation but also by political shifts, the effects of which are yet to be fully understood. In January 2025, Donald Trump assumed office as President of the United States. He issued an executive order that specifically targeted what he described as "radical and wasteful government DEI programs" (White House, 2025). This action raised concerns regarding his Executive Orders affecting diversity, equity, inclusion, and accessibility (DEIA), particularly regarding who would benefit from technology and who might be excluded.

When systems fail to be inclusive of diverse backgrounds, the risk of a digital divide increases. Social inequalities can create barriers for marginalized communities, leaving vulnerable populations—such as individuals with disabilities—without access to essential services, information, and opportunities. Before 1990, there were no laws in the US protecting the rights of people with disabilities. The Americans with Disabilities Act (1990) mandated accessibility in employment, public spaces, transportation, and telecommunications (Anti-Defamation League, 2024).

A significant amount of federal funding is allocated for research related to diversity, equity, inclusion, and accessibility, and this funding is now at risk.

Generative Applications and Experiences

As we consider the current spatial computing landscape, there is much discussion about the possibility (or inevitability) of applications and experiences generated by AI based on prompts given by a user. Jasmine Roberts, an AR and VR developer whose work often showcases forward-looking use cases, posted on Twitter in October of 2022 by integrating OpenAI's GPT3 into a real-time Unity 3D scene. What she shows is an early demonstration of generating three-dimensional objects and moving them around in a three-dimensional environment using only speech-to-text prompts from a user. Roberts's (2022) early demo scene offers a small glimpse into what may be possible in the future as generative AI systems continue to make strides toward being capable of generating full three-dimensional scenes. A user wearing a VR headset may at some point be able to tell the operating system what they want to experience and have it come into view before them. Users could compose a piece of music and ask for it to be performed by an orchestra, talk to a fictional character about their love life, imagine what life might be like on an alien world, collaboratively dream up an adventure with a friend, or imagine an erotic experience like the Singapore-based company Lovense, a sex toy company which integrated its device with the Vision Pro to create a more immersive form of virtual intimacy for long-distance couples using intuitive hand gestures (Forlini, 2024). Spatial computing offers immersive experiences that transport us to new realities and integrates seamlessly with the systems we use daily. AI assistants now routinely manage our schedules, personalize our news feeds, and even anticipate our needs before we express them.

While these systems will most likely enter ours and work in mundane ways—such as using ChatGPT to write emails and assist with clerical work (as it is already is)—we should be mindful of the ways all this will change the way that we think, imagine, dream, and interact with one another. If we obtain the ability to visualize a multitude of interactive worlds in our homes, how will that change our desire to interact with the physical world? If we have artificial digital companions that know more about us than anyone else because they have access to all that we write—text messages, email, our photos and videos—then will we feel a deeper connection with them than with our friends, coworkers, and family? If users can conjure pornography of any variety, which is not only embodied but interactive, how will that change sexual relationships, desires, and expectations in ways that we haven't anticipated?

As we sit on the cusp of substantive changes in human–computer interaction, we are directly confronted with the question "What does it mean to be human?" This is a question with a deeply troubling past that has often been answered loudest and most violently by those who wish to define their subgroup as somehow the *true* humans and to use their own specific characteristics to define others as less worthy. Skin color, neurodiversity, height, eye color, educational level, religion, language, geographical origin—and anything else we become insecure about or obsessed with enough—can turn into hate. As we seek to develop computing tools that are more *human*, we must be very careful about how we define "human," who we exclude from that definition, and how the systems we build may reinforce existing biases and build greater divides between users and nonusers. There is also the question of how we define our relationship with artificial digital entities as they start to take on traits and forms that make us more prone to treat them not just like an appliance, but as peers. We define ourselves through our relationships, and our relationship with computers (a term that itself can already seem quite outdated) will continue to become increasingly definitional as more and more of our personal activity takes place with their assistance.

We can also expect that there will be some amount of significant resistance to the adoption of these technologies—attempts by governments to regulate them, coalitions that form to combat the rise of AI-generated content—as well as those who will seek to use these tools to create misinformation and to harm others. Expect that, as these technologies mature and expanded use cases become clear, the leadership of the companies controlling them will be working toward the advancement of their own power and revenue generation for their stakeholders, and that most other concerns will remain secondary. The billionaire class is not incentivized to align itself with the interests of the working class.

Sensor Data and Contextual Awareness

As spatial computing devices continue to include more capable and high-resolution external sensors (cameras, microphones, light detection and ranging (LiDAR), etc.) and internal and biometric sensors (face tracking, eye tracking, heart rate, temperature, etc.), they will feed data into increasingly powerful software systems that will be able to develop a full model of your environment and you within it. These systems will know your body position and be able to monitor your physical state at a deeply personal level. How much of this data users are willing to let companies have access to will dictate how these applications continue to develop. Studies show that 97% of people aged 18–34 do not read terms of service, highlighting a concerning lack of public awareness regarding the privacy and safety implications of the information we share. This finding, reported by Guynn in 2020, highlights the importance of understanding what we're agreeing to when we use online services. It is also important to consider how these systems will interact with present nonusers—someone who is not wearing the device, and may not even be aware of the device, but is present in the same physical environment as the device.

Our future presents a complex relationship with technology and privacy that builds on current concerning trends. The widespread practice of sharing photos of others without consent is a troubling example of our diminishing privacy boundaries. This behavior has become normalized despite the serious ethical implications. When people casually share images of friends, family members, or even strangers, they are making unilateral decisions about others' digital presence and potential data exposure.

This connects to broader concerns about consent in our digital ecosystem. As AI advances, we are seeing the exploitation of personal data in increasingly invasive ways. The proliferation of pornographic deepfakes demonstrates how innocuous photos can be weaponized through technology, creating false but convincing sexual content of real people without their knowledge or permission. In a film *Another Body*, a documentary about college students seeking justice after their faces were used without consent for deepfake pornography, highlights disturbing statistics that 95% of deepfakes are non-consensual and 90% target women (Viola, 2024). The tension between rapid technological advancements and the slower development of laws and regulations may seem insurmountable. Without deliberate intervention, we may witness a further erosion of privacy boundaries as technology advances more quickly than our ethical frameworks can adapt.

There are questions worth asking about level of data integration, storage, and synthesis we allow spatial computing devices to access:

- Will users want to store conversations between them, other users, and nonusers who are perceived in the same physical space? This would function as a sort of indexable embodied memory storage device.

- How do we manage consent for users and nonusers? Many users and nonusers may not want to have three-dimensional depth data, audio, video, and other sensor information that captures them recorded (for any purpose even if data is only processed on a device and not pushed out to a cloud service) and potentially augmented in some way. This becomes especially important when we consider younger users and nonusers who may not be able to consent to this in the first place.

- If spatial computing devices become stable and reliable in outdoor settings, will we leave them unregulated in their use or will they become as ubiquitous as smartphones but with their sensors always on and potentially always recording?

- While there are many privacy and safety concerns that arise from the always-on sensors, there are also interesting design opportunities to consider if they become the norm. If a user can give direct access to all the sensor data, what sort of applications and features might designers be able to develop? With so much additional information, there are opportunities to overlay more contextual information, to understand the environment and the objects in it, and to create the opportunity for a digital layer over in-person conversations.

- Thinking about two people wearing the same devices in a shared physical space that has contextual awareness of both users, how much data can or should be shared between devices and how that data is stored? What level of transparency into this data is given to the developer to incorporate into their application? What level of control do users have to choose how their data is handled?

Connecting Over Distance

People have grown even more accustomed to connecting from a distance—often through immersive video and mixed-reality platforms.

What began with the 2020 COVID-19 pandemic has evolved into a seamless blend of remote and in-person interaction, now common not only in workplaces but also in homes, classrooms, community events, and virtual gathering spaces worldwide. A global crisis forced everyone to ask, "How do we do online all the things we used to do in person?" Karl et al. (2022) highlight the rapid growth of the use of video calling during the start of the pandemic: "Zoom, for instance, had 10 million daily meeting participants in December 2019, but by April 2020, that number had risen to over 300 million." Their research found that "many employees were unaware of social norms or meeting etiquette" (Karl et al. 2022) while participating in video meetings as opposed to in-person meetings. Many of our long-held social norms did not translate to mass adoption of video calling, with people eating in front of the camera, talking to family members at home without muting their microphone during the meeting, or in some cases forgetting to turn off the camera or mute when doing or saying something inappropriate on camera. During the height of the pandemic, the authors of the book advised students to turn off their cameras and microphones during breaks. This recommendation was made because there were instances of inappropriate behavior. For example, a colleague reported seeing two students in bed with each other during a Zoom class. While the shift to virtual platforms like Zoom highlighted connections across physical distances, the parallel in VR technology transformed how we connect meaningfully in immersive worlds.

We also saw a rise in the adoption rates of VR headsets and their use during the COVID-19 pandemic. Ball et al. (2021) confirmed what the press had been theorizing—that the pandemic had directly contributed to the adoption of VR headsets and a rise in use related to these circumstances. People were looking for new ways to connect across distances.

The Metaverse

Around this same time, we saw a doubling down by some major companies on the idea of building a "metaverse"—a digital world where we all spend time and do things together. The company Meta describes the

Metaverse on its website: "The metaverse is the next evolution in social connection and the successor to the mobile internet."

Meta has positioned itself at the front of the race toward whatever the spatial version of the Internet will be. Its approach assumes—and demands—that the current state of the Internet (mostly accessed through smartphones) gives way to a new three-dimensional, spatial, and social platform. Meta has yet to prove that this is something that users want, that it is feasible, or that it can accommodate the variety of applications users will expect from a new computing platform. It now faces fierce competition from both Apple and Google as Apple's VisionOS and Google's Android XR already have a large suite of mature consumer applications available.

In an interview, Meta CEO Mark Zuckerberg said, "in 2020 it is a lot easier to move bits around than atoms. So I'd much rather have us teleport by using virtual reality or video chat than sit in traffic" (Newton, 2020). As the world continues to grapple with the realities of global health crises and the effects of climate change, there is a need to pursue alternative forms of connection that bridge the gaps left by videoconferencing. To do this Meta needs to drive mass adoption to make meeting with people using a spatial computing device compelling enough to consider forgoing travel in a variety of instances. In *The Immersive Enclosure: Virtual Reality in Japan*, Paul Roquet (2022) offers an important warning:

> VR offers Facebook the chance to become the virtual landlord of digital transit, work, and recreational infrastructures set to replace physical travel and real estate. In other words, Zuckerberg is interested in VR not just as a new communications platform but as a virtual substitute for basic spatial infrastructure as well.

There is no certainty that spatial computing systems will become the ubiquitous device that replaces smartphones as our new constant companion. If you are someone actively engaged in the development of tools, content, applications, hardware, or anything else in this space you have the opportunity, and the responsibility, to look ahead to the ways that whatever the next computing platform is will change the next generation of humanity. Living behind the question "Will we *all* live in the meta-verse?" is "Do we all *want* to live in the metaverse?" At the heart of this is a still deeper question: "Who do we want to become?" Do we, all together, want to build deeper and more personal connections with computers?

Technology and Power Dynamics

As many of the major tech companies look for an economic driver to replace the revenue lost in the battle to the bottom over digital ads (i.e., the way many of them make their money) we are seeing them all move in different directions over how they see the future of computing and their ability to capitalize on it. How companies make money from spatial computing platforms will be one of the strongest determining factors in what gets built, by who, and how users will get to interact with it.

The power dynamics of technology and its creation are closely linked to who builds it, what is built, and how users engage with it. People often hold more power than they realize. In 2018, Google employees protested, successfully gathering over 4,000 signatures on a petition to halt the company's contract with the Pentagon for Project Maven, an AI program for analyzing drone footage (Conger, 2018). This was one of the first instances of employee activism compelling a major corpo-ration to decline a lucrative government contract. Advocacy, lobbying, legislation, and organizational involvement are particularly important for causes people believe in.

Government and user advocacy efforts have made significant progress in protecting users online and on mobile devices, especially in the EU and regions where the General Data Protection Regulation (GDPR) has become enforceable law. As we anticipate the emergence of various new consumer technologies that foster deep personal connec-tions in the coming years, regulating these technologies will become in-creasingly challenging. Lawmakers already struggle to fully understand the complex systems that have become widespread.

Access to spatial computing devices will suffer from many of the same issues current for mobile phone users. Will we see a fracturing of user groups: While there will be those who can afford premium devices that offer higher levels of user privacy and safety, other groups will have to opt in to some sort of user-fueled platform that relies on ads or some other sort of user-based economic system we haven't yet seen. With mobile devices, Apple is currently positioning itself against most other major tech companies to make high-quality privacy- and health-focused products that are prohibitively expensive for many people who still need capable devices. When devices become necessary to engage in modern society (as the smartphone has debatably become) accessibility becomes imperative. Note that the economic model of a platform has a direct impact on how accessible it is—and how exploitative it is. As companies like Apple drive further toward premium products that are privacy and quality focused, many of its competitors look for ways to create cheaper, or even free, products and services that turn the users into a product themselves—selling user data, serving ads, or employing other forms of user-based economies.

There is no way to predict the future, but we can learn from our past. In the 21st century, we have seen advancements in technology that positively and negatively impact culture, society, politics, and our behavior. We have seen improvements in communication with people worldwide through immersive experiences, VR helping people with palliative care, and the harm social media has had on individuals and government entities. The responsibility for creating ethical spatial computing lies with its creators, as well as the government, the industry, and the public.

Big tech companies have significantly transformed modern industries. For example, the military has integrated AI for various defense purposes, and large institutions have also adopted these advanced tools. In the realm of spatial computing, we have witnessed notable advancements in military training, where virtual environments are utilized to reduce costs related to weapons, travel, and physical risks, all while simulating real-world scenarios.

The US military is employing immersive technologies for several applications, including tactical augmented reality (TAR), which enables soldiers to see the precise locations of both allied and enemy forces without the need to look down at a GPS device (NSTXL, 2023). In the medical field, AR applications allow medical students and professionals to participate in realistic surgical simulations, train for patient care, practice emergency responses, and engage in rehabilitation programs, all without putting real patients at risk (Makarevych & Diachenko, 2024).

Spatial audio technology enables users to experience sound in a more immersive way. Samsung is collaborating with Google on a project called Eclipsa Audio, which is a three-dimensional audio framework designed for creation, delivery, and playback (Roth, 2025). Even when users remain stationary, the sounds in their environment create the illusion that they have moved to a different location. As spatial audio transforms the experience of sound, a similar evolution is happening across various ecosystems where technology, business, and culture converge to create new modes of interaction.

Examining different ecosystems—such as individual, societal, political, and cultural perspectives—allows us to identify areas for improvement and develop ideas to create a more inclusive, ethical, accessible, and equitable future.

Who are the gatekeepers of spatial computing? Regardless of our location, the gatekeepers are those who control internet speed, determine what content is accessible, and set the prices for products and services. Much of the focus in the technology world takes a Western perspective, but there is a vast world out there that is changing how technology is approached. TikTok was banned in India in June 2020 following a military clash with China, with the government citing privacy concerns and national security threats (Pathi, 2024). India had about 200 million TikTok users at the time, the largest market outside China. After the ban, competitors like YouTube Shorts and Instagram Reels quickly filled the void, capturing most of TikTok's former market (Pathi, 2024). The gatekeepers are governments and corporations who control the distribution and access to technology and the cost of products and services.

A growing movement of content creators, particularly in underrepresented communities, is working to change the dominant narrative and approach to technology. Black content creators play a crucial role in shaping digital history by challenging traditional narratives, promoting inclusivity, and redefining online communities across platforms such as YouTube, Instagram, and TikTok. Despite encountering issues like algorithmic biases and disparities in pay, these creators demonstrate significant cultural influence through trends, dialogues, community building, and economic empowerment via brand partnerships. They also contribute to innovation in content creation and exhibit originality in storytelling (Victoria, 2024). Use of technology to tell their stories and share their perspectives is making a significant impact in shaping that technology's future, to be more inclusive and representative of diverse voices. For example, Indigenous people work to tell their stories by partnering with corporations (see Chapter 3).

The reality of life is that everything is a remix. We use the technology of the past to create our present and future. Understanding our past helps us to understand harms as well as benefits.

One of the significant successes of spatial computing is the development of global navigation satellite systems (GNSS) such as BeiDou (China), QZSS (Japan), IRNSS/NavIC (India), GLONASS (Russia), GPS (United States), and Galileo (Europe). Spatial computing not only helps us navigate to our desired locations but also offers new opportunities through VR, AR, and other immersive technologies (Taoglas, 2024). However, along with the benefits these technologies bring, it is important to acknowledge the potential drawbacks. These government-funded and -operated systems provide strategic control over critical infrastructure while ensuring global coverage, which has resulted in substantial investments to maintain and expand these satellite constellations across multiple nations.

To address the vulnerabilities associated with satellite-based navigation, several complementary technologies have emerged. These include low earth orbit (LEO) satellite systems that offer reduced latency and improved accuracy (Fox, 2024), as well as terrestrial-based networks like enhanced long range navigation (eLoran) that operate independently of satellite signals. Additionally, alternative technologies leverage cellular networks, Wi-Fi, and other terrestrial transmitters (Stanford GPS Research Center, n.d.). These backup systems, developed through collaborations among government agencies, private companies, and research institutions, enhance resilience against signal interference, jamming, and other GNSS vulnerabilities, while extending navigation capabilities to previously challenging environments.

The Collingridge Dilemma

Spatial computing can bring people closer together or push them apart. The Collingridge dilemma is when it is difficult to fully predict a new technology's impacts early in its development, but once those effects become clear, the technology is often too entrenched to easily alter or govern. First, the advancement of spatial computing needs to be sufficiently predicted. Nevertheless, we can change the direction the technology can go in from a social, cultural, political, and public perspective. The real question to ask concerning our technology is: Who has the power? Is it an organization, or is it the public?

When considering the positive impact of spatial computing, we should examine the technologies that have gained prominence in the 21st century, such as brain–computer interfaces (BCIs), electroencephalograms (EEGs), and advanced AR and VR experiences. These technologies allow individuals to experience a sense of their body in a different space. Non-invasive, EEG-based BCIs are progressing toward practical applications due to improvements in materials, miniaturization, and advancements in AI algorithms (Hsieh et al., 2025).

BRAIN–COMPUTER INTERFACES

The integration of BCIs with AR and VR platforms represents a significant advancement, creating immersive environments where users can control digital spaces using their brain signals. This is particularly beneficial for neuro-rehabilitation. The combination of BCIs and spatial computing facilitates more intuitive interactions between humans and computers, potentially transforming healthcare through closed-loop systems that utilize neuroplasticity for recovery and enhancement.

With the ongoing development of wearable and comfortable BCIs, along with advances in machine learning, this technology is becoming increasingly accessible for both clinical applications and everyday use. This suggests a future where thought-controlled spatial computing could become commonplace (Hsieh et al., 2025).

A study (Slater, et al., 2020) investigated how touch and visual input can alter the brain's perception of limb ownership. Researchers found that when a person observed a rubber hand being touched while their real hand was hidden, they began to feel the sensation of touch in their own hidden hand. This phenomenon, known as the "rubber hand illusion," illustrates how the brain combines sensory information to establish a sense of body ownership.

Spatial computing can give people powerful experiences that seem impossible and feel very real to the person's brain, whether in a VR like a cube or using an HMD.

BCIs are an innovative way of connecting the human mind to technology. By creating a direct link between our cognitive processes and the digital world, BCIs can potentially transform the lives of people who struggle with communication. For example, individuals who have lost the ability to speak due to injury or illness can use BCIs to translate their neural signals into digital commands, which are then transmitted to devices like computers or speech synthesizers. UCSF (University of California, San Francisco) neurosurgeon Edward Chang has made a significant technological breakthrough that allows people to communicate through technology by establishing a direct neural link. This innovation mainly benefits individuals who experience speech impediments, allowing them to bridge the communication gap and interact with others.

Although BCIs offer hope for enhanced communication and connectivity, they have positive and negative consequences. On one hand, individuals previously marginalized by their inability to communicate can now interact with others, share ideas, and participate in social interactions. This newfound empowerment promotes inclusion and enriches their quality of life. However, the cost of installing BCIs remains a significant barrier that prevents individuals from lower economic backgrounds from accessing this technology. Moreover, BCIs may not work for everyone, as individual brain structures and functions differ. Certain physical limitations may also hinder the successful implementation of the technology for individuals with severe neurological conditions or other constraints. Additionally, BCIs may not address different dimensions of daily life, such as mobility.

BCIs and spatial computing complement each other and provide new possibilities for individuals with disabilities. Spatial computing is a versatile tool that transcends barriers, offering navigation, transportation, and communication avenues that cater to unique needs. Through spatial computing, individuals can interact with the world innovatively, using AR overlays for navigation assistance or creating immersive environments that facilitate meaningful interactions. However, ensuring that spatial computing solutions are designed with inclusivity and accessibility is critical to prevent the emergence of new barriers or biases.

Integrating BCIs and spatial computing is a groundbreaking convergence that holds promise for transforming the lives of individuals with disabilities. Chang's pioneering work exemplifies the potential of BCIs to restore communication while spatial computing expands the horizons of accessibility. As these technologies evolve, a collaborative effort to mitigate challenges and ensure universal access becomes essential, marking a pivotal step toward a more inclusive and interconnected world.

Artificial Intelligence

AI presents both positive and negative outcomes. On one hand, it is increasingly integrated into everyday life, enhancing efficiency in various systems such as healthcare, education, sports, and the judicial system. On the other hand, there is a significant concern regarding implicit bias present in AI, particularly with spatial computing. Harding (2023) highlights that facial recognition technologies often struggle to accurately detect darker skin tones due to biased training datasets and technical calibrations primarily designed for lighter skin tones.

Organizations like the Algorithmic Justice League, founded by Dr. Joy Buolamwini, aim to raise awareness about algorithmic bias by combining research with art and developing practices for creating more equitable AI. Striving for an equitable future is both challenging and complex. However, if we fail to address the inherent biases in AI systems, their benefits will be inaccessible to certain populations, ultimately reinforcing existing hierarchies of race, class, and power (Algorithmic Justice League 2025).

AI is increasingly being integrated into various products, with significant advancements in spatial computing. As a result, people around the world are becoming more familiar with this technology. However, there is considerable anxiety regarding its uses and effects, and significant gaps in trust highlight disparities that need to be addressed. According to McKinsey's 2024 Global Survey on AI, 72% of surveyed organizations are utilizing AI, which marks a roughly 50% increase from the previous year. Additionally, nearly 65% of organizations regularly use generative AI, nearly double the percentage from just 10 months earlier. This substantial growth in generative AI adoption is primarily seen in marketing and sales, product development, and information technology. Despite this progress, many organizations still face challenges related to data governance when operating their data models. As the growth of this technology continues, it is essential for humans to prepare for the future.

Beauty or Nightmare?

Our brains are hardwired to survive, and because of that, we often think the worst of a situation and can have a dystopian worldview. We all have biases, and our negativity bias can impact how we see a problem. Spatial computing can be used in various ways and industries. Whether a beautiful experience or a nightmare is provided can all be changed through lines of code. For example, some practitioners use a risk register in project management. This risk register will list everything that can go wrong with a project. What might that look like if a risk register was made of all the things that could go wrong with spatial computing projects?

In the *Black Mirror* episode titled "PlayTest," the main character, Cooper, is an American traveling in London who undergoes an implant procedure, referred to as a "mushroom," at the back of his neck. He agrees to test an AR game based on whack-a-mole and becomes increasingly involved in additional tests (Black Mirror, 2021).

What starts as an enjoyable experience quickly turns into a nightmare as Cooper begins to see spiders—his greatest fear—and hears the footsteps of a childhood friend, which intensifies his sense of dread. Eventually, he becomes engulfed in doubt and uncertainty until he wakes up back in reality. However, after waking, he receives a call from his mother that inadvertently triggers the chip in his head, leading to his demise.

Many Viewers interpret *Black Mirror* as a glimpse into a dystopian future, highlighting that our limited understanding of technology often leads us to envision the worst possible outcomes. Some potential dangers include privacy issues, health and safety risks, security vulnerabilities, and ethical implications. By identifying these risks and working to mitigate them, we can create a better future by understanding our past and anticipating where we might be heading.

Spatial computing holds the potential to create a more utopian world by offering immersive experiences that are tailored to individual needs. It utilizes AR and VR to develop environments that cater specifically to users, providing access to necessary resources and tools.

The future is here with smart glasses that use AI to recognize people, places, and objects. Glasses like Meta's Ray-Bans can assist blind individuals in navigating their surroundings, but they can also be misused for facial recognition without the consent or knowledge of those being recorded. In this envisioned future, we may connect to an AR environment through wearable technologies, such as contact lenses or clothing equipped with haptic feedback. These innovations could enhance our daily interactions, allowing for health monitoring and creating immersive spatial computing experiences that improve our lives.

BUILDING A BETTER FUTURE

Moving forward, we must adopt spatial computing technologies inclusively and ethically. We must consider this transformative wave's potential benefits and risks as significant corporations invest in supplanting existing computing paradigms. While some pursue it for financial gain or to manifest science-fiction dreams, others view it as an incremental stride, like previous technological advancements.

However, not all actors operate with benevolent intentions or a thorough understanding of the consequences. There is a risk of misuse, profit-driven exploitation, and disregard for consequences. We need critical voices that can shed light on shortcomings and guide us toward leveraging these new tools to foster the best aspects of our collective nature.

As we navigate the uncharted waters of spatial computing, we must acknowledge its potential and address its pitfalls together. With vigilance, ethical consciousness, and a shared commitment to human well-being, we can ensure that the power of technology serves as a force for good.

Balancing ethics, safety, privacy, and usability in a capitalist society requires a combination of individual empowerment, corporate responsibility, and advocacy for stronger regulations. By adopting these strategies, both individuals and corporations can contribute to a more human-conscious digital ecosystem.

As we think about who we want to become, it is important to work on framing what positive, inclusive, and ethical mass adoption of these technologies might look like. The hope of all the major companies investing into spatial computing is that it will one day replace other forms of computing—their hope being that they get there first and that they can control the largest piece of that new form. It is important to acknowledge that for many this is a pursuit of profit, for others a pursuit of escapism, for some it is a realization of a fantasy born from science fiction, and for others it is just another step no different than those taken before.

Not everyone developing these technologies does so with good intentions, with an eye on the future of humanity, or with the consequences in mind. As some companies, bad actors, governments, and others will inevitably seek to use these tools for greater profit and increased control, and will ignore the consequences, we must embrace those who can help us to be critical of these developments, who can highlight their failings and help us direct ourselves toward a way of using these new tools that encourages the best in us. We can build a more inclusive, delightful, and safe future, but it will take hard work and intention. Let us try and build it together.

ACKNOWLEDGMENTS

FROM REGINÉ GILBERT

I want to express my sincere gratitude to my collaborator Doug North Cook, and to editor Sarah Schweppe, whose guidance and teachings were invaluable during the writing of this book. Thank you to Brett Gary, PhD for your editorial support.Completing this book would not have been possible without the relentless efforts of my research assistants, Asad Mahmood, Blessing Emole, Cindy Liu, Isabella Lopez, Janvi Patel, Jin Li, Kaiyou Liu, Lauren Chun, Rebecca Huang, Saki Asakawa, and Spandita Sarmah.I owe a debt of gratitude to my friends and family who stood by me throughout the creation of this book, including Allen Gilbert, Corey Gilbert, Deon Lambert, Reginald Gilbert, Winnie Gilbert, Lucille Stelly, and Juanita Holdsworth. Thank you to Christophe Drayton, Angela Fludd, Barbara Jackson, Christina Morillo, Dian Holton, Gerald Glackin, Indira Knight, Thomas Logan, Estella Tse, Kamilah Cole, Kojo Boatang, Tanasha Brown, and Angelica Schott.Lastly, I want to thank my colleagues and students, who continue to inspire me and remind me of the boundless possibilities in this world.

FROM DOUG NORTH COOK

To my wife Rose for keeping me sane, editing my early drafts, and encouraging me to the end.

To Jazmin Cano—who provided so much constructive feedback on one of my chapters and helped me think through how better to address some critical issues.

To Kate Romane for giving me a quiet place to finish my writing.

To my mom, Anne, for instilling in me the sense of wonder that has let me explore the world in the way that I do.

And of course, to my collaborator Reginé, who worked graciously by my side as we tackled a very difficult project at a very difficult time.

Much love to you all.

REFERENCES

CHAPTER 1

Apple (2025) "Privacy control," Apple.com. Available at: https://www.apple.com/privacy/control/ (Accessed: 15 January 2025).

Baba, Y. (2023) "The potential impacts of virtual reality (VR) on social norms and culture," *Capsule Sight*, April 14. Available at: https://capsulesight.com/vrglasses/the-potential-impacts-of-virtual-reality-vr-on-social-norms-and-culture/.

Belamare, J. (2016) "My First Virtual Reality Sexual Assault," *Medium*. Available at: https://medium.com/athena-talks/my-first-virtual-reality-sexual-assault-2330410b62ee (accessed October 4, 2022).

Crawford, P. & Smith, A. (2022) "Metaverse app allows kids into virtual strip clubs," BBC News. Available at: https://www.bbc.com/news/technology-60415317 (accessed December 3, 2022).

Dornhege, M. (2019) "Uchi and Soto in architecture: The Japanese concept of inner and outer worlds," *Rethink Tokyo*. Available at: https://www.rethinktokyo.com/uchi-soto-architecture-japanese-concept (accessed January 10, 2025).

Dower, J.W. (1986) *War without mercy: Race and power in the Pacific War*. New York: Pantheon.

Fleming, P., Bayliss, A.P., Edwards, S.G. et al. (2021) "The role of personal data value, culture and self-construal in online privacy behavior," *PLoS One*, 16(7), p. e0253568. doi: 10.1371/journal.pone.0253568 (accessed December 29, 2024).

Future of Privacy Forum (2024) "How manipulative design patterns may develop in immersive environments." Available at: https://www.freevacy.com/news/future-of-privacy-forum/how-manipulative-design-patterns-may-develop-in-immersive-environments/5205 (accessed February 16, 2025).

Gayle, G. (2021) "Facebook aware Instagram harmful effect teenage girls, leak reveals," *The Guardian*. Available at: https://www.theguardian.com/techology/2021/sep/14/facebook-aware-instagram-harmful-effect-teenage-girls-leak-reveals (accessed January 2023).

GDPR.EU (2024) "What is GDPR, the EU's new data protection law?." Available at: https://gdpr.eu/what-is-gdpr/.

Grother, P. & Ngan, M. (2023) "Face recognition vendor test (FRVT) Part 3: Demographic effects," National Institute of Standards and Technology, IR-8280, December. Available at: https://www.bfdi.bund.de/SharedDocs/Downloads/

EN/Berlin-Group/20230608_WP-Facial-Recognition-Tech-EN.pdf?__blob=publicationFile&v=2.

Guynn, J. (2020) "Not reading the small print is privacy policy fail," *USA Today*. Available at: https://www.usatoday.com/story/tech/2020/01/28/not-reading-the-small-print-is-privacy-policy-fail/4565274002/ (accessed January 4, 2021).

Haidt, J. (2024) *The anxious generation: How the great rewiring of childhood is causing an epidemic of mental illness*. New York: Penguin.

Japan Center for International Cooperation in Conservation (n.d.) Act on the protection of cultural properties. Available at: http://www.tobunken.go.jp/~kokusen/ENGLISH/DATA/Htmlfg/japan/japan01.html (accessed December 30, 2024).

Kroeber, A.L. & Kluckhohn, C. (1952) "Culture consists of patterns, explicit and implicit, of and for behavior acquired and transmitted by symbols," in E.E. Bosch (ed.), *Culture: A critical review of concepts and definitions*. Springer, pp. 29–39. Available at: https://link.springer.com/chapter/10.1007/978-3-642-84497-3_4 (accessed September 15, 2022).

Lakshmanan, R. (2024) "Clearview AI faces €30.5M fine for violating EU privacy laws," *The Hacker News*, September. Available at: https://thehackernews.com/2024/09/clearview-ai-faces-305m-fine-for.html (accessed February 1, 2025).

Milmo, D. (2021) "Frances Haugen: 'I never wanted to be a whistleblower. But lives were in danger,'" *The Guardian*, October 24. Available at: https://www.theguardian.com/technology/2021/oct/24/frances-haugen-i-never-wanted-to-be-a-whistleblower-but-lives-were-in-danger (accessed January 22, 2025).

Mishra, S. & Basu, S. (2014) "Family honor, cultural norms and social networking: Strategic choices in the visual self-presentation of young Indian Muslim women," *Cyberpsychology* 8(2), Article 3. doi: 10.5817/CP2014-2-3.

Norwegian Consumer Council (2018) *Deceived by design: How tech companies use dark patterns to discourage us from exercising our rights to privacy*, June 27. Available at: https://storage02.forbrukerradet.no/media/2018/06/2018-06-27-deceived-by-design-final.pdf.

Outlaw, J. & Duckles, B. (2017) "Why women don't like social virtual reality: A study of safety, usability, and self expression in social VR," https://static1.squarespace.com/static/60e8ceb4ae52881d57698bf6/t/6164b95156a52d3614c29e82/1633990999726/The-Extended-Mind_Why-Women-Don%27t-Like-Social-VR_2017.pdf.

Song, V. (2024) "College students used Meta's smart glasses to dox people in real time," *The Verge*, October 2. Available at: https://www.theverge.com/2024/10/2/24260262/ray-ban-meta-smart-glasses-doxxing-privacy.

Thompson, N. (2018) "Inside the two years that shook Facebook—and the world," *Wired*, February 12. Available at: https://www.wired.com/story/inside-facebook-mark-zuckerberg-2-years-of-hell/.

Virilio, P. (1999). *Politics of the very worst: An interview by Philippe Petit* (ed. S. Lotringer, trans. M. Cavaliere). Semiotexte.

Vivek, N., Garrido, G.M., Song, D., et al. (2023) "Exploring the privacy risks of adversarial VR game design," ResearchGate. Available at: https://www.researchgate.net/publication/374355789_Exploring_the_Privacy_Risks_of_Adversarial_VR_Game_Design (accessed June 2023).

World Bank (2018) "What Kenya's mobile money success could mean for the Arab world," World Bank, October 3. Available at: https://www.worldbank. org/en/news/feature/2018/10/03/what-kenya-s-mobile-money-success-could-mean-for-the-arab-world (accessed January 16, 2025).

CHAPTER 2

Barfield, W. & Furness, T.A. (1995) *Virtual environments and advanced interface design*, New York: Oxford University Press.

Bishop, C. (2006) *Participation: Documents of contemporary art*. Cambridge, MA: MIT Press.

Brownlee, M. (2023) [Twitter] June 5. Available at: https://twitter.com/MKBHD/status/1665786283296210956?s=20 (Accessed 25 June 2023).

Cunningham, J.A. & Link, A.N. (2021) *Technology and innovation policy: An international perspective*. Cheltenham: Edward Elgar.

Emmer, M. (1993) *The visual mind: Art and mathematics*. Cambridge, MA: MIT Press.

Forster, E.M. (1909) "The Machine Stops," in *The Oxford and Cambridge Review*. London: Stephen Swift.

Gibson, W. (2000) *Neuromancer*. New York: Ace Books.

Goldstine, H. (2001) *The Computer: From Pascal to von Neumann*. Princeton, NJ: Princeton University Press.

Harding, S. (2022) "US Army soldiers felt ill while testing Microsoft's HoloLens-based headset," *Ars Technica*. Available at: https://arstechnica.com/gadgets/2022/10/microsoft-mixed-reality-headsets-nauseate-soldiers-in-us-army-testing/ (accessed June 4, 2023).

Harris, B.J. (2019). *The history of the future: Oculus, Facebook, and the revolution that swept virtual reality*. New York: Dey St., an imprint of William Morrow.

Haupt, J. (2014) Available at: https://www.flickr.com/photos/51764518@N02/15751836930. Licensed under a Creative Commons Attribution-ShareAlike 2.0 Generic (CC BY-SA 2.0).

Holmes, O.W. (1859) *The Atlantic Monthly*, 3(20). Available at: https://onlinebooks. library.upenn.edu/webbin/gutbook/lookup?num=11751 (accessed May 27, 2023).

Jordan, K. & Packer, R. (eds) (2002) *Multimedia: From Wagner to virtual reality* (expanded edition). New York: W.W. Norton & Co.

Lanier, J. (2010) *You are not a gadget*. London: Knopf Doubleday Publishing Group.

Murray, J.H. (1997) *Hamlet on the holodeck: The future of narrative in cyberspace*. New York: Free Press.

Olson, J.L., Krum, D.M., Suma, E.A., et al. (2011) "A design for a smartphone-based head mounted display." Presented at the 2011 IEEE Virtual Reality Conference, pp. 233–234. Available at: https://doi.org/10.1109/VR.2011.5759484.

Osthoff, S. (1997) "Lygia Clark and Hélio Oiticica: a legacy of interactivity and participation for a telematic future." *Leonardo* 30, pp. 279–289.

Stephenson, N. (2000) *Snow Crash*. New York: Bantam Books.

Sutherland, I.E. (1965) "The ultimate display." Presented at the IFIP Congress, pp. 506–508.

Wheatstone, C. (1838) "Contributions to the physiology of vision—Part the first."*Philosophical Transactions of the Royal Society of London* 128, pp. 371–394.

Williamson, J. & Palmer, C. (2018) *Virtual reality blueprints: Create compelling VR experiences for mobile and desktop.* Birmingham: Packt Publishing.

IMAGE REFERENCES

"File:2Holmes Stereoscope 1861.png" by Nieborak is marked with CC0 1.0. To view the terms, visit https://creativecommons.org/publicdomain/zero/1.0/deed. en?ref=openverse.

CHAPTER 3

Andrey, V. (2025) *What is calligraphy? Discover different types of writings.* Artsper, 22 April. Available at: https://blog.artsper.com/en/a-closer-look/art-movements-en/ calligraphy-definition/ (accessed September 5, 2025).

Encyclopaedia Britannica (2020) "Hula" definition. Available at: https://www. britannica.com/art/hula.

Brown, J., Bailenson, J., & Hancock, J. (2023) "Misinformation in Virtual Reality," *Journal of Online Trust and Safety*, 1(5). https://doi.org/10.54501/jots.v1i5.120.

Cornell College of Arts & Sciences (2020) "Professor shares immersive VR project to fight racism." Available at: https://as.cornell.edu/news/professor-shares-immersive-vr-project-fight-racism.

Coyle, J. (2023) "In Hollywood writers' battle against AI, humans win (for now)," AP News, September 27. Available at: https://apnews.com/article/hollywood-ai-strike-wga-artificial-intelligence-39ab72582c3a15f77510c9c30a45ffc8 (accessed February 13, 2025).

Cleveland Clinic (2023) *Auditory processing disorder.* Available at: https://my. clevelandclinic.org/health/diseases/24938-auditory-processing-disorder (last reviewed April 21, 2023; accessed February 14, 2025).

Ebeyer, T. (2025) *Expanding Aphantasia Definition: Researchers Propose New Boundaries.* Available at: https://aphantasia.com/article/science/aphantasia-definition/ (accessed January 18, 2025).

Ferretti, F., Adornetti, I., Chiera, A., et al. (2018) "Time and narrative: An investigation of storytelling abilities in children with autism spectrum disorder," *Frontiers in Psychology*, 9. Available at: https://www.frontiersin.org/journals/psychology/ articles/10.3389/fpsyg.2018.00944.

Flores Camas, R.A. & Leon-Rojas, J.E. (2023) "Specific language impairment and executive functions in school-age children: A systematic review," *Cureus*, 15(8), e43163. doi: 10.7759/cureus.43163. https://pmc.ncbi.nlm.nih.gov/articles/ PMC10484522/.

Fortis, S. (2022) "Island nation turns to metaverse to preserve its disappearing heritage." *Coin Telegraph.* Available at: https://cointelegraph.com/news/island-nation-turns-to-metaverse-to-preserve-its-disappearing-heritage.

Grover, S., Nguyen, J.A., & Reinhart, R.M.G. (2021) "Synchronizing brain rhythms to improve cognition," *Annual Review of Medicine*, 72, pp. 29–43. doi: 10.1146/annurev-med-060619-022857. https://pmc.ncbi.nlm.nih.gov/articles/PMC10068593/.

Lewis, S. & Tolla, J. (2003) "Creating and using tactile experience books for young children with visual impairments," *Teaching Exceptional Children*, 35(3), pp. 22–28. https://www.pathstoliteracy.org/creating-and-using-tactile-experience-books-for-young-children-with-visual-impairments/.

Mendoza, M. (2015) "The evolution of storytelling," *Reporter*. Available at: https://reporter.rit.edu/tech/evolution-storytelling.

Myers, A. (2022) *The science behind storytelling: When you give a brain a story*. Available at: https://storysoft.io/the-science-behind-storytelling/ (accessed February 3, 2025).

National Institute on Aging (2024) "Coping with grief and loss," viewed February 21, 2025, https://www.nia.nih.gov/health/grief-and-mourning/coping-grief-and-loss.

NHS (2024) *Face blindness (prosopagnosia)*. Available at: https://www.nhs.uk/conditions/face-blindness/ (accessed December 29, 2024).

NLI Staff (n.d.) *The neuroscience of storytelling*. Available at: https://neuroleadership.com/your-brain-at-work/the-neuroscience-of-storytelling/ (accessed January 15, 2025).

Ortutay, B. (2023) "What you should know about Section 230, the rule that shaped today's internet," *PBS NewsHour*, February 21. Available at: https://www.pbs.org/newshour/politics/what-you-should-know-about-section-230-the-rule-that-shaped-todays-internet (accessed February 24, 2025).

Oswalt, W.H. (1964) "Traditional storyknife tales of Yuk girls," *Proceedings of the American Philosophical Society*, 108, pp. 310–336.

Princeton University Art Museum (n.d.) *Untitled object 36798*. Available at: https://artmuseum.princeton.edu/collections/objects/36798 (accessed December 12, 2024).

Rantanen, S. (2020) "Why our brains need a good story," Modern Employer Brand. Available at: https://modernemployerbrand.com/brains-and-story/.

Royal, T.A.C. (n.d.) "Māori creation traditions: Te Ara," *The Encyclopedia of New Zealand*. Available at: https://teara.govt.nz/en/maori-creation-traditions (accessed December 27, 2024).

Rutledge, P. (2022) "Story power: The psychology of story," (online). Available at: https://www.pamelarutledge.com/story-power-the-psychology-of-story/ (accessed July 9, 2023).

de Souza, C.S., Salgado, L.C., Leitão, C.F., et al. (2014) "Cultural appropriation of computational thinking acquisition research: Seeding fields of diversity," *Proceedings of the 2014 Conference on Innovation & Technology in Computer Science Education (ITiCSE '14)*, Uppsala, Sweden, June 21–25. New York: Association for Computing Machinery, pp. 117–122. Available at: https://doi.org/10.1145/2591708.2591729.

Tribeca Festival (n.d.) "1,000 Cut Journey," viewed January 21, 2025. Available at: https://www.tribecafilm.com/films/1000-cut-journey-2018.

Vim & Vibe (n.d.) *Storytelling & memory retention.* Available at: https://vimandvibe.com/blog/storytelling-memory-retention/ (accessed February 1, 2025).

Zhang, S., Yang, Y., Li, J., et al. (2018) "Physiological diversity of orchids," *Plant Diversity* 40(4), pp. 196–208, doi:10.1016/j.pld.2018.06.003.

CHAPTER 4

Center for Universal Design (n.d.) College of Design. Available at: https://design.ncsu.edu/research/center-for-universal-design/ (accessed June 25, 2023).

Curtis, A. (2015) "Rhetoric of flat design and skeuomorphism in Apple's iOS graphical user interface," Open-access master's thesis. Available at: https://doi.org/10.23860/thesis-curtis-ambrose-2015.

Lovell, S. (2011) *Dieter Rams: As little design as possible.* New York: Phaidon.

Pallasmaa, J. (2005) *The eyes of the skin: Architecture and the senses.* Hoboken, NJ: Wiley & Son.

Stevens, J.E., Robinson, A., & MacEachren, A. (2013) "Designing map symbols for mobile devices: Challenges, best practices, and the utilization of skeuomorphism," GeoVISTA Center, Department of Geography, Pennsylvania State University.

Su, S. (2019) Reproduced from https://www.pexels.com/photo/stairs-and-ramps-11441014/. Licensed under Pexels Free Use License.

Watanuki, K. (2010) "Development of virtual reality-based universal design review system." *Journal of Mechanical Science and Technology,* 24, pp. 257–262. https://doi.org/10.1007/s12206-009-1156-z.

CHAPTER 5

Reproduced from Jean-Pierre Dalbéra (2016). https://www.flickr.com/photos/72746018@N00/28099682105. Licensed under a Creative Commons Attribution 2.0 Generic (CC BY 2.0).

Billinghurst, B., Belcher, D., Gupta, A., et al. (2003) "Communication Behaviors in Colocated Collaborative AR Interfaces," *International Journal of Human-Computer Interaction,* 16(3), pp. 395–423. doi:10.1207/S15327590IJHC1603_2.

Bray, K.E., Diakhate, N., Grimes Parker, A., et al. (2022) "Radical futures: Supporting community-led design engagements through an Afrofuturist speculative design toolkit," Available at: https://www.researchgate.net/publication/360263287_Radical_Futures_Supporting_Community-Led_Design_Engagements_through_an_Afrofuturist_Speculative_Design_Toolkit.

CCS Insight (2021) "Virtual reality gets a boost during the pandemic." Available at: https://www.ccsinsight.com/company-news/virtual-reality-gets-a-boost-during-the-pandemic/.

Deb, S., Suraksha, & Bhattacharya, P. (2018) "Augmented sign language modeling (ASLM) with interaction design on smartphone: An assistive learning and communication tool for inclusive classroom," *Procedia Computer Science,* 125, pp. 492–500. Available at: https://doi.org/10.1016/j.procs.2017.12.064.

Ethnologue (n.d.) Available at: https://www.ethnologue.com/ (accessed February 24, 2025).

Franken, R.E. (1994) *Human motivation* (3rd edn.). Belmont, CA: Brooks/Cole Publishing Co.

Immordino-Yang, M.H., & Damasio, A., (2007) "We feel, therefore we learn: The relevance of affective and social neuroscience to education," *Mind, Brain, and Education* 1(1), pp. 3–10.It

Ramirez, E. (2021) "It's dangerous to think virtual reality is an empathy machine," *Aeon*. Available at: https://aeon.co/ideas/its-dangerous-to-think-virtual-reality-is-an-empathy-machine.

Tonkinwise, C. (2014) "How we intend to future: Review of Anthony Dunne and Fiona Raby, *Speculative Everything: Design, Fiction, and Social Dreaming*," *Design Philosophy Papers*, 12, pp. 169–187. Available at: https://doi.org/10.2752%2F144871314X14159818597676.

World Health Organization (2023) "Autism." Available at: https://www.who.int/news-room/fact-sheets/detail/autism-spectrum-disorders.

Zheng, Q., Do, T.N., Wang, L., et al. (2022) "Facing the illusion and reality of safety in social VR," *ArXiv*. Available at: https://www.researchgate.net/publication/359971361_Facing_the_Illusion_and_Reality_of_Safety_in_Social_VR.

CHAPTER 6

Cinque, T., & Vincent, J.B. (eds.) (2022) *Materializing digital futures: touch, movement, sound and vision*. Bloomsbury Academic.

Cebolla, A., Herrero, R., Ventura, S., et al. (2019) "Putting oneself in the body of others: A Pilot study on the efficacy of an embodied virtual reality system to generate self-compassion," *Frontiers in Psychology*, 10. Available at: https://doi.org/10.3389/fpsyg.2019.01521.

Dekker, A., Wenzlaff, F., Biedermann, S.V., et al. (2021) "VR porn as 'empathy machine'? Perception of self and others in virtual reality pornography," *The Journal of Sex Research*, 58, pp. 273–278. Avaible at: https://doi.org/10.1080/00224499.2020.1856316.

Humes, L.E., Busey, T.A., Craig, J., et al. (2013) "Are age-related changes in cognitive function driven by age-related changes in sensory processing?" *Attention, Perception & Psychophysics*, 75, pp. 508–524. Avaiable at: https://doi.org/10.3758/s13414-012-0406-9.

Lawson, B.D., & Stanney, K.M. (2021) "Editorial: Cybersickness in virtual reality and augmented reality," *Frontiers in Virtual Reality*, 2. https://doi.org/10.3389/frvir.2021.759682. (accessed July 5, 2022).

Lombard, M. & Ditton, T. (1997) "At the heart of it all: The concept of presence," *Journal of Computer-Mediated Communication*, 3. Available at: https://doi.org/10.1111/j.1083-6101.1997.tb00072.x.

Di Luca, M., Seifi, H., Egan, S., et al. (2021) "Locomotion vault: The extra mile in analyzing VR locomotion techniques." In *CHI '21: Proceedings of the 2021 CHI Conference on Human Factors in Computing Systems*. Association for Computing Machinery. Available at: https://doi.org/10.1145/3411764.3445319.

Matamala-Gomez, M., Donegan, T., Bottiroli, S., et al. (2019) "Immersive virtual reality and virtual embodiment for pain relief," *Frontiers in Human Neuroscience*, 13, p. 279.

NASA (2019) Reproduced from NASA Goddard Photo and Video (2019). Available at: https://www.flickr.com/photos/24662369@N07/49467767318. Licensed under a Creative Commons Attribution 2.0 Generic (CC BY 2.0).

Noll, J.G., Shenk, C.E., Barnes, J.E., et al. (2013) "Association of maltreatment with high-risk internet behaviors and offline encounters," *Pediatrics*, 131, pp. e510–e517. https://doi.org/10.1542/peds.2012-1281.

Outlaw, J. (2018) "Survey of social VR users," *The Extended Mind*. Available at: https://www.extendedmind.io/2018-survey-of-social-vr-users (accessed July 24, 2022).

Slater, M., Gonzalez-Liencres, C., Haggard, P., et al. (2020) "The ethics of realism in virtual and augmented reality," *Frontiers in Virtual Reality*, 1, pp. 1–13.

Teixeira, J., Miellet, S., & Palmisano, S., (2022) "Unexpected vection exacerbates cybersickness during HMD-based virtual reality," *Frontiers in Virtual Reality*, 3, pp. 1–14.

Weber, S., Weibel, D., & Mast, F.W. (2021) "How to get there when you are there already? Defining presence in virtual reality and the importance of perceived realism," *Frontiers in Psychology*, 12, pp. 1–10.

CHAPTER 7

Çamci, A. (2019) "Exploring the Effects of diegetic and non-diegetic audiovisual cues on decision-making in virtual reality." University of Michigan Department of Performing Arts Technology.

Durt, C., Brinck, I., Fuchs, T., et al. (2017) *Embodiment, enaction, and culture: Investigating the constitution of the shared world*. Cambridge, MA: MIT Press.

Game Developer Staff (2018) "Game design deep dive: Creating comfortable UI for VR strategy in Skyworld." Available at: https://www.gamedeveloper.com/design/game-design-deep-dive-creating-comfortable-ui-for-vr-strategy-in-i-skyworld-i- (accessed December 6, 2022).

Game Press (2022) "Gorilla Tag now available in the Meta Quest store." Available at: https://www.gamespress.com/de/Gorilla-Tag-now-available-in-the-Meta-Quest-store (accessed January 14, 2023).

Gibson, J. (2015) *The ecological approach to visual perception*. New York: Psychology Press.

Gottsacker, M., N. Norouzi, K. Kim, et al. (2021) "Diegetic representations for seamless cross-reality interruptions." 2021 IEEE International Symposium on Mixed and Augmented Reality, pp. 310–319.

Norman, D. (2013) *The design of everyday things* (revised and expanded edition). Boulder, CO: Basic Books.

Oliver, M. (2005) "The problem with affordance," *E-Learning and Digital Media*, 2, pp. 402–413.

Zizioulas, J.D. (2010) *The one and the many: Studies on god, man, the church, and the world today*. Alhambra, CA: Sebastian Press.

CHAPTER 8

Bruschetta, A., De Luca, R., Calabrò, R.S., et al. (2022) "Demographic and clinical variables associated with recovery of cognitive function in traumatic brain injury patients after well-validated virtual reality training," cited in Calderone et al. (2023).

Calderone, A., Carta, D., Cardile, D., et al. (2023) "Use of virtual reality in patients with acquired brain injury: A systematic review," *PMCID: PMC10743630.*

Daniels, J.K., & Vermetten, E. (2016) "Odor-induced recall of emotional memories in PTSD: Review and new paradigm for research," *Experimental Neurology*, 284, pp. 168–180.

Dellwo, A. (2024) *Anatomy and function of abducens nerve.* Verywell Health, December 13. Available at: https://www.verywellhealth.com/abducens-nerve-anatomy-4783613.

Dewan, M.C., Rattani, A., Gupta, S., et al. (2018) "Estimating the global incidence of traumatic brain injury," *Journal of Neurosurgery*, 130(4), pp. 1080–1097. doi: 10.3171/2017.10.JNS17352.

Farnsworth, B. (2022) "What is VR eye tracking? And how does it work?" *iMotions.* Available at: https://imotions.com/blog/learning/best-practice/vr-eye-tracking/.

French, M.A., Roemmich, R.T., Daley, K., et al. (2022) "Precision rehabilitation: Optimizing function, adding value to health care," *Archives of Physical Medicine and Rehabilitation*, 103(6), pp. 1233–1239. doi: 10.1016/j.apmr.2022.01.154.

Gino, F., & Coffman, K. (2021) "Unconscious bias training that works." Available at: https://hbr.org/2021/09/unconscious-bias-training-that-works.

Gomez, J., Barnett, M., & Grill-Spector, K. (2019) "Stanford researchers identify brain region activated by Pokémon characters," *Nature Human Behavior*, published online May 6.

Hefferman, A., Abdelmalek, A., & Nunez, D.A. (2021) "Virtual and augmented reality in the vestibular rehabilitation of peripheral vestibular disorders: Systematic review and meta-analysis." Available at: https://www.ncbi.nlm.nih.gov/pmc/articles/PMC8426502/.

Houston, K. (2025) *Head-Cancelled Virtual Reality for Ocular Cranial Nerve Palsies (OCNP)* (clinical trial). University of Massachusetts Chan Medical School. Retrieved from https://ctv.veeva.com/study/head-cancelled-virtual-reality-for-ocular-cranial-nerve-palsies.

Javanbakht, A., Hinchey, L., Gorski, K., et al. (2024) "Unreal that feels real: Pioneering technology developed at Wayne State to treat PTSD uses augmented reality and artificial intelligence," *European Journal of Psychotraumatology*, November 14. Available at: https://www.starclab.org/projects (accessed February 14, 2025).

Kim, S.Y., Motlagh, M., & Naqvi, I.A. (2022) "Neuroanatomy, cranial nerve 4 (Trochlear)." StatPearls. Available at: https://www.ncbi.nlm.nih.gov/books/NBK537244/ (accessed December 5, 2022).

Kim, S.Y., & Naqvi, I.A. (2022) "Neuroanatomy, cranial nerve 12 (Hypoglossal)." StatPearls. Available at: https://www.ncbi.nlm.nih.gov/books/NBK532869 (accessed December 5, 2022).

Kolko, J. (2015) "Design thinking comes of age," *Harvard Business Review.* Available at: https://hbr.org/2015/09/design-thinking-comes-of-age.

Lapinski, S. (2022) "Who was Phineas Gage?" Countway Library, Harvard Medical School (online). Available at: https://asklib.hms.harvard.edu/faq/153359 (accessed February 14, 2025).

Mühling, T., Späth, I., Backhaus, J., et al. (2023) "Virtual reality in medical emergencies training: Benefits, perceived stress, and learning success," *Multimedia Systems,* 29(4), pp. 2239–2252.

Murray, L., & Shmidheiser, M. (2024) "Virtual reality immerses you in your mind: The experience and stress-reduction benefits of VR mindfulness modules in persons with TBI," *Brain Injury,* 38(5), pp. 335–360. https://doi.org/10.1080/02699052.2024.2311334.

National Eye Institute (n.d.) "How the eyes work." Available at: https://www.nei.nih.gov/learn-about-eye-health/healthy-vision/how-eyes-work.

Nicholls, M. (2018) "Neurosurgery taught via virtual reality," Available at: https://healthcare-in-europe.com/en/news/neurosurgery-taught-via-virtual-reality.html (accessed December 6, 2022).

Ricci, F. S., Rizzo, J.-R., Porfiri, M., et al. (2024) "New virtual reality-tested system shows promise in aiding navigation of people with blindness or low vision." NYU Tandon School of Engineering. December 16.

Shen, V., Shutlz, C., & Harrison, C. (2022) "Mouth haptics in VR using a headset ultrasound phased array," Available at: https://dl.acm.org/doi/abs/10.1145/3491102.3501960.

Shih, J.J., Krusienski, D.J., & Wolpaw, J.R. (2012) "Brain-computer interfaces in medicine," *Mayo Clinic Proceedings,* 87(3), pp. 268–279.

Słowiński, P., Grindley, B., Muncie, H., et al. (2022) "Assessment of cognitive biases in augmented reality: Beyond eye tracking," *Journal of Eye Movement Research,* 15(3), p. 4.

Tewfik, T.L. (2017) "Vagus nerve anatomy," Medscape. Available at: https://emedicine.medscape.com/article/1875813-overview (accessed January 2, 2023).

Värbu, K., Muhammad, N., & Muhammad, Y. (2022) "Past, present, and future of EEG-based BCI applications," *Applied Sciences,* 12(10), p. 5194. https://doi.org/10.3390/app12105194.

Voise Foundation (2024) "The surprising link between virtual reality and improving memory loss. July 1." Available at: https://voisefoundation.org/the-surprising-link-between-virtual-reality-and-improving-memory-loss/.

Yoo, H., & Mihaila, D.M. (2022) "Neuroanatomy, vestibular pathways." In StatPearls. StatPearls Publishing, November 7.

Zanier, E., Di Lernia, D., Zoerle, T., et al. (2018) "Virtual reality for traumatic brain injury," *Frontiers in Neurology,* 9. Available at: https://www.academia.edu/70814169/Virtual_Reality_for_Traumatic_Brain_Injury.

CHAPTER 9

Algorithmic Justice League (2025) *Algorithmic Justice League.* Available at: https://www.ajl.org/ (accessed February 21, 2025).

Allen, B.D. (2021) "Digital twins and living models at NASA," ASME Digital Twin Summit (keynote presentation), November 3. Available at: https://ntrs.nasa.gov/api/citations/20210023699/downloads/ASME%20Digital%20Twin%20Summit%20Keynote_final.pdf.

Anti-Defamation League (2024) *A brief history of the Disability Rights Movement.* Available at: https://www.adl.org (accessed February 15, 2025).

Ball, C., Huang, K. T., & Francis, J. (2021) "Virtual reality adoption during the COVID-19 pandemic: A uses and gratifications perspective," *Telematics and Informatics*, 65, doi: 10.1016/j.tele.2021.101728.

Barron's (2024) "The next wave of AI could be led by Nvidia and Pokémon Go," Available at: https://www.barrons.com/articles/nvidia-pokemon-go-ai-geospatial-models-accf82f1 (accessed February 20, 2025).

Black Mirror (2011–present) Created by Charlie Brooker. London: Zeppotron/House of Tomorrow/Netflix.

Conger, K. (2018) "Google employees resign in protest against Pentagon contract." Available at: https://gizmodo.com/google-employees-resign-in-protest-against-pentagon-con-1825729300.

Fox, E. (2024) "Low earth orbit satellite: Achieving fast-speed connectivity." MetTel. Available at: https://www.mettel.net/blog/low-earth-orbit-satellite/ (Accessed: 15 February 20, 2025).

Gelernter, D. (1991) *Mirror worlds: Or the day software puts the universe in a shoebox … How it will happen and what it will mean.* New York: Oxford University Press.

Hsieh, J., Alawieh, H., Millán, J., et al. (2025) "The evolving landscape of non-invasive EEG brain-computer interfaces," *Device*, January 2. Available at: https://www.bme.utexas.edu/news/the-evolving-landscape-of-non-invasive-eeg-brain-computer-interfaces (accessed February 26, 2025).

Jonze, S. (dir.) (2013) *Her.* Warner Bros. Pictures.

Karl, K.A., Peluchette, J.V., & Aghakhani, N. (2022) "Virtual work meetings during the COVID-19 pandemic: The good, bad, and ugly," *Small Group Research*, 53, pp. 343–365.

Makarevych, N. & Diachenko, A. (2024) "How AR & VR in healthcare enhances medical training?" Available at: https://onix-systems.com (accessed February 19, 2025).

McKinsey & Company (2024) "The state of AI in early 2024: Gen AI adoption spikes and starts to generate value." McKinsey & Company, May 30. https://www.mckinsey.com/capabilities/quantumblack/our-insights/the-state-of-ai (accessed February 22, 2025).

Myers, J. (2022) "Artifiticial intelligence: 5 charts that show what people around the world think about AI." Available at: https://www.weforum.org/agenda/2022/01/artificial-intelligence-ai-technology-trust-survey/.

Newton, C. (2020) "Mark Zuckerberg on taking his massive workforce remote." The Verge. Available at: https://www.theverge.com/2020/5/21/21265780/facebook-remote-work-mark-zuckerberg-interview-wfh (accessed January 27, 2023).

NSTXL (2023) "Immersive technologies in the US military." Available at: https://nstxl.org/immersive-tech-in-the-military/ (accessed February 19, 2025).

Pathi, K. (2024) "Here's what happened when India banned TikTok," Associated Press, April 24. Available at: https://www.pbs.org/newshour/world/heres-what-happened-when-india-banned-tiktok (accessed February 20, 2025).

Roberts, J. (2022) Twitter post, October 20. Available at: https://t.co/4xg0FKYkEk.

Roquet, P. (2022) *The immersive enclosure virtual reality in Japan*. New York: Columbia University Press.

Roth, E. (2025) "Samsung and Google's new spatial audio format will take on Dolby Atmos this year," The Verge. Available at: https://www.theverge.com/2025/1/3/24335170/samsung-google-eclipsa-spatial-audio-format-2025-tvs (accessed February 13, 2025).

Smith, G.J. (2011) "Augmented (hyper)reality: An interview with Keiichi Matsuda." Berfrois. Available at: https://www.berfrois.com/2011/01/augmented-hyperreality/ (accessed January 27, 2023).

Stanford GPS Research Center (n.d.) "Enhanced long range navigation (eLoran)." Available at: https://gps.stanford.edu/research/early-gpspnt-research/enhanced-long-range-navigation-eloran (accessed February 15, 2025).

Taoglas (2024) "GNSS constellations: Exploring GPS, GLONASS, Galileo, Bei-Dou, NavIC, and QZSS." Available at: https://www.taoglas.com/blogs/gnss-constellations-exploring-gps-glonass-galileo-beidou-navic-and-qzss/ (accessed February 21, 2025).

Tilt Labs (2024) "Mixed reality, wearable tech, and AI: 2024—the year spatial computing takes off." Available at: https://tiltlabs.medium.com/mixed-reality-wearable-tech-and-ai-2024-the-year-spatial-computing-takes-off-26f80f131179 (accessed February 20, 2025).

Victoria, K. (2024) "Black content creators are at the forefront of digital history," *Essence*, May 1. Available at: https://girlsunited.essence.com/feedback/news/black-content-creators-digital-history/ (accessed February 20, 2025).

Viola, K. (2024) "'Another Body' documentary exposes harm of deepfake technology." Cornell University College of Arts & Sciences, January 25. Available at: https://as.cornell.edu/news/another-body-documentary-exposes-harm-deepfake-technology.

White House (2025) "Ending radical and wasteful government DEI programs and preferencing" (Executive Order), January 20. Available at: https://www.whitehouse.gov/presidential-actions/2025/01/ending-radical-and-wasteful-government-dei-programs-and-preferencing/.

XR Today (2024) "6 spatial computing trends to watch in 2024," Available at: https://www.xrtoday.com/mixed-reality/6-spatial-computing-trends-to-watch-in-2024 (accessed February 20, 2025).

Figures and Boxes are indicated by an italic *f* and *b*.

For the benefit of digital users, indexed terms that span two pages (e.g., 52–53) may, on occasion, appear on only one of those pages.

abducens nerve (CN VI), 211
ability, 129–133
ableism, 123
accessibility, 123, 210–211
accessory spinal nerve (CN XI), 214
Act on the Protection of Cultural
    Properties (Japan), 28–29
actual and perceived
    affordances, 182–183
adaptable affordances, 183
ADHD, 207
aerial drones, 114–115
affordances,
   defined, 175–178
   definitional relationships, 194–195
   developing new, 185–187
   digital *versus* physical and virtual, 187
   mapping, 187–195
   method for understanding, 191–193
   perceived and actual, 182–183
   project, 195*b*
   questions for reflection, 194*b*
   representative, 184–185
   and signifiers, 178–182
age, and sensory processing, 152
agency, sense of, 168–169
age requirements, 4
AI. *See* artificial intelligence (AI)
algorithmic bias, 80–81, 246–247

Algorithmic Justice League, 246
Americans with Disabilities Act
    (1990), 233
anchoring bias, 219
Another Axiom, 181
Another Body, 236
Anxious Generation, The (Haidt), 32–33
aphantasia, 75
Apple, 26, 59–60, 112–113, 232, 240–241
Apple Vision Pro, 59–60, 232–234
appropriation, 80–81
App Tracking Transparency (ATT), 26
Arataki Systems, 91
Army (US), 42, 60
artificial intelligence (AI), 31, 98–99,
    141, 228–229, 231–235, 246–247
Art of War, The (Sun Tzu), 18–19
Asher, Tobin, 70–71
ATT (App Tracking Transparency), 26
attribution bias, 219–220
audio, 154–155
auditory processing and language, 76
auditory processing disorders, 76
augmented reality (AR). *See also* affor-
    dances; body as input device; brain
    and biases
   aerial drone example, 114–115
   and AI, 141

augmented reality (AR) (*Continued*)
  BCIs, 198–199, 244–246
  Black Mirror, 247–248
  communication with, 134–135
  deaf community, 142–143
  Human Spatial Computing course
    (NYU), 147–148
  lack of ethical guidelines for, 22
  Matsuda and *Hyper-Reality*, 120–121,
    229–230
  in military and medical field, 241–242
  Ngā Atua Māori, 92–93
  privacy concerns, 13, 36
  projects for consideration, 38*b*
  safety challenges, 13
  sense of realism, 24
  and storytelling, 84–86
autism, 76, 135–136, 207
Autismity, 136
availability bias, 220
avatars, 73, 133–134

Bailenson, Jeremy, 70–71, 90
Ball, C., 238
BCIs (brain-computer in-
    terfaces), 198–199,
    244–246
Belamire, Jordan, 10
Bharatanatyam, 84–85
biases, 218–223, 246–247
Bill, Max, 55–56
Billinghurst, B., 134–135
Black content creators, 242–243
Black Mirror, 247–248
blind and visually impaired
    users, 130–132, 210–211
blink movement, 160
blocked affordances, 183
body as input device, 151
  embodiment, 161, 167–170
  immersive sexual
    experiences, 171–172
  physical effort, 120
  presence, 151–152, 161–167
  questions and project, 173*b*
  senses, 152–161

settling into, 172–174
  tolerance for error, 117–118
body ownership, 169
Bolas, Mark, 58–59
bottom-up information, 169
brain and biases, 197
  biases, 197–198, 218–223
  EEG and BCIs, 198–199
  functions, 204–207
  multiple senses working
    together, 200–201
  nervous system. *See* nervous system
  new ways of learning, 217–218
  promise, 197
  questions and projects, 223–224*b*
  stories' effect on, 73–80
  TBI, 199–200, 202–204
brain chemicals, 78–79
brain-computer interfaces
    (BCIs), 198–199, 244–246
Bray, K.E., 147
Brignull, Harry, 30
Brown, J., 90
Brown, Tanasha, 221–222
Building Utopia toolkit, 147
Buolamwini, Joy, 246
ByteDance, 61

Calderone, A., 202
calligraphy, 85
Calypso music, 84
Çamci, Anil, 180
capitalistic systems, 3–4
Cebolla, A., 151–152
Chang, Edward, 245–246
ChatGPT, 231
child safety, 10
"Chocolate" (Hurd), 151
choices, 133–134
Clark, Lygia, 55
Clearview AI, 8
Cogburn, Courtney, 70–71
cognitive biases, 218–223
cognitive processing variations, 76
collectivist cultures, 26–28

Collingridge dilemma, 244
colors, 117
communication, 134–135
Communications Decency Act (1996), 81
compassion, 135–137
complex systems, 47
computer hats, 43
cortisol, 78–79
COVID-19 pandemic, 90, 127, 172–173, 237–238
cranial nerves. *See* nervous system
creativity, 137–139
critical design, 146
cross-cultural exchange, 93–96
Cubism (Van Bouwel), 164–165
cultural appropriation, 80–81
"Cultural Appropriation in Computational Thinking Education" (de Souza), 81–82
cultural exchange, 80–83
cultural sensitivity, 16
culture, 16–17, 20–21, 22–23, 24–29, 124, 170
culture bias, 221–222
curiosity, 68–73, 139
curiosity gap theory, 69
Curiosity VR, 139
customizing avatars, 133–134
cybersickness and vection, 159–161

DALL-E, 231
data collection, 31, 34
Dataglove, 56–58
data protection, 14–15
da Vinci. *See* Leonardo da Vinci
Deb, S., 142–143
deceptive patterns, 29–32
deepfakes, 236
definitional relationships, 194–195
DEIA (diversity, equity, inclusion, and accessibility), 35–37, 232–233
Dekker, A., 171
design considerations, 146–149
Design of Everyday Things, The (Norman), 176, 178

de Souza, C.S.: "Cultural Appropriation in Computational Thinking Education," 81–82
diegetic design, 180–182
digital twins, 87–89, 230–231
Di Luca, M., 161
disability, 129–133
discouraged affordances, 183
Ditton, Theresa, 166–167, 169–170
diversity, equity, inclusion, and accessibility (DEIA), 35–37, 232–233
dopamine, 78–79, 80
drones, 114–115
Duckles, Beth, 11
Dunne, Anthony, 146–147

EAA (European Accessibility Act), 34–35
Eclipsa Audio, 242
Ecological Approach to Visual Perception, The (Gibson), 175–177, 184, 193
education, 82
EEG (electroencephalography), 198–199, 204, 205*f*
embodiment, 161, 167–170
emotions, 140
Eng, Catherine, 97–98
environment, size of, 121–122
Equal Entry, 130
equitable use, 104–108
error, tolerance for, 117 119
Escape Fake, 89
ethical behavior, development of, 14
ethics, 1
    deceptive user experiences, 29–32
    DEIA, 35–37
    emerging technologies, 33–35
    human experience, 22–24
    innovation *versus* responsibility, 6–12
    minimizing uncertainty, 33
    progress and culture, 24–29
    questions and project, 37–38*b*

ethics (*Continued*)
    reasons to care, 1–6
    social impact, 12–22
    virtual spaces, 32–33
European Accessibility Act (EAA), 34–35
Extended Reality Safety Intelligence
        (XRSI), 19–20
extended reality (XR), 97–98, 159
EyePhone, 56–58
eye tracking, 215

face blindness (prosopagnosia), 75
Facebook. *See* Meta
facial recognition technology, 6–8
fail states, 118–119
false affordances, 182
fiction/literature, 48–56, 120–121, 228,
        229–230, 247–248
filters, 69, 99
Fleming, P., 27–28
flexibility, 108–111
Forster, E.M., 44–46
frontal lobe, 200
Furness, Tom, 53–54
future of spatial computing. *See* spatial
        computing, potential of

Gage, Phineas, 199–200
games, 17–19
gatekeepers, 242
General Data Protection Regulation
        (GDPR), 14–15, 27, 34
Gibson, James J., 175–177, 184, 193
Gibson, William, 46
Gilbert, Reginé, 93
global navigation satellite systems
        (GNSS), 243
global perspective, 124
Global Survey on AI (2024), 246–247
Godot, 98
Google, 137, 240, 242
Gorilla Tag, 181
Gravity Sketch, 232
grief, 65–67
griots, 85
groundedness

in reality, 163–164, 165
in VR, 166–167
Guynn, J., 235–236

hackathons, 7
Hackett, Patrick, 137
Haidt, Jonathan, 32–33
halo effect, 220
Hamlet on the Holodeck (Murray), 44, 48
Hancock, J., 90
haptics, mouth, 213
harassment, prevalence, 171–172
Harding, X., 246
harmful behaviors, 14
Harmon, Jalaiah, 81
Harris, Blake, 58–59
Haugen, Frances, 29–30, 32
head-mounted displays, 52–53. *See also*
        VR headsets
headsets. *See* VR headsets
hearing, 154–155
Hefferman, A., 212
Heilig, Morton, 52–53
Her (Jonze), 228
hidden affordances, 183
history of spatial computing. *See*
        human-computer interaction
History of the Future, The (Blake), 58–59
HMD (head-mounted displays). *See* VR
        headsets
Holmes, Oliver Wendell, Sr., 51
hula, 86
human computation, 42–43
human-computer interaction, 41
    arrival of spatial computing, 59–60
    dawn of Oculus, 58–59
    EyePhone, 56–58
    painting for presence, 48–56
    questions and project, 62*b*
    search for a new reality, 61–62
    stories, 43–48
    Western influence and shifting
        culture, 60–61
    why we built computers, 41–43
Human Spatial Computing course
        (NYU), 147–148

human traits, 127
  ability, 129–133
  choices, 133–134
  communication, 134–135
  compassion, 135–137
  creativity, 137–139
  curiosity, 139
  and design considerations, 146–149
  emotions, 140
  intelligence, 140–142
  language, 142–143
  lenses to apply, 128
  questions and projects, 149–150*b*
  social interaction, 143–145
Hurd, Tyler, 151
Hyper-Reality (Matsuda), 120–121,
    229–230
hypoglossal nerve (CN XII), 213

identity, 73
Immersive Enclosure, The (Roquet), 239
immersive environments, 10–12, 30–31,
    74–75, 79, 121, 201, 244. *See also*
    augmented reality (AR); virtual
    reality (VR)
immersive sexual experiences, 171–172
immersive theater, 71–72
impact, achieving, 149
impassable fail states, 118–119
"In Bloom" (Tse), 64–68, 100–101
Indigenous storytelling, 91–93, 97–98
individualistic cultures, 26
information perception and
    processing, 116–117
input devices. *See* body as input device
input methods, 110–111
Instagram Teen Annotated Research, 32
intelligence, 140–142
intention, designing with,
interfaces, 116. *See also* affordances;
    BCIs (brain-computer interfaces);
    body as input device; universal
    design (UD)

Internet, lack of access to, 15–16, 98
*Introduction to Virtual Environments
    and Advanced Interface Design*
    (Furness), 53–54
I-XRAY project, 13

Japan, 20, 28–29
Javanbakht, Arash, 209
Jobs, Steve, 112
Jonze, Spike, 228
joystick-controlled locomotion
    systems, 158

Karl, K.A., 237–238
Kofe, Simon, 87
Kolko, J., 223
Krum, David M., 58

language, 142–143
language impairments, 76
language processing, 76
Lanier, Jaron, 56–58
Lattin, Kilma, 97–98
Lawson, B.D., 159
legislation, 47–48
Leonardo da Vinci, 48–51
Leon-Geyer, Andres, 93
limitations, 16–17
literature/fiction, 48–56, 120–121, 228,
    229–230, 247–248
Loewenstein, George, 68–69
Lombard, Matthew, 166–167, 169–170
Lovense, 233–234
low physical effort, 119–120
Luckey, Palmer, 58–59

Mace, Ronald, 104
"Machine Stops, The" (Forster), 44–46
magnetic resonance imaging (MRI), 204
Māori, 91–93
Māori Studios, 92–93
Matamala-Gomez, M., 152
Matsuda, Keiichi, 120–121, 229–230
McKinsey, 246–247
meditation, 216
memory processing conditions, 76

Meta, 13, 14–15, 59–60, 91, 93, 227, 238–240, 248
Meta Quest headsets, 56, 188, 210–211
Metaverse, 238–240
Microsoft, 60
Midjourney, 231
military (US), 241–242
misinformation, 89–90
mixed reality, 18–19, 164–165
Möbius strip, 56
motion data, 8–9
motion-tracking telemetry, 8–9
mouth haptics, 213
move fast and break things, 3–4
M-Pesa, 26
Mühling, T., 217
Murray, Janet Horowitz, 44, 48
Murray, L., 203–204

National Institute of Standards and Technology (NIST), 7–8
nature, 125
nervous system, 207–216
  abducens nerve, 211
  accessory spinal nerve, 214
  hypoglossal nerve, 213
  olfactory nerve, 209
  optic nerve, 214–215
  trigeminal nerve, 215–216
  trochlear nerve, 210–211
  vagus nerve, 216
  vestibular neurons, 212–213
neural coupling, 77
neurodiversity, 74–76, 205–207
Neuromancer (Gibson), 46
neurons, 204–205, 212–213
neuroscience of stories, 48–56
neurotypical thinking, 74–75, 205–206
New York University (NYU), 93–96
Ngā Atua Māori AR experience, 92–93
Nichols, Teff, 70–71
1996 Communications Decency Act, 81
NIST (National Institute of Standards and Technology), 7–8
Norman, Don, 176, 178
Notre-Dame Cathedral, 28

occupation, 164–166
Oculus Rift, 59f
Ogle, Elise, 70–71
Oiticica, Hélio, 55
olfactory nerve (CN I), 209
Oliver, Martin, 177–178
Olson, J. Logan, 58
"1,000 Cut Journey" (Cogburn, Ogle, and Bailenson, Asher, and Nichols), 70–71
Open Brush, 137
OpenXR, 98
optic nerve, 214–215
Osthoff, Simone, 55
OurWorlds, 97–98
outgroup bias, 220
Outlaw, Jessica, 11
overconfidence bias, 220
oxytocin, 78

painting and visual art, 48–56
Pallasmaa, Juhani, 103
perceived and actual affordances, 182–183
perceptible information, 115–117
Personal Information Protection Law, 27
physical effort, 119–120
place illusion, 167
"PlayTest" (Black Mirror), 247–248
PlutoVR survey, 171–172
Pokémon GO, 207–209
poker analogy, 17–18
Pontificia Universidad Católica de Perú (PUCP), 93–96
positive impact, 149
post-traumatic stress disorder (PTSD), 209
potential of spatial computing. See spatial computing, potential of
power dynamics, 240–243
precision rehabilitation, 207
presence, 151–152, 161–167
preservation, 87–89
privacy and privacy concerns, 13, 20–22, 25, 27–28, 36, 107, 235–236
privacy regulations, 25, 27

proprioception, 158–159
prosopagnosia (face blindness), 75
"Psychology of Curiosity, The"
    (Loewenstein), 68–69
PTSD (post-traumatic stress
    disorder), 209
PUCP (Pontificia Universidad Católica
    de Perú), 93–96

Quest headsets, 56, 188, 210–211

Raby, Fiona, 146–147
Ramirez, Erick, 136
Rams, Dieter, 112
Ray-Bans, 248
reactive synaptogenesis, 202
rehabilitation, precision, 207
representative affordances, 184–185
representativeness bias, 220
responsive design, 122
risk registers, 33, 247
risks, addressing, 9, 19, 31, 153. *See also*
    universal design (UD)
Roberts, Jasmine, 233–234
Roquet, Paul, 239
rubber hand illusion, 244–245
Rutledge, Pam, 80

safety, 28, 107
Samsung, 242
scalable game design (SGD)
    projects, 81–82
selection bias, 220
self-location, 168
self-serving bias, 221
sense of agency, 168–169
sense of embodiment (SoE), 168–170
senses, 116, 152–161
Sensorama, 52–53
sensor data and contextual
    awareness, 235–237
sensory processing, 74
sexual experiences, 171–172
shadow puppetry, 85–86
Shakespeare, William, 72
Shen, V., 213
Sherwood, Jess, 3

Shmidheiser, M., 203–204
signifiers, 178–182
simple and intuitive use, 112–115
size and space, 121–122
skeuomorphic design, 112–113, 180
Skillman, Drew, 137
Slater, M., 167–169
Słowiński, P., 222
smart glasses, 13
smartphones, 43, 47
smell and taste, 155–156
Smith, Greg, 230
Snapchat, 23–24
Snow Crash (Stephenson), 46
social desirability bias, 221
social interaction, 143–145
social media, 89
social presence, 169–170
social VR, 20, 33, 73, 93–96, 127, 133,
    144–145, 171–172
Song, V., 13
spatial audio, 154, 242
spatial computing
    affordances. *See* affordances
    and the body as input device. *See* body
        as input device
    brain and biases. *See* brain and biases
    ethics. *See* ethics
    history of. *See* human-computer
        interaction
    and human traits. *See* human traits
    storytelling. *See* storytelling
    universal design. *See* universal design
        (UD)
spatial computing, potential of, 227
    AI, 228–229, 231–235, 246–247
    AR and digital twins, 229–231
    BCIs, 244–246
    beauty or nightmare, 247–248
    building a better future, 248–249
    Collingridge dilemma, 244–247
    connecting over distance, 237–240
    and power dynamics, 240–243
    sensor data and contextual
        awareness, 235–237

spatial interfaces, 116. *See also* affordances; BCIs (brain-computer interfaces); body as input device; universal design (UD)
spatialized text, 105–106
speculative design, 146–148
SPOSA, 136
Stable Diffusion, 231
Stanney, K.M., 159
status-quo bias, 221
Stephenson, Neal, 46
stereoscope, 50–51
stereotyping bias, 221
stories, of machines, 48–56
storytelling, 63
    around the world, 83–86
    cross-cultural exchange, 93–96
    cultural exchange, 80–83
    and curiosity, 68–73
    digital twins, 87–89
    expanding access through, 96–101
    "In Bloom" (Tse), 64–68, 100–101
    Indigenous, 91–93, 97–98
    intrinsic to human experience, 63–64
    misinformation, 89–90
    questions and projects, 100–101*b*
    shaping the mind, 73–80
Strivr, 217
Suma, Evan A., 58
Sun Tzu, 18–19
survivorship bias,
Sutherland, Ivan, 52–53, 55, 58
Sword of Damocles, 53, 54*f*

tactical augmented reality (TAR), 241–242
Tallon, Andrew, 28
taste and smell, 155–156
TBI (traumatic brain injury), 199–200, 202–204
Teixeira, J., 160
telekinesis, 185–186
teleportation, 160
Tempest, The (Shakespeare), 72
Tender Claws, 72

terms of service, 5, 6*f*, 235–236
three-dimensional object scaling, 109
three-dimensional problems, 115
TikTok, 242
Tilt Brush, 137, 138*f*
Timutimu, Lee, 91–93
tolerance for error, 117–119
tongue, 213
top-down information, 169
touch, 156–157
training programs, 217–218
traits. *See* human traits
traumatic brain injury (TBI), 199–200, 202–204
A Treatise on Painting (Leonardo da Vinci), 48–51
trigeminal nerve (CN V), 215–216
trochlear nerve (CN IV), 210–211
true affordances, 182
Trump, Donald, 232–233
Tse, Estella, 64–68, 100–101
Tuvalu, 87–88
2024 Global Survey on AI, 246–247
2023 Writers' Strike, 98–99

uchi/soto, 20
Ultimate Display, The (Sutherland), 53
uncertainty, minimizing, 33
Under Presents, The (Tender Claws), 72
United States, 60–61
universal design (UD), 103
    additional considerations, 123–126
    building experiences for everyone, 122–123
    equitable use, 104–108
    flexibility in use, 108–111
    low physical effort, 119–120
    perceptible information, 115–117
    questions and project, 125*b*
    simple and intuitive use, 112–115
    size and space for approach and use, 121–122
    tolerance for error, 117–119
US Army, 42, 60
US military, 241–242

vagus nerve (CN X), 216
Van Bouwel, Thomas, 164–165
van der Meer, Paul, 179–180
vection, 160
verisimilitude, 167
vestibular neurons, 212–213
vestibular rehabilitation, 212
vestibular sense, 157–158
vestibulocochlear nerve (CN VIII), 212
Vickers, John, 230–231
Virilio, Paul, 24
virtual environments, 10–13, 130–132, 205, 216, 218. *See also* affordances; body as input device; immersive environments; presence
"Virtual Reality Immerses You in Your Mind" (Murray and Shmidheiser), 203–204
virtual reality (VR). *See also* affordances; body as input device; brain and biases; VR headsets
    and AI, 141, 232–234
    BCIs, 198–199, 244–246
    for blind and visually impaired users, 130–132
    environment size, 121–122
    harassment in, 10–12
    lack of ethical guidelines for, 22
    Luckey and, 58–59
    Metaverse, 238–240
    and misinformation, 90
    motion data, 8–9
    for physically disabled users, 132
    projects for consideration, 38b
    safety challenges, 3–4, 13
    sense of realism, 24
    social VR. *See* social VR
    and storytelling, 70–71, 84–86
vision, 153–154, 214–215

Vision Pro, 59–60, 232–234
visual impairments, 75–76, 210–211
visually impaired and blind users, 130–132, 210–211
visual processing differences, 75
VR. *See* virtual reality (VR)
VRChat, 3
VR headsets, 51
    in architecture firms, 138
    during COVID-19 pandemic, 238
    dawn of Oculus, 58–59
    Meta Quest, 56, 188, 210–211
    Meta's vision for, 227
    Microsoft, 60
    Vision Pro, 59–60, 232–234
VR motion data, 8–9

WalkinVR, 132
Walmart, 217
web development and usage, 34–35
Western influence, 60–61
Wheatstone, Charles, 49–51
women, social VR experiences, 11
World Health Organization (WHO), 135–136
Writers Guild of America, 98–99

XR (extended reality), 97–98, 159
XRSI (Extended Reality Safety Intelligence), 19–20

Yeo, S., 88
You Are Not a Gadget (Lanier), 57
Yupik story knife, 86

Zheng, Q., 144–145
Zizioulas, John, 194
Zoom, 237–238
Zuckerberg, Mark, 3–4, 239

The manufacturer's authorised representative in the EU for product safety is
Oxford University Press España S.A. of el Parque Empresarial San Fernando de
Henares, Avenida de Castilla, 2 – 28830 Madrid (www.oup.es/en or product.
safety@oup.com). OUP España S.A. also acts as importer into Spain of products
made by the manufacturer.